Creating a Healing Community

A Training Manual for Healing Centers
in the Higher Life/Alliance Heritage

BY PAUL L. KING, D.MIN., TH.D.

Founder of
Higher Life/Alliance Heritage Renewal Network
& Higher Life/Alliance Healing Centers

Endorsements

"You have inspired me! It was your writing and passion that was part of God igniting a fresh spark in my soul. Bless you. I am delighted to endorse this training manual. You are gift to your Alliance family."

—Rev. David Hearn, President,
The Christian and Missionary Alliance
in Canada

"I am very excited about Paul King's new book about "Healing Communities." In the early days of the C&MA, "Houses Of Healing" were a powerful part of our ministry. I hope this book will be used of God to spark an interest in this much-needed ministry, and give guidance to those led of God to launch into it. I urge everyone in Christian Ministry to read this book!"

—Rev. Dick Sipley, Associate Evangelist,
Canadian Revival Fellowship,
Alliance pastor,
author of *Understanding Divine Healing*

"Paul King is a wonderful Alliance historian. More than that he is passionate to see the original vision of the early Alliance leaders restored in our day. This analysis of healing homes is insightful and helpful. It is more than a history though. It is a helpful, practical guide on the practice of prayer for healing, and of our need to boldly pray for the healing ministry to become a common practice today. Read this to both learn and be refreshed."

—Rev. Dr. David Chotka, Chair,
Alliance Pray!Team (C&MA Canada);
Lead Pastor, Heritage Park Alliance Church
(Windsor, Ontario); Conference Speaker;
Author, *Power Praying, Discerning The Voice,
Sifting Our Discerning*.

ISBN - 978-1-940931-14-2

Library of Congress catalog card number: 2015948787

Printed in the United States of America

Table of Contents

Acknowledgements

Many people have helped to make this manual happen. Steve Peterson, a member of IT staff at the Christian and Missionary Alliance National Office in Colorado Springs first placed this idea in my mind and heart. Dialoguing with Dr. Jennifer Miskov about healing homes as she was writing her doctoral dissertation on Carrie Judd Montgomery, stirred my heart further.

Our church, Higher Life Fellowship, implemented the Healing Rooms ministry of International Association of Healing Rooms (IAHR), which is a prototype of the broader Healing Center ministry concept. Rev. Jerry Fidler and his wife Kelly have directed our monthly Higher Life Healing Rooms, putting into practice the principles of this manual. They have also provided insights and stories of the results of healing prayer.

When I shared this vision with Dr. John Stumbo, the new president of the Christian and Missionary Alliance, he encouraged me and suggested we could implement the Healing Homes in Alliance District Campgrounds. Jake MacPeek, Director of Pinecrest Camp, the Southwestern District C&MA campground caught this vision and desires to implement the healing center concept at the campground. Rev. David Hearn, president of the C&MA in Canada, and Dr. David Chotka, director of the Prayer Mobilization ministry of the C&MA in Canada brainstormed together with me how we might implement this concept in Canada.

Darlene Kipling, also a Canadian and one of my mentors, encouraged me to pursue this vision. She had worked in conjunction with

Kathryn Kuhlman ministries, has been an oncology nurse, and was part of my SWAT team when I had cancer in 2007. Becky Duncan, who has assisted in our Higher Life Healing Rooms and Freedom in Christ Ministries, provided insights and editorial assistance.

Foreword

Paul King has a masterful way of drawing from the well of history to bring fresh water into our present reality. His training manual for "creating a healing community" is another inspiring example of this. Paul immediately captures our imagination by demonstrating the dynamic connection between the higher life and the healing home movement. It was a desperately longing after the manifest presence of Jesus that was the revolutionary atmosphere, the air that filled these healing communities. Healing was a by-product of deep spiritual renewal and healing homes became centers of restoration and transformation. It is time for a fresh expression of this ministry to flood our continent again. I want to challenge you not only to read this book, but to be engaged by it. Your own soul is longing for "more"—I dare you.

Rev. David Hearn

President of the Christian & Missionary Alliance in Canada

CHAPTER 1

Introduction to Higher Life/Alliance Healing Centers

This manual has grown out of Chapter 40 of my book *God's Healing Arsenal* on "Developing a Community of Healing: How to Implement a Healing Ministry in Your Church." In one sense, this manual is Volume 2 of *God's Healing Arsenal*. I have designed this manual so the two can be used in tandem to develop a healing center ministry through your church or ministry.

Creating Communities of Healing

Hobart Mowrer in the 1960s asserted that the church "ought to be a 'therapeutic community.'"[1] Calling the church a "community of healing," James McGilvray, Director of the Christian Medical Council, urged, "The healing role is given to the congregation, the people of God, who must exercise this dimension of their calling to the sick world in which they live."[2]

Drawing upon their challenges, Frank Bateman Stanger, former president of Asbury Seminary, wrote a book in the 1980s entitled *God's Healing Community*, reaffirming, "The local congregation must rediscover the concept that the church is a community of healing."[3] He laid down a theology of healing and an embryonic plan to develop the church as a healing community. He emphasized the importance of the church creating an atmosphere and expectancy of healing as well as a providing a variety of healing practices on a regular and repeated basis. This manual takes up the challenge for the church to become a community of healing.

Overview — What Are Healing Centers?

Christian Healing Centers exist in many forms and methodologies. Even New Age and psychic groups have types of healing centers or methodologies. This makes it all the more important to establish Christ-centered, Bible-based healing centers, which are clearly distinguished from such healing counterfeits. Christian Healing Centers are based upon biblical concepts and practices and historic Christian Healing Home models. Many Christian healing centers today are identified with Pentecostalism. However, the original 19th century healing homes predated the Pentecostal movement by more than half a century.

Healing homes were created out of the New Testament concept that homes are places where Christian faith is nurtured and strengthened, where pastoral care and healing can take place: "breaking bread from house to house" (Acts 2:46). Several people in the Bible were healed in a home setting: the widow's dead son brought back to life by Elijah, Peter's mother-in-law, the servant at home of the centurion, the paralyzed man let down through roof of a home, the young, dead girl at the synagogue leader's home, Dorcas brought back to life by Peter, and the healing of Saul's eyes through the prayers of Ananias.

The intent of Christian Healing Centers is to provide a pastoral environment of faith in which healing can be fostered. One scholar has called this an "incubational" healing model, meaning that it is a place to nurture life. Early Higher Life leader William Boardman called healing homes "nurseries for faith."

Healing Centers are flexible and can be established in a variety of ways and settings. They can be short-term or long-term; they can be operated in a designated room or time of ministry in a church, a house or building set aside for ministry, a campground or retreat center, or even in a tent or a booth at a community festival.

What Are Higher Life/Fourfold Gospel/ Alliance Healing Centers?

Patterned after the early Healing Homes of the 19th and early 20th century, especially in the Higher Life movement and the early Christian and Missionary Alliance, Higher Life/Fourfold Gospel Healing Centers are intended to equip believers to work as a team to impart the healing presence and power of God into their community. Anyone with a physical, emotional, or spiritual need is invited to Healing Centers for prayer sessions with a team of trained workers.

The Fourfold Gospel as outlined by A.B. Simpson emphasizes exalting Jesus Christ as Savior, Sanctifier, Healer, and Coming King. Higher Life/Fourfold Gospel Healing Centers are uniquely designed to present this Fourfold Gospel, especially in the dimension of Jesus Christ as Healer. At the same time, all four dimensions of the Fourfold Gospel are interrelated and intertwined. A.B. Simpson intended that the healing homes he founded were to be a place of:

- fellowship—where people of like mind can share together in their faith and the Spirit
- instruction—on the Word, faith, healing, holiness, the baptism in the Spirit, the authority of the believer
- rest, peace, and waiting on God through the power of stillness
- modeling truth and principles of healing through saturation with the Word of God, testimony, and example
- sending for sowing seed and multiplying fruit in others—impartation of the presence and power of God to impart to others
- providing an atmosphere of faith
- providing wholeness for the whole person—body, soul, and spirit

- preparing people to be able to receive healing
- "rest for those who wish to wait on God for a deeper spiritual life and physical strength. . . . the hallowed atmosphere of a Christian Home and a Father's house."[4]

Goals of Higher Life/ Fourfold Gospel/ Alliance Healing Centers

Mission Statement. The Mission of Higher Life/Fourfold Gospel/Alliance Healing Centers is to provide a community of healing, a safe environment with an atmosphere of faith, rest, peace, and love to foster healing of the whole person—spirit, soul, and body—in the spirit and heritage of the 19th-early 20th century Higher Life/Fourfold Gospel/Alliance Healing Homes.

Vision of Higher Life/Fourfold Gospel/Alliance Healing Centers

- To provide opportunities beyond the regular church service setting for people to come for extended times of prayer for healing of body, soul, and spirit
- To be an evangelistic outreach tool to those who need a touch from God, but who may not come to a church service
- To establish Healing Centers in and through C&MA churches, campgrounds, and ministries throughout the US and Canada and internationally, as well as with other churches and ministries inter-denominationally who believe in the Higher Life and Fourfold Gospel message
- To train workers and prayer teams in Higher Life/Fourfold Gospel/Alliance healing principles
- To provide a training manual for workers and prayer teams
- To provide a network of Higher Life/Fourfold Gospel/Alliance healing ministries
- To provide testimonies of God's healing power

- To provide an atmosphere of faith and peace conducive to releasing God's healing power

It is our vision to welcome various streams of healing ministry in the Higher Life/Fourfold Gospel/Alliance spirit of openness and loving acceptance with discernment and balance. This means accepting the insights, blessings, and benefits of each stream which are in harmony with Higher Life/Fourfold/Alliance heritage and mission, but without one stream dominating and without necessarily embracing every facet, teaching, or practice of those streams, and integrating those streams with balance, love, wisdom, discernment, and maturity with Higher Life and Fourfold Gospel C&MA distinctives. We seek to exercise sound faith and healing principles based on historic Higher Life and C&MA Fourfold Gospel teaching and practice. This includes a healthy theology of suffering and death. We embrace the good of renewal movements and avoiding the excesses and building bridges of balance between streams.

What Is the Higher Life?

The Upward Call. The Apostle Paul's passion for more of Jesus is the foundation of the Higher Christian Life: *"I press on toward the goal for the prize of the upward call of God in Christ Jesus" (Phil 3:14).* Based on this Scripture, Jonathan Oatman's classic 19th century song "Higher Ground" was the theme song of the Higher Life Movement:

I'm pressing on the upward way
New heights I'm gaining every day
Still praying as I onward bound
Lord, plant my feet on higher ground.

Chorus:
Lord, lift me up and let me stand
By faith on heaven's table land
A higher plane than I have found
Lord, plant my feet on higher ground.

My heart has no desire to stay
Where doubts arise and fears dismay
Tho' some may dwell where these abound
My prayer, my aim is higher ground.

I want to live above the world
Tho' Satan's darts at me are hurled
For faith has caught the joyful sound
The song of saints on higher ground.

I want to scale the utmost height
And catch a gleam of glory bright
But still I'll pray till heaven I've found
"Lord, lead me on to higher ground."

Throne Life—In Heavenly Places. The theme of Throne Life was an ancient biblical truth based on Paul's grand words in Ephesians 2:6, *"God . . . seated us with Him in the heavenly places in Christ Jesus."* Through identification with Christ we are seated with Him on the right hand of the throne of God in the heavenly places. This was known as the "higher life" or "throne life," living life on a higher plane as royal children of the King of Kings. A.B. Simpson explains:

> This is much more than resurrection. It is ascension. It is taking the place of accomplished victory and conceded right, and sitting down in an attitude of completed repose, from henceforth expecting with Him until all our enemies be made our footstool. . . . It is throne life. It is dwelling with Christ on high, your head in the heaven even while your feet still walk the paths of the lower world of sense and time. This is our high privilege.[5]

These concepts were taught in various ways and terminology throughout church history, but became a lost treasure. The concepts were rediscovered and taught in some ways among the Puritans in the 17th and 18th centuries and were especially recovered and popularized in the late 19th and early 20th centuries, permeating the Scotch and Dutch Reformed Covenant Theology, Keswick, Higher Life, and Overcomer movements. These principles of throne life applied especially to the ministry of healing.

The Higher Life Movement. The Higher Life movement appears to have begun with a book written in 1858 by Presbyterian minister William Boardman, entitled *The Higher Christian Life.* That book impacted Quaker evangelists Pearsall and Hannah Whitall Smith, the latter who wrote the classic *The Christian's Secret of a Happy Life* in the 1870s. Boardman, the Smiths, and others gathered together for a faith and holiness convention in the town of Keswick, England, in 1874. Thus, the Keswick holiness movement emerged from that meeting focusing on sanctification, the deeper and higher life, faith, and later on healing.

A.B. Simpson, another former Presbyterian minister, was profoundly impacted by Boardman's book. Simpson founded The Christian and Missionary Alliance (C&MA) in 1887, as a Higher Life movement emphasizing a Fourfold Gospel of Jesus Christ as Savior, Sanctifier, Healer, and Coming King. A.B. Simpson wrote *The Highest Christian Life*, an exposition on Ephesians, as well as other books with related themes such as *In Heavenly Places, A Larger Christian Life,* and *Land of Promise.*

George Peck, who was a Methodist friend of Simpson and Baptist pastor A.J. Gordon and a leader in the early C&MA, wrote his book *Throne-Life, or The Highest Christian Life*, in which he wrote concerning "throne-power," or the "command of faith." This appears to be the premier book on the concept of Throne Life.

Andrew Murray, a Dutch Reformed missionary to South Africa, wrote about this higher Christian life, what he called "the power of an endless life," in *The Holiest of All*, his great devotional exposition of the book of Hebrews. Based on Reformed Covenant theology, Murray and Simpson, as well as Swiss healing leader Dorothea Trudel, and the famed Scottish preacher and hymn writer Horatius Bonar, taught that believers are kings and priests.

Several Baptists leaders alluded to themes of Throne Life, or the higher Christian life, including Charles Spurgeon, British Keswick leader F.B. Meyer, American Baptists A.J. Gordon and E.W. Kenyon. Oswald Chambers taught principles of the higher Christian life in *My Utmost for His Highest* and other works, although he also warned of dangers and imbalances that can accompany the Higher Life movement.

Other leaders in the Keswick movement, cousins of the Higher Life movement, taught elements of Throne Life, such as Presbyterian preacher A.T. Pierson, who served as interim pastor of Spurgeon's Metropolitan Tabernacle, after Spurgeon's death. In 1906, Keswick and Overcomer movement leader Jessie Penn-Lewis (known as the "little apostle of England") wrote a booklet entitled *Throne Life of Victory*, which was hailed as "God's answer to powers of darkness." Keswick missionary to India Amy Carmichael alludes to the concepts of Throne Life, as also do T. Austin Sparks, Norman Grubb, and Watchman Nee in his books *Sit, Walk, Stand* and *God's Plan and the Overcomers*.

Higher Life and the Authority of the Believer. John A. MacMillan, a missionary and professor with The Christian and Missionary Alliance, wrote the classic book *The Authority of the Believer*, based on the principles of Throne Life. MacMillan's principles on the authority of the believer have been applied by a wide diversity of Christian leaders, including Kenneth Hagin, Billye Brim, and Kenneth Copeland in the Word of Faith movement, Wesleyan holiness leader Paul Billheimer, Foursquare leader Jack Hayford, and Freedom in Christ Ministries founder Dr. Neil T. Anderson.

Higher Life and Healing

One vital aspect of Throne Life/Higher Life teaching and practice is that we can begin to experience the heavenly life to a greater measure in the here-and-now in our physical bodies. Healing of the whole person is a part of the Higher Life message. Freedom from demonic oppression through exercising our authority as a believer is also a part of the Higher Life message.

George Eldon Ladd expressed this in the phrase, "the kingdom of God is here now, but not fully here yet." Decades earlier, A.B. Simpson understood this concept, calling it the "overlapping of the ages":

> As in the past God was always overlapping the coming age, so is He today overlapping the next age. . . . The coming of the Lord is to bring the resurrection of these mortal bodies. Surely we may expect some earnests in the last days. . . . Healing of the body is an actual earnest and firstfruit of the future resurrection. . . . The healing of disease through the indwelling life of Christ is simply the beginning of the resurrection. . . . We shall find nothing awaiting us yonder that we have not begun to find in our experience here.[6]

Healing as Living Under the Powers of the Age to Come—The Border Zone. A.B. Simpson further explains, "Just as these ancient saints looked forward, and overlapped and got into the age to come in some measure by their faith, so God permits us to live under the powers of the age to come, and come into the border zone, where our feet are yet on earth, and our heads, our eyes, and our hearts are in the coming kingdom. Divine healing is one of the overlappings of this coming age."[7]

What Is the Fourfold Gospel?

A.B. Simpson, the Presbyterian minister who founded the Christian and Missionary Alliance, coined the term "Fourfold Gospel," emphasizing a Christ-centered message of four major roles of Jesus Christ as Savior, Sanctifier, Healer, and Coming King. Simpson explained it this way:

> What do we mean by the four-fold gospel? . . . . In one sense it is a manifold gospel with countless blessings and ever higher and higher stages of spiritual privileges and attainment. . . . There are four messages in the gospel that sum up in a very complete way the blessings which Christ has to offer us: Jesus Christ as Savior,

Sanctifier, Healer, and Coming King. . . . Is not this great blessing of the *full gospel* worth believing, receiving and telling?"[8]

It Is the Full Gospel. Notice that Simpson clarifies that there is much more to Christ and the gospel than these four messages—he calls it a "manifold gospel"—but that these four emphases sum up the whole gospel. In fact, he calls it the "full gospel," the term coined by William Boardman in his 1858 book *The Higher Christian Life.* The four-fold gospel is a full gospel—a full-orbed gospel centered on Jesus Christ. It is the gospel of the Higher Life.

- *Jesus Christ as Savior—A Gospel of Full Salvation.* Simpson explains, "This glorious gospel of full salvation. . . . Jesus, a complete Savior for body, soul and spirit."[9] He wrote a hymn, "Jesus Only," on each of the four themes of the of the Fourfold Gospel, beginning with Jesus Christ as Savior:

  Jesus only is our Savior,
  All our guilt He bore away,
  He, our righteousness forever,
  All our strength from day to day.

- *Jesus Christ as Sanctifier—The Gospel of a Supernatural, Consecrated, Overflowing Life.* "The Highest Christian Life is the supernatural life . . . the consecrated life . . . the overflowing life of love and service."[10] For Simpson and Higher Life leaders, this included the sanctifying baptism with the Holy Spirit. Boardman had written: "The higher Christian life . . . full trust and full salvation . . . a deeper life attained after conversion. . . . the full gospel. . . . the baptism of the Holy Spirit is a reality and a more glorious one." A.B. Simpson's hymn "Jesus Only" includes two verses on Christ as Sanctifier:

  Jesus is our Sanctifier,
  Saving us from self and sin,
  And with all His Spirit's fulness,
  Filling all our hearts within.

Jesus only is our Power,
He the gift of Pentecost;
Jesus, breathe Thy pow'r upon us,
Fill us with the Holy Ghost.

- *Jesus Christ as Healer—The Gospel of Wholeness for the Whole Person.* Simpson closely connected healing and the higher Christian life: "There is a still higher phase of this precious truth [Divine Healing] . . . 'Your youth is renewed like the eagle's' (Psalm 103:5). This is the quickening life of Christ in our mortal flesh, giving vitality and spring to the body. . . . This is more than being healed of disease and redeemed from death. It is being quickened in the higher life and filled with the vigor and energy of our Lord." A.B. Simpson wrote another verse on Jesus Christ our Healer:

Jesus only is our Healer,
All our sicknesses He bare,
And His risen life and fulness,
All His members still may share.

- *Jesus Christ as Coming King—The Full Restoration of Holy Spirit Power in the Latter Days.* A.B. Simpson connects all of the Fourfold Gospel together in Christ's coming: "Just as the coming of Jesus brought the Holy Spirit, so the coming of the Holy Spirit in the fullness of His power will bring the second coming of Christ; and as that advent approaches, His power will be more gloriously manifested."[11] His final verse and chorus sum up this Fourfold Gospel:

And for Jesus we are waiting,
List'ning for the Advent Call;
But 'twill still be Jesus only,
Jesus ever, all in all.

Jesus only, Jesus ever,
Jesus all in all we sing,

Savior, Sanctifier, and Healer,
Glorious Lord and coming King.

The Alliance Was Founded as a Full Gospel Movement.
Announcing plans to found the Alliance in 1887, A.B. Simpson proclaimed, "The time has come and the way is clear for a simple, spiritual and undenominational movement to send the *full gospel* . . . to the neglected millions of heathen lands. . . Is it not fitting that the great multitude whom the Holy Spirit has called in these days into a closer union with Jesus, and a deeper revelation of His fullness, should unite in some work for the evangelization of others which would be a worthy expression of their gratitude and love, and in turn a bond of delightful union and a means of yet higher blessing to their own soul.[12] The Higher Life and the Fourfold Gospel are a movement of the Full Gospel centered on Jesus Christ in all His dimensions and roles.

Simpson sums up the message of the Alliance and the Fourfold Full Gospel as "the promotion of a higher Christian life and full salvation for both soul and body, and the evangelization of the world and its preparation for the Master's coming."[13] George Müller, the great Apostle of Faith who started "faith homes" in London to care for orphans, endorsed Simpson's Fourfold Gospel, telling Simpson "that this arrangement of truth was most evidently 'of the Lord' and suggested that he never change its mold."[14]

Higher Life/Fourfold Gospel Leaders and Teachers

Among the Higher Life leaders and teachers cited in this manual include the following:

- **Ethan O. Allen**—Methodist/Brethren leader who became known as the father of the healing movement in America.

- **Paul Billheimer**—Wesleyan author of books on Higher Life themes such as *Destined for the Throne, Destined for the Cross, Destined to Overcome, Don't Waste Your Sorrows.*

- **William Boardman**—Presbyterian founder of the Higher Life movement with the publication of his book *The Higher Christian Life* in 1858. Helped to found Bethshan Healing Home in London.

- **F.F. Bosworth**—C&MA pastor and evangelist who wrote the classic book *Christ the Healer.*

- **Johannes Blumhardt**—German Lutheran pastor who founded the first healing home.

- **Russell Kelso Carter**—associate of A.B. Simpson, author of the hymn "Standing on the Promises."

- **Oswald Chambers**—Baptist author of the classic devotional *My Utmost for His Highest,* he affirmed principles of faith and healing.

- **Charles Cullis**—Physician who became a healing home pioneer and impacted A.B. Simpson.

- **Armin Gesswein**—Norwegian C&MA revival evangelist.

- **A.J. Gordon**—Baptist pastor, friend of A.B. Simpson, founder of what today is known as Gordon College and Gordon-Conwell Seminary, and author of numerous books, including *The Ministry of Healing* and *The Ministry of the Spirit.*

- **Sarah Lindenberger**—deaconess of Berachah Healing home of the C&MA.

- **William T. MacArthur**—C&MA leader and associate of A.B. Simpson who was mentored in healing and deliverance by Ethan O. Allen.

- **John A. MacMillan**—Canadian Presbyterian lay elder who became a missionary with the C&MA to China and the Philippines, instructor at Nyack College, and was a pioneer in spiritual warfare and wrote the original book *The Authority of the Believer.*

- **Dr. T.J. McCrossan**—Presbyterian Greek scholar who became a C&MA pastor, professor, traveled with healing evangelist Charles Price, and wrote the book *Bodily Healing and the Atonement.* His daughter was a life-long friend of Kathryn Kuhlman.

- **F.B. Meyer**—British Baptist Higher Life leader who taught on faith and healing.

- **George Müller**—Known as the "apostle of faith," he founded a faith home for orphans. He affirmed A.B. Simpson's Fourfold Gospel.

- **Carrie Judd Montgomery**—close friend and associate minister of A.B. Simpson, a founding Vice President of the C&MA, who founded healing homes and was a bridge-builder between Pentecostals and non-Pentecostals.

- **Andrew Murray**—Dutch Reformed missionary to South Africa and author of numerous books on Higher Life and healing themes, including: *Abide in Christ, With Christ in the School of Prayer, Divine Healing, Waiting on God, Holiest of All.*

- **A.B. Simpson**—Presbyterian minister who founded the Christian and Missionary Alliance and coined the "Fourfold Gospel" of Jesus Christ as Savior, Sanctifier, Healer and Coming King.

- **William C. Stevens**—early Alliance leader and Dean at Nyack Missionary Training Institute (Now Nyack College and Alliance Theological Seminary).

- **R.A. Torrey**—associate of evangelist Dwight L. Moody, founder of Bible Institute of Los Angeles (now Biola University), wrote a book on healing.

- **A.W. Tozer**—C&MA pastor, author of numerous books, including the classics *The Pursuit of God* and *Knowledge of the Holy.*

Similarities to and Differences from International Association of Healing Rooms

The International Association of Healing Rooms (IAHR) was established by Cal Pierce out of Bethel Church in Redding, California, based on the healing room ministries of John G. Lake in the early 20th century. The Higher Life/Alliance Healing Centers have some similarities in concepts and methodologies and some IAHR practices have been adapted. However, the Higher Life/Alliance Healing Centers are based not on IAHR, but primarily on the principles and patterns of healing home ministries from the late 19th and early 20th centuries. More specifically, these principles and practices emerge from the Higher Life, healing and holiness movements, and of A.B. Simpson and the early Christian and Missionary Alliance. These homes predate the John G. Lake healing room ministries by decades.

Further, IAHR is mostly Pentecostally-oriented. They stipulate that trained leaders speak in tongues and hold to the belief that tongues is the evidence of the baptism in the Spirit. While Alliance and Higher Life leaders do believe in speaking in tongues, we do not require healing center team members to speak in tongues, nor do we believe that a person has to speak in tongues to be filled with the Spirit.

The IAHR Healing Rooms focus only on a 20-30 minute healing prayer time after listening for the voice of the Lord. While this type of short-term prayer ministry is included in Higher Life Alliance Healing Centers, the Higher Life Alliance Healing Centers provide for a broader and more extensive time of prayer ministry as well as more follow-up and pastoral care.

Additional Resources on the Higher Life

Boardman, W.E. *The Higher Christian Life*. Ft. Washington, PA: CLC Publications, 2007. An updated language version of the original book published in 1858.

King, Paul L. *Come Up Higher: Rediscovering Throne Life—The Highest Christian Life for the 21st Century*. Tulsa, OK: Timothy Publishing, 2013.

McIntyre, Joe. *Throne Life*. Bothel, WA: Empowering Grace Ministries, 2011. A contemporary summary of the principles from the original book *Throne Life* by C&MA/Higher Life leader George Peck originally published in 1889.

Murray, Andrew. *Holiest of All*. New Kensington, PA: Whitaker House, 1996. A devotional deeper, higher life commentary on Hebrews and the spiritual typology of the tabernacle—entering into the Holy of Holies.

Simpson, A.B. *In Heavenly Places*. Harrisburg, PA: Christian Publications, 1958. A study of what it means to be seated in the heavenly places in Christ. Out of print, but used copies available on Amazon.com.

—*Days of Heaven on Earth*. Camp Hill, PA: Christian Publications, 1984. A daily devotional on the Higher Christian Life.

—*The Fourfold Gospel*. Harrisburg, PA: Christian Publications, n.d.

—*The Highest Christian Life*. Harrisburg, PA: Christian Publications, 1966. Messages from Ephesians, the epistle of the Higher Life.

—*The Land of Promise*. Harrisburg, PA: Christian Publications, 1969. A typological study of the believer's spiritual journey to the Promised Land of the Higher Christian life, based on Israel's journey from Egypt to Canaan.

—*A Larger Christian Life*. Harrisburg, PA: Christian Publications, n.d., accessed via website: http://online.cbccts.sk.ca/alliances-tudies/simpson/larglife.html. Calling believers to more—a larger, higher, deeper, fuller life.

—*The Supernatural*. Harrisburg, PA: Christian Publications, 1967. Original published as *Present Truths or the Supernatural*.

—*Seeing the Invisible*. Camp Hill, PA: Christian Publications, 1994. Messages based on Hebrews 11 on walking by faith.

CHAPTER 2

A Brief History of Healing Homes

The First Healing Homes—Established in Europe

The first healing home was opened in 1843 in Bad Boll, Germany, by Rev. Johannes Christoph Blumhardt, a Lutheran pastor who experienced a revival and began a healing and deliverance ministry. A woman who had been oppressed by demons was set free over a two-year period of time. When she was finally liberated totally, revival broke out and people swarmed to his church for healing prayer. However, his superiors objected to his healing ministry in the church and told him he could no longer hold healing services in the church. He obtained a house where people could come for healing prayer. As a result, other homes were opened by Otto Stockmayer in Germany, Dorothy Trudel in Switzerland, and Elizabeth Baxter in London, England.

Establishment of Healing Homes in America

Charles Cullis, an Episcopalian homeopathic physician, began one of the earliest "faith" homes in America in Boston in 1864, before completely understanding divine healing, and later introduced the

James 5 prayer with anointing oil. In 1882, after visiting the faith works of George Muller, Trudel, and Blumhardt, he opened a "Faith Cure House" patterned on Trudel's healing home in Männedorf, Switzerland.

The Higher Life movements of the second half of the 19th century, by and large, embraced healing belief and practice, though to varying degrees. Presbyterian minister, William Boardman, who is considered the Father of the Higher Life movement, wrote the seminal book *The Higher Christian Life* in 1858. He later wrote *The Great Physician* and assisted Elizabeth Baxter in developing her healing home in London. A.B. Simpson was strongly impacted by Boardman and his books.

After a miraculous healing in 1880 through the ministry of African-American healing evangelist Mrs. Elizabeth Mix, Carrie F. Judd began a healing home called Faith Rest Cottage or Faith Sanctuary in Buffalo, New York, as a place of rest, prayer, and an atmosphere of faith conducive to receiving healing. She also set aside a consecrated space called "The Prophets Room" for guests briefly visiting their city. Books and literature on faith and healing were made available. She would visit her guests several times a day. "Faith meetings" included a Thursday night prayer meeting from 7:30-9:00 p.m. and a Tuesday Bible study at 3:00 p.m.

A year later she became editor of a monthly periodical about faith and healing entitled *Triumphs of Faith*. Her book on faith and testimony of healing had an impact on Simpson, and she became a frequent convention speaker for the C&MA. In 1890 she married George Montgomery and they founded another healing home in Oakland, California, called "Home of Peace." George later became a Vice President of the C&MA and continued in that role until his death in 1930.

Healing Homes of A.B. Simpson and the C&MA

In 1882 former Presbyterian minister A.B. Simpson, founder of The Christian and Missionary Alliance (C&MA) in 1887, began Friday afternoon healing meetings with 500-1000 in attendance. These meetings provided an atmosphere for teaching and for faith and hope, continuing for more than thirty years. The following year, in May 1883, Simpson established Berachah Healing Home (first known as the "Home for Faith and Physical Healing"). He called Berachah "a place of healing and a gateway to holiness and higher Christian living." Simpson was influenced by Cullis and Judd. He coined the phrase, "the Fourfold Gospel of Jesus Christ as Savior, Sanctifier, Healer, and Coming King" (reflected in the logo of the cross, laver of cleansing, pitcher of anointing oil, and crown).

The Pitcher of Anointing Oil represents Christ as Healer

Sarah Lindenberger served as the resident director/deaconess of the Berachah Healing Home for forty years. Healing homes in the C&MA were started in many other locations around the nation:

- *Beulah Healing Home, Grand Rapids, Michigan.* Dora Griffin Dudley, who received healing in 1885 and was influenced by Carrie Judd's book *The Prayer of Faith*, established the Beulah Healing Home in Grand Rapids, Michigan, in 1887. Carrie Judd was the guest speaker at the dedication of the home. Many manifestations of healing took place. In similar fashion, the home included prayer, Bible reading, anointing with oil, listening for the voice of God.[15]

- *Fourfold Gospel Mission, Troy, New York.* Sara M.C. Musgrove (1839-1933) also founded a healing home following her own healing. Musgrove had been an invalid for four years before she was healed in January of 1882 after Ethan O. Allen traveled from Massachusetts to New York to pray for her. Following this account, she actively followed the James 5 prescription of anointing with oil when she prayed for the sick. Allen encouraged her to open her healing home in 1883. She pastored her Fourfold Gospel Mission in Troy, New York, for forty-one years.

- *Alliance Home, Pittsburgh, Pennsylvania.* E. D. Whiteside, known as "The Praying Man of Pittsburgh," himself had experienced a dramatic healing and was asked by Simpson to become the superintendent of the Alliance work in the Western Pennsylvania area. He founded the Alliance Home in Pittsburgh as a place of rest and healing.

- *Home of Peace, Oakland, California*—Carrie Judd married George Montgomery and they moved to Oakland, where they founded the Home of Peace, which functioned as an active healing ministry through the Salvation Army, Christian and Missionary Alliance, and Assemblies of God.

- *Shiloh Chapel Faith Home, Springfield, Massachusetts*—founded through the ministry of Ethan O. Allen. Mrs. Mary Shoemaker became the patroness of the home for many years.

- *Hebron Home, Philadelphia, Pennsylvania*—founded by Pastor Frederick Senft, who later served as a C&MA president.

- *Bethany Home, Toronto, Ontario*—founded by Pastor John Salmon, C&MA Vice President and founder of the C&MA in Canada.

- *Faith Mission, Trenton, Ontario*—Pastor Mary Gainworth founded Faith Mission after she was healed and then established a strong healing and prophetic ministry.

- *Healing Home, Atlanta, Georgia.*

- *Hebron House*—Rev. & Mrs. Frederick Senft (Rev. Senft was later the 3rd C&MA president).

- *Kellogg Home, Utica, New York*—Mrs. J. P. Kellogg.

- *Kemuel House, Germantown/Philadelphia, Pennsylvania*—Mrs. Sarah Beck.

- *Alliance Home, Santa Barbara, California*—Mrs. Scudder.

- *El-Shaddai, Cleveland, Ohio*—David Wesley Myland (C&MA State Supt.).

Healing Rooms of John G. Lake

John G. Lake had been introduced to healing home ministry through the Zion Healing Community of John Alexander Dowie in Illinois. He opened Healing Rooms in Spokane, Washington, in 1915. In their first 5 years of operation, they had 100,000 documented healings and Spokane was declared "The Healthiest City in America." The Healing Rooms eventually closed down with Lake's passing. Cal Pierce, an elder at Bethel Church in Redding, California, was led by the Lord to re-open the Healing Rooms in Spokane in 1999. Since that time, Healing Rooms has expanded world-wide with more than 1850 healing rooms in 52 countries.

Decline and Revival of Healing Home Concepts

Healing homes, for the most part, faded from the scene in the 1920s and following for several reasons. Prayer for healing became much more accepted and common in local churches. Longer-term healing ministry was replaced by healing evangelism crusades, by such people as Aimee Semple McPherson, F.F. Bosworth, Raymond Ritchey, Charles Price, Maria Woodworth-Etter, and many others. Some healing ministries did not want to be identified with Pentecostal excesses, and toned down or ceased their ministries. In the 1940s and following, a resurgence of healing crusades by William Branham (accompanied for a time by F.F. Bosworth), Gordon Lindsay (founder of Christ for the Nations Bible Institute), T.L. Osborne, Oral Roberts, Kathryn Kuhlman, and others.

With the charismatic movement came the healing ministries of Francis MacNutt and Tommy Tyson, who reintroduced the healing home concept of longer prayer ministry, calling it "soaking prayer." Kenneth Hagin, often known as the father of the modern word of faith movement, reintroduced many of the faith and healing principles of Higher Life leaders like A.B. Simpson and John MacMillan. Charles and Frances Hunter, their daughter Joan, and many other healing ministries emerged. The Third Wave Movement which wanted to be identified more with evangelicals than with Pentecostals and charismatics included healing ministries of Peter Wagner, John Wimber, and others. More recent healing ministries have included Rodney Howard-Browne, Randy Clark, Bill Johnson, and others. Wimber, Johnson, and Clark especially embraced many of the earlier healing home concepts.

Inner healing ministries, such as those of John Wimber, Francis and Judith MacNutt, David Seamands (Methodist), John and Paula Sandford (Elijah House), Neil T. Anderson (Freedom in Christ Ministries), and Ed Smith (Theophostic) brought back the healing home emphases on whole person healing and root causes behind sicknesses.

Additional Resources on Healing Homes and Ministries

Bosworth, F.F. *Christ the Healer.* Grand Rapids, MI: Fleming H. Revell, 1973.

Hardesty, Nancy A. *Faith Cure: Divine Healing in the Holiness and Pentecostal Movements* (Peabody, MA: Hendrickson Publishers, 2003. (Contains a section on healing homes. Hardesty has some background in the C&MA, and her grandmother told her of the healing ministries of F.F. Bosworth and the early Alliance).

Kydd, Ronald A.N. *Healing Through the Centuries.* Peabody, MA: Hendrickson, 1998. (contains a section on healing homes and "incubational" healing prayer).

Miskov, Jennifer A. *Life on Wings: The Forgotten Life and Theology of Carrie Judd Montgomery (1858-1946).* Cleveland, TN: CPT Press, 2012.

Pierce, Cal. *Healing Rooms Ministry Teams Training Manual.* Spokane, WA: IAHR (International Association of Healing Rooms).

Zuendel, Friedrich. *The Awakening: One Man's Battle with Darkness.* Farmington, PA: Plough Publishing House, 1999. (on the healing and deliverance ministry of Johann Blumhardt).

CHAPTER 3

Higher Life/ Fourfold Gospel/ Alliance Principles of Healing

Higher Life and Fourfold/Alliance beliefs and practices of healing are anchored in Scripture. At least ten Scriptural principles have been identified and promoted in Higher Life and Fourfold Gospel/Alliance healing ministries and are foundational to Higher Life and Fourfold Gospel/Alliance Healing Centers today. Every worker in Higher Life/Fourfold Gospel/Alliance Healing Centers should be trained in these principles and should thoroughly embrace them as well as impart them to the people coming for prayer. If workers have doubts about these principles, faith will falter and their healing ministry will be less effective.

Biblical Principle 1:
Jesus Christ Is the Same Yesterday, Today, Forever

"Jesus Christ is the same yesterday and today and forever"
(Heb. 13:8, NIV).

The Higher Life healing and holiness movements and such classic faith leaders as George Müller, A.J. Gordon, Charles Spurgeon, A.B.

Simpson, and Andrew Murray took to heart literally the Scripture in Hebrew 13:8, "Jesus Christ is the same yesterday and today and forever" (Heb. 13:8, NIV). The understood implication was that all of God's power, gifts, and promises are therefore applicable for all times. As Jonathan Goforth, Presbyterian missionary to China, put it, "All the resources of the Godhead are at our disposal!"[16] A.B. Simpson explained, especially regarding healing, "Our Lord's ministry began . . . in the manifestation of His healing power, and He is still the 'same yesterday, today, and forever.'"[17] They believed He is the Great I AM, not "the great I was."

Jesus Will Do for His Disciples Today What He Did for His Disciples in His Time. Following in this Higher Life understanding of Scripture, A.W. Tozer declared, "In view of much of today's dispensational teaching about Bible interpretation, the apostles, miracles of God, and the fullness of the Spirit, I must remind you that the Lord Jesus Christ is the same yesterday, today and forever. . . . There is nothing that Jesus has ever done for any of His disciples that He will not do for any other of His disciples! Where did the 'dividers-of-the-Word-of-Truth' get their teaching that all the gifts of the Spirit ended when the last apostle died? . . . When some men beat the cover off their Bible to demonstrate how they stand by the Word of God, they should be reminded that they are only standing by their own interpretation of the Word."[18]

Therefore, the Christianity of Christ Is the Same Yesterday, Today, and Forever. A.B. Simpson makes the logical conclusion, "In every age it ought still to be true, God also bearing them witness both with signs and wonders and with diverse miracles and gifts of the Holy Spirit according to His own will. If the Christ of Christianity is the same yesterday, today and forever, the Christianity of Christ ought also to be the same yesterday, today, and forever." A.B. Simpson wrote a song:

> Still He loves to save the sinful, heal the sick and lame
> Soothe the mourner, still the tempest, glory to His name.
> Yesterday, today, forever, Jesus is the same.
> All may change, but Jesus never, glory to His name.

In Higher Life/Fourfold Gospel/Alliance Healing Centers today, we believe that Jesus Christ has not changed and that the Christianity of Jesus Christ has not changed. We believe in and expect the healing power of Jesus to be manifested today.

What Jesus Did, He Continues through the Church. Higher Life leaders would assert that what Jesus did, He continues to do through the Church. For example, Simpson declared according to Acts 1:1 that what Jesus began to do and teach during His life on earth, "He continued to do and teach after His ascension" through the Church.[19] In other words, the Church as the Body of Christ is the extension of Jesus' life to carry on His supernatural ministry. Simpson viewed this as a fulfillment of Jesus' words: "Truly, truly, I say to you, he who believes in Me, the works that I do shall he do also; and greater works than these shall he do; because I go to the Father" (John 14:12).

Biblical Principle 2:
All Gifts of the Spirit Are in Operation Today and Are Needed for Effective Ministry

"The Kingdom comes not in word, but in power"
(1 Corinthians 4:20)

The C&MA statement on "Spiritual Gifts: Expectation without Agenda" states, "Every believer can expect the Holy Spirit to minister through him or her with spiritual gifts. Now **to each one** the manifestation of the Spirit is given for the common good . . . *(1 Corinthians 12:7; emphasis added)*. This protects us from a static view of spiritual gifts and leads into a more dynamic relationship with the Holy Spirit where we can expect Him to move through us in multiple ways for His Glory as He sees fit."

We Believe in All of the Charismata. The founder of the Healing Home movement, Johannes Blumhardt believed in and yearned for all of the gifts of the Spirit to be restored to the church: "The gifts and powers of the early Christian time—oh, how I long for their return! And I believe the Savior is just waiting for us to ask for them."[20] Historically, the C&MA, as well as many other Higher Life leaders, believed that all of the gifts of the Spirit are to continue in the church until Christ's coming. This is called a "continuist" view, as opposed to a "cessationist" view that believes that the supernatural gifts ceased with the apostolic age of the first century church. If a person or church believes that supernatural gifts no longer exist today, that limits healing ministry to an occasional sovereign work of God to heal.

In contrast, A.B. Simpson asserted, "The Alliance Movement stands for all the scriptural manifestations of the Holy Spirit since Pentecost. Its unique testimony has ever been for the supernatural."[21] Simpson affirmed belief in operation of *all* of the supernatural gifts of the Spirit for today:

> A common objection is observed in this way—Christ's last promise in Mark embraces much more than healing; but if you claim one, you must claim all. If you expect healing of the sick, you must include the gift of tongues and the power to overcome malignant poisons; and if the gift of tongues has ceased, so in the same way has the power over disease. We cheerfully accept the severe logic, we cannot afford to give up one of the promises. We admit our belief in the presence of the Healer in all the charismata of the Pentecostal church.[22]

All Gifts Are Still Needed Today. A.B. Simpson affirms, "Were these [supernatural gifts] meant merely to be transitory and special and temporary signs in connection with the introduction of Christianity into the world? Or were they part of the permanent enduement of the church? Does not the apostle tell us that these gifts and ministries were bestowed 'till we all come into the unity of the faith and the knowledge of the Son of God unto a perfect man, unto the measure of the stature of the fulness of Christ'? Certainly the church has not yet reached that maturity and if these gifts were need then they are needed still."[23]

All the gifts are needed because oftentimes various gifts or manifestations of the Spirit operate in conjunction with one another. A gift of faith enhances healing power to be manifest. A prophecy, word of wisdom or word of knowledge often provides illumination and revelation into a person's needs for healing, hindrances and obstacles, and what is needed to prepare for healing. Discernment of spirits can reveal any demonic influences causing sickness or preventing healing. Praying supernaturally in tongues when we don't know how to pray empowers and guides our prayers through the Holy Spirit. Interpretation of tongues provides to our understanding the sense of what was prayed through the Holy Spirit. Dreams and visions provide supernatural illumination and vision.

All of the Gifts Are Still in Effect Until the Second Coming of Christ. Paul prayed of the Corinthians, "so that you are not lacking in any gift, awaiting eagerly the revelation of our Lord Jesus Christ" (1 Corinthians 1:7). Inspired by the Holy Spirit, Paul desires that all of the gifts be operational until Christ's return.

Missing Gifts Are a Tragedy in the Church. A.W. Tozer proclaimed that missing gifts are "A tragedy in the church," avowing, "Much of the religious activity we see in the churches is not the eternal working of the Eternal Spirit, but the mortal working of man's mortal mind—and that is a raw tragedy! . . . About ninety percent of the religious work carried on in the churches is being done by ungifted members. . . . There has never been a time in the history of the Christian church that some of the gifts were not present and effective. Sometimes they functioned among those who did not understand or perhaps did not believe in the same way that we think Christians should believe."[24]

The Supernatural Life of Heaven Begins Now. Classic Higher Life faith leaders often noted that Paul writes in Ephesians that we are seated together in Christ in the heavenly places, so the heavenly supernatural life begins in the here and now, not just in the sweet by-and-by. Simpson wrote, "We anticipate in the present life to a certain extent the power of our future resurrection, and that we have a foretaste of this part of our salvation here even as we have a foretaste of heaven."[25]

George Eldon Ladd would later describe it as a partially realized eschatology—the "already here now, but not yet (fully)" status of the kingdom of God.[26]

Jesus Promised We Would Do Greater Works. Higher Life leaders frequently cited John 14:12; "Truly, Truly, I say unto you, he that believes on me, the works that I do shall he do also, and greater works than these shall he do because I go to the Father." Commenting on this verse, early Alliance leader William T. MacArthur explained, "This is perhaps the most encouraging promise of all the promises of our Lord as regards works of power. This is a promise of, let it be noted, of works, the *same* works. We must understand this to mean the same kind of works that Jesus did, only greater than those which He performed. . . . We have such power manifested in the person of Peter that the sick were carried to the streets in order that His shadow might fall across them, and heal their diseases. Wonderful works of power were manifested in Jesus Christ Himself, but nothing so great as this is recorded."[27]

The Gifts of Healing Are Operational in the Church Today. Paul writes of "gifts of healing" in 1 Corinthians 12:9. In the Higher Life and Alliance movements, we believe that these gifts of healing continue to function in the church today. A.B. Simpson and early Alliance churches recognized that the Holy Spirit would grant the gift of healing to some: "Just as God gives to some the special ministry of leading souls to Christ, so He gives to others as distinct a ministry in leading sufferers to receive the healing power of the Great Physician."[28]

Mrs. Etta Wurmser, Alliance pastor and Bible Institute Superintendent testified: "A great part of the flocks [Alliance branches] . . . received the baptism in the Holy Spirit with signs following. . . . , one would have the gift of healing, another the gift of interpretation, and we would be amazed at the wisdom given. Children began to open the Scriptures and old men and old women received the Holy Spirit."[29]

It is not so much that a person is a gifted healer, but rather that the Holy Spirit operates His gifts through whomever is available to be used by the Holy Spirit in healing ministry. A. B. Simpson, for example, never claimed to have a gift of healing; however, he did speak of how the Holy Spirit would work through him supernaturally: "Dear friends, I never feel so near to the Lord . . . as when I stand with the Living Christ, to manifest His personal touch and resurrection power in the anointing of the sick."[30]

Any of the gifts of the Spirit can be manifested through any consecrated person who is available to the Holy Spirit. The more that we pray for people to be healed, the more we will be used in a healing ministry, and the greater the healing anointing will flow. In order for a healing center ministry to be effective, we must not doubt that God intends for all gifts of the Spirit to be in operation today, and further to have an expectant attitude that those gifts will be manifested.

Note also that the text says, "gifts of healing," indicating that a multiple healing gifts may be manifested. One person may be used more effectively to pray for people with cancer, another more effectively to heal heart disease, another more effectively to heal mental illness. In all cases, the gift is a gift of healing to the person being healed.

Dispensationalism Diminishes the Power of the Holy Spirit. Dispensationalism is a form of cessationism, believing that the supernatural gifts of the Spirit belonged only to the apostolic dispensation of the first century. C&MA evangelist Armin Gesswein describes the destructive effects of dispensationalism to faith and the power of the Spirit:

Those who taught us the combination key [of dispensationalism] say, 'God doesn't do those things now. God doesn't work like that any more.'. . . Dispensationalism does not open the book of Acts and the power of God; it closes them. . . . it is arbitrarily superimposed by man. . . . Wherever dispensationalism gets in, it kills the deep spirit of prayer and revival. . . . But how bracing in this day of need to know that we are still in the dispensation of the Holy Spirit just as in the Acts, and that God can baptize and fill believers with His Spirit, set churches on fire, and through them bring sinner to repentance and to Christ. . . . For neither the promise of the Holy Spirit nor the promised

Holy Spirit has been withdrawn, except where men no longer want Him as the first Christians did.[31]

Biblical Principle 3:
It Is God's Will to Heal

"I am the Lord who heals you" (Exodus 15:26)

Along with Principles 1 and 2, this principle is foundational to effective Healing Center ministry. Much healing does not take place because people doubt it is God's will to heal. They will acknowledge, yes, God can heal; yes, God sometimes heals; but we cannot know if it is God's will to heal. If we don't believe that it is God's will to heal when we pray for a person, the faith level or expectation is lowered, and the likelihood of healing occurring is greatly diminished. However, we *can* know it is God's will to heal.

Because It Is His Nature to Heal and Restore. One of the primary names of God is Yahweh Ropheka, The Lord Our Healer (Exodus 15:26). God reveals that it is His nature and character to heal. He is a restoring and healing God. He is the Divine Physician. A.B. Simpson notes that God has made healing a part of His redemptive plan from the very start: "The Indians have a tradition that wherever the rattlesnake is found there always grows in the neighboring forests a little plant which is a certain antidote to the fatal sting. And so redemption springs in all its healing power amid the very earliest seeds of sin and misery, and God prepares His balm of healing even before the serpent has time to strike his fatal blow. How marvelous His resources! How wonderful His love!"[32]

Because Sickness Is Contrary to God's Kingdom. Jesus came to heal all who are oppressed by the devil (Acts 10:38). He told the disciples, "As you go, preach, saying the kingdom of heaven is at hand, heal the sick, raise the dead, cleanse, the lepers, and cast out demons" (Matthew 10:7-8). Healing was part and parcel of the Kingdom gospel message.

William C. Stevens, Early Alliance leader and Dean at Nyack Missionary Training Institute (Now Nyack College and Alliance Theological Seminary) asserted, "Sickness is contrary to the kingdom of heaven. . . . Disease is interference with His original and established laws. It is the sign of an invader somewhere in His kingdom. . . . God's answer is the restoration of His law from this daring infringement. . . . He treated sickness as a disorder in His kingdom, a menace to His honor and authority."[33]

Because God Is More Glorified by Sanctified Health. When Andrew Murray, a Scotch Dutch Reformed missionary to South Africa, lost his voice for two years, he struggled for quite some time over whether he should even pray for healing, wondering if the infirmity was more of a blessing than health. Eventually, though, Murray became convinced that it is God's will to heal. That is a vital key, Murray realized, to appropriating healing. Later, after his healing at Bethshan Healing Home in London, he wrote in reference to his former belief:

> It is a prevalent idea that piety is easier in sickness than in health, and that silent suffering inclines the soul to seek the Lord more than the distractions of life. For these reasons, sick people hesitate to ask for healing from the Lord. They believe that sickness may be more of a blessing to them than health. To think thus is to ignore that healing and its fruits are divine. . . . Although many sick people may have glorified God by their patience in suffering, He can be still more glorified by a health which He has sanctified.[34]

He found from his own experience that passively praying "if it be God's will" can sometimes hinder God's will from being done.[35]

Because Healing Is God's Normal Provision—A Redemption Right for the Believer. Jesus called healing "the children's bread," the provision that belongs to the children of God (Matthew 15:26; Mark 7:27). A.B. Simpson declared, "Divine healing . . . is His normal provision for the believer. It is something that is included in our redemption rights, something that is part of the gospel of His grace, something that is

already recognized as within His will and not requiring a special revelation to justify us claiming it."[36]

Biblical Principle 4:
Healing Is a Provision of the Atonement

"By His stripes you were healed" (Isaiah 53:5).

"Provision is made in the redemptive work of the Lord Jesus Christ
for the healing of the mortal body. Prayer for the sick
and anointing with oil are taught in the Scriptures
and are privileges for the Church in this present age."
—C&MA Statement of Faith

The last point of Biblical Healing Principle 3 leads into Principle 4:
Healing is a provision of the New Covenant, a right of redemption
through the atonement of Christ for our sins. "Atonement" is the theological word to express the work of Jesus Christ to die for or atone for
our sins on the Cross. Some have expressed its meaning simply as "at-
one-ment," meaning made one with God, reconciled with God,
redeemed from our sins. While that is the primary purpose of Christ's
atonement, many other effects or benefits result from what Christ has
done for us. Healing is one of those provisions of the redemptive work
of Christ on the Cross. The doctrine of healing in the atonement is
based upon three chief interrelated passages of Scriptures:

Surely our griefs [margin, "sickness"] *He Himself bore,*
And our sorrows [margin, "pains"] *He carried;*
Yet we ourselves esteemed Him stricken,
Smitten of God, and afflicted.
But He was pierced through for our transgressions,
He was crushed for our iniquities;
The chastening for our well-being fell upon Him,
And by His scourging we are healed (Isaiah 53:4-5).

And when evening had come, they brought to Him many who were demon-possessed; and He cast out the spirits with a word, and healed all who were ill; in order that what was spoken through Isaiah the prophet might be fulfilled, saying, "He Himself took our infirmities, and carried away our diseases" (Matthew 8:16-17).

He Himself bore our sins in His body on the cross, that we might die to sin and live to righteousness; for by His wounds you were healed (1 Peter 2:24).

This teaching recognizes that the Hebrew words for "griefs" and "sorrows" can carry the meaning of sicknesses and pains, and thus believes that healing is a privilege of believers through the Atonement, and can be claimed as a redemption right according to these passages of Scripture.

The Cross Is the Remedy for Both Sin and Sickness—A Redemption Right. A.B. Simpson explains, "If sickness has come into the world through sin, which is conceded, it must be got out of the world through God's great remedy for sin, the cross of Jesus Christ. . . . If healing is provided for by Jesus Christ, then it is a redemption right which we may humbly yet boldly claim while walking obediently with the Lord."[37]

Andrew Murray relates this redemption right to the New Covenant privileges we have in the New Covenant we have with Christ: "It is His Word which promises us healing. The promise of James 5 is so absolute that it is impossible to deny it. This promise only confirms other passages, equally strong, which tell us that Jesus Christ has obtained for us the healing of our diseases, because He has borne our sicknesses. According to this promise, we have right to healing, because it is a part of the salvation which we have in Christ."[38]

Healing Is the Children's Bread. When the Phoenician woman from Tyre brought her demonized daughter to Jesus, she asked Jesus to heal her daughter. Jesus responded that healing was "the children's bread," for those under God's covenant with Israel (Matthew 15:21-28). Because of her appeal and great faith, Jesus healed her daughter anyway, out of His mercy. The significance of Jesus' statement is that healing is "the children's bread"—a provision of being a child of God. I appropriated this truth during my cancer ordeal. Daily I proclaimed, "By His stripes I am healed." Over and over again every day, I played a Jewish song based on Isaiah 53, letting my mind soak with this truth of the Word of God. And I was healed!

Forgiveness and Healing Go Hand-in-Hand. We see this interconnection in Psalm 103:2-5: "Bless the Lord, O my soul, and forget not all His benefits: who forgives all your iniquities, who heals all your diseases, who redeems your life from destruction, who crowns you with loving kindness and tender mercies, who satisfies your mouth with good things, so that your youth is renewed like the eagle's." A.B Simpson comments on this: Why does he use the word 'redeem?' Simply because he is thinking . . . the healing of his diseases is through the redemption."[39]

By His Stripes We Are Healed from Both Sin and Sickness. A.B. Simpson declared, "As He has borne our sins, so Jesus Christ has borne away our sicknesses, yes, and even our pains, so that abiding in Him, we may be fully delivered from both sickness and pain. Thus 'For by His stripes we were healed!'"[40] Russell Kelso Carter, an associate of Simpson and author of the hymn "Standing on the Promises" further explains, "The clear meaning is, that Jesus did take upon Himself our diseases and mental trouble in precisely the same way that 'He bore our sins in His own body upon the tree.'"[41]

Christ Is the Sickness Bearer as Well as the Sin Bearer—Matthew 8:16-17. William C. Stevens declared that Matthew 8:1-17 is the "Magna Charta of divine healing."[42] A.B. Simpson affirmed, "Matthew's translation [of Isaiah 53:4] bears out in every part the application of this verse to the healing of the body."[43] A.J. Gordon asserted, "In the atonement of Christ there seems to be a foundation laid for bodily healing. . . . We have Christ set before us as the sickness bearer as well as the sin bearer of His people. . . . Something more than sympathetic fellowship with our suffering is evidently referred to here. The yoke of His cross by which He lifted our iniquities took hold also of our diseases. . . . The passage seems to teach that Christ endured vicariously our diseases as well as our iniquities."[44]

Jesus Suffered, Bled, and Died for Our Sickness as Well as Our Sins—1 Peter 2:24. Dr. T.J. McCrossan, C&MA pastor, professor, and Greek scholar, presented the biblical exegesis for this Scripture: "Here note two facts: (1) That the word for 'healed' here, both in the Septuagint and in the Greek New Testament is *iaomai*, a verb that always speaks of physical healing in the New Testament. . . . Yes, Peter here (1 Peter 2:24) clearly teaches that Christ not only suffered, bled, and died for our sins, but also for our physical healing."[45]

We Are Redeemed from the Curse of the Law—Galatians 3:13. In addition to the three interrelated passages, other Scriptures can be identified as well. F.F. Bosworth comments:

> In Gal. 3:13 we read: "Christ has redeemed us from the curse of the law, being made a curse for us.". . . What was the curse of the law? In Deut. 28 God names the blessings promised to the obedient, and then enumerates the curses that will fall upon those who will not hearken unto His voice and do all His commandments. He names the diseases which are known as 'the curse of the law.' . . . When Jesus redeemed us from the curse of the law, He redeemed us from . . . the whole list of diseases named in that curse. . . . Tell me the name of your disease and I will tell you one from which you have been redeemed and can be healed.[46]

A.B. Simpson explains further, "Of course we know that it was a far-reaching and eternal curse, but it was also a temporal curse, a physical curse, a curse involving sickness, suffering, infirmity, disease, pain. . . . Read Deut. 28:15-22. Therefore, it is perfectly scriptural to say Christ has redeemed us from consumption, fever, inflammation, having been made curse for us."[47]

A Balanced View of Healing in the Atonement. Some people erroneously come to the conclusion that since healing is provided in the atonement, full healing is guaranteed in this life. Some go so far as to claim that if people are not healed, they must be in sin or lack faith. Although these could be reasons why a person might not be healed, it unscriptural to blame all lack of healing on lack of faith or sin. While we believe that it is God's nature and will to heal, Simpson explains, "Divine healing fully recognizes the sovereignty of God and the state and spiritual attitude of the individual."[48]

Further, sanctification, or holiness, is also a provision in the atonement. But just as complete sanctification or sinlessness does not occur in this life, complete healing cannot be expected in this life. Higher Life leader R.A. Torrey, a friend of evangelist Dwight Moody and A.B. Simpson, explains:

> But while we do not get the full benefits for the body secured for us by the atoning death of Jesus Christ in the life that now is but when Jesus comes again, nevertheless, just as one gets the first fruits of his spiritual salvation in the life that now is, so we get the first fruits of our physical salvation in the life that now is. We do get in many, many, many cases of physical healing through the atoning death of Jesus Christ even in the life that now is.[49]

More will be discussed on this in Chapter 10 on "Pastoral Care for Those Who Are Not Healed."

For more on a balanced view on healing in the atonement, see Chapter 18 of *God's Healing Arsenal* on "Putting on the Breastplate of Righteousness," and Chapter 14 of my book *Only Believe* on "Faith and Healing in the Atonement." For Additional Resources on Healing in the Atonement, see Appendix 3.

Biblical Principle 5:
Faith Plays a Role in Healing

"Your faith has healed you."
(Matt. 9:22; Mark 10:52; Luke 7:50; 17:19; 18:42)

The author of Hebrews assures us, "Without faith it is impossible to please God" (Hebrews 11:6). The Apostle John declares, "This is the victory that overcomes the world—even your faith." (1 John 5:4). When we study the healing ministry of Jesus, we find that faith is mentioned about one-third of the time in relationship to healing. Faith is thus a vital component contributing to healing.

Higher Life and Alliance teaching recognized the importance of this principle. Simpson emphasized the real-life manifestation of the supernatural presence of God according to this Scripture, "I am courage in your difficulties . . ."[50] He believed, "All difficulties and dangers must give way before the omnipotence of faith. . . . Faith is . . . one of the attributes of God Himself. . . . There is no doubt that while the soul is exercising, through the power of God, the faith that commands what God commands, a mighty force is operating that moment upon the obstacle. God has put into our hands one of His own implements of omnipotence and permitted us to use it in the name of Jesus, according to His will and for the establishment of His Kingdom."[51]

Faith Is a Live Point of Contact with a Living Savior. A.B. Simpson explains, "Faith in connection with our healing. . . .[is] this point of contact, this organ of receptiveness, this open mouth of the soul—confidence in God, appropriating faith."[52] Simpson further asserts, "There is no power in prayer unless it is the prayer of God Himself. Unless you are in contact with Christ the living Healer, there is no healing. . . . Faith is more than believing; it is a living contact with a living Savior."[53]

God Is the Source of Healing; Faith Is the Channel. It is important to understand that faith is not the source of our healing. There are some who erroneously teach that it is our faith that heals. Rather, we need to be clear to understand that God is the Source; faith is the channel or conduit through which healing is obtained. Simpson explains: "It is not the faith that heals. God heals, but faith receives it."[54] Some people tend to call such belief in healing as "faith healing," but Simpson clarifies, "We are not advocates of 'faith healing' and never used that term. We do believe God heals His sick and suffering children when they can fully trust Him."[55]

Our Confidence Must Be in Christ and God's Character, Not in Our Faith. A.W. Tozer advises, "I cannot recommend that anyone have faith in faith. . . . Our confidence must not be in the power of faith but in the Person and work of the Savior Jesus Christ. . . . I have been memorizing the Scripture ever since I was converted, but my faith does not rest on God's promises. My faith rests upon God's character. Faith must rest in confidence upon the One who made the promises."[56]

Don't Have Faith in Your Own Faith. Some people claim you should have faith in your own faith. However, Higher Life faith leaders did not consider this biblical. A.B. Simpson cautioned, "Faith is hindered most of all by what we call 'our faith.'"[57] A.W. Tozer likewise warned, "Faith in faith is faith astray."[58]

Don't Try to Work Up Your Faith. A.B. Simpson testifies from his own experience: "If I need faith for anything, I don't try to work up faith, I don't agonize in prayer until I get a certain degree of faith; I just say, 'It is Your faith, not mine; You have it for me, just as You have the blood, and the power, and the cleansing, It is all Yours, and I just borrow it for the time. Lend me Your faith for this hour,' and I take His faith, and depend upon it to be mine, I go forward and act as if I had it, and I find that He meets me and gives me the blessing of confidence in His healing and His power."[59]

Claim the Faith of God. A.B. Simpson clarifies that "Jesus does not say to us, 'Have great faith yourselves.' But He does say, 'have the faith of God.'"[60] The faith of God is a perfect faith, mountain-moving faith, not an everyday faith. Thus, as Simpson counsels, we cannot just passively assume we have this kind of faith, but rather, "We must claim the faith of God, letting the Spirit of Jesus sustain our faith with His strong faith."[61]

Pray for Special Faith. A.B. Simpson advises us further, "If you have any question about your faith for this, make it a special matter of preparation and prayer. Ask God to give you special faith for this act. All our graces must come from Him, and faith among the rest. We have nothing of our own, and even our very faith is but the grace of Christ

Himself within us. We can exercise it, and thus far our responsibility extends; but He must impart it, and we simply put it on and wear it as from Him."[62] Simpson affirms, "This faith [Mark 11:22-24 and James 1:6-7] is a special work of the Holy Spirit."[63]

Let Jesus Work His Faith into Us. Carrie Judd Montgomery reminds us, "Jesus is the author and finisher of our faith, and He will work *His own faith* in our hearts. Let us give up our own poor attempts at faith and take the faith of the Son of God. The Lord Jesus has faith in His own power to make good all His promises."[64]

Then Act in Faith. Once we have claimed and prayed for this God-kind of faith, then we need to act our faith, Simpson asserts: "We believe that God is healing before any evidence is given. It is to be believed as a present reality and then ventured on. We are to act as if it were already true."[65]

But Act Only with Clear Assurance from God—Not on Human Faith or Word. Lest anyone misunderstand, Simpson further cautions, "Act your faith . . . not to show your faith, or display your courage, but *because* of your faith, begin to act as one that is healed. . . . But it is most important that you should be careful that you do not do this on any other human faith or word. Do not rise from your bed or walk on your lame foot because somebody tells you to do so. That is not faith, but impression."[66]

Faith Is Activated by Connecting with God. Simpson stresses the importance of personally connecting with God: "We must trust as if all depended upon God and we must work as if all depended on us. . . . The blessings which God has to impart to us through the Lord Jesus Christ do not wait upon some sovereign act of His will, but are already granted, completed and prepared and simply awaiting the contact of a believing hand to open all the channels of communication."[67]

These are principles that can help stir a sick person's faith to be increased, but even more to enhance the faith of those who are praying for and ministering to the sick. We must never make a person feel guilty for lack of faith. We must be careful not to tell people that they are sick or are not healed because they lack in faith.

We must recognize that when a person is not feeling well, they are not at the top of their game. Their faith is not going to be at its peak. To tell them they don't have enough faith to be healed will further discourage them. It also makes them think that their healing depends upon their performance.

Community Faith Enhances Healing; Community Unbelief Hinders Healing. In reality, people need the faith of others to bolster their own faith for healing. They need the Aarons and Hurs to lift up their hands when they are too weak to do so. It was the faith of the people who tore open the roof and lowered the paralyzed man down to Jesus who provided the environment for healing. Instead of pointing to the sick person for their lack of faith, the church community needs to point a finger at ourselves for our corporate lack of faith.

The chief reason for lack of supernatural signs and power acknowledged for centuries by evangelical leaders is unbelief. Consider the many voices who have acknowledged this:

- Lutheran 18th century Greek scholar Johann Bengel: "The reason why many miracles are not now wrought is not so much because faith is established, as that unbelief reigns."[68]

- German 19th century theologian Theodore Christlieb, professor of Bonn University: "It is the want of faith in our age which is the greatest hindrance to the stronger and more marked appearance of that miraculous power which is working here and there in quiet concealment. Unbelief is the final and most important reason for the retrogression of miracles."[69]

- Presbyterian/C&MA A.B. Simpson: "The signs of healing do not follow all believers, but they follow those who believe for the signs."[70]

- Dutch Reformed Andrew Murray: "If divine healing is seen but rarely in our day, we can attribute it to no other cause than that the Spirit does not act with power. The unbelief of worldlings and the want of zeal among believers stop His working."[71]

- <u>Baptist A.J. Gordon</u>: "Faith for healing cannot rise above the general level of the Church's faith."[72]

Simpson sums up the tenor of all these leaders, proclaiming, "We need a larger faith. . . . We need a faith that will personally appropriate all that we understand, a faith so large that it will reach the *fullness* of God's great promises. A faith so large that it will rise to the level of each emergency that comes into our lives."[73] Corporate faith will foster an environment in which God's healing power can be manifested more frequently and fully.

How to Implement This Principle of Faith in Your Healing Ministry. Encourage those to whom you minister to take these Higher Life steps of faith as led by the Holy Spirit. It is important to understand and communicate that these steps are not a formula, but tools by which God works, and conduits through which our faith is activated and exercised.

- *Believe it before you feel it.* Simpson explains, "It is not enough to think it, to feel it, to resolve it; we must say it. . . Speaking of the woman who touched Jesus' garment (Luke 8:48): "She did not feel first and then believe, but she believed and then she felt. But her blessing must be confessed. Christ will not allow us to hold His gifts without acknowledgement."[74]

- *Confess it before you see it.* Again, Simpson urges, "We must confess Him in order to be saved; so we must receive and keep our sanctification, our healing, and the answers to our prayers by acknowledging God, even before we see His working."[75]

- *Refuse the sickness.* John MacMillan exhorts, "We should claim this gracious relationship to the fullest degree for our own flesh and bones, and refuse the sicknesses that seek to fasten upon our physical frames."[76]

- *Take hold of your healing.* A.B. Simpson and Andrew Murray wrote about exercising a "faith that takes." By this, they meant that is not merely passively receiving healing, but actively taking hold of our healing. Simpson expressed this in his hymn:

> I clasp the hand of Love divine,
> I claim the gracious promise mine,
> And add to His my countersign,
> "I take"—"He undertakes."

> I take Him for this mortal frame,
> I take my healing through His Name,
> And all His risen life I claim,
> "I take"—"He undertakes."

> I simply take Him at His word,
> I praise Him that my prayer is heard,
> And claim my answer from the Lord,
> "I take"—"He undertakes."

- *Look to Jesus, not at your symptoms.* F.F. Bosworth illustrates:

God told Moses to lift up the brazen serpent, which was a type of Christ. Those who were dying were carried to where they could look at the type of Christ, and all who looked received the double cure and were healed (Numbers 21). . . . If the children of Israel could look at the type of Christ and received healing, why can not we look at the antitype, Christ Himself, and be healed? . . . Everyone who looked at the brazen serpent was healed. They didn't get healed looking at their swollen bodies that had been bitten by the serpents, but by looking at the type of Christ. You can never get faith by looking at symptoms or at yourselves, but you can look to Jesus, and meditate on God's faithfulness, until faith will come into existence without an effort, and then your diseases will evaporate like a mist before the sun.[77]

- *Draw your life from Jesus.* Mary Gainsworth, an Alliance pastor in Trenton, Ontario, who had a healing home and ministry endorsed by A.B. Simpson, shared her secret of health and healing: "I find that healing, like salvation, is retained by constantly looking to Jesus, drawing our life from Him moment by moment. Oh, it is a blessed experience to be leaning on His breast, breathing our very life from Him."

Biblical Principle 6:
Attitude Plays a Role in Health and Healing

"As a man thinks in his heart, so is he" (Proverbs 23:7).

Higher Life leaders were especially concerned about how our thoughts and words affect our health, citing the Scripture above. The context of the verse is that the self-centered thoughts of a greedy or selfish man cause him to become what he is—a self-centered person. Negative thoughts and attitudes adversely affect our behavior and character. Conversely, God-centered thoughts cause a person to be godly in nature and character. A.W. Tozer explained it this way: "To be right we must think right."[78] This verse can appropriately be applied to health as well. As our attitude is, so is our health. Many other Scriptures uphold the idea that our attitudes can influence and even determine the state of our health:

A joyful heart is good medicine, But a broken spirit dries up the bones (Proverbs 17:22).

For those who are according to the flesh set their minds on the things of the flesh, but those who are according to the Spirit, the things of the Spirit. For the mind set on the flesh is death, but the mind set on the Spirit is life and peace (Romans 8:5-6).

Finally, brethren, whatever is true, whatever is right, whatever is pure, whatever is lovely, whatever is of good repute, if there is any excellence and if anything worthy of praise, let your mind dwell on these things (Philippians 4:8).

Negative Attitudes and Words Can Affect Health. A.B. Simpson emphasized this biblical principle:

If you want to keep the health of Christ, keep from all spiritual sores, from all heart-wounds and irritations. One hour of fretting will wear out more vitality than a week of work, and one minute of malignity, or rangling jealousy or envy will hurt more than a drink of poison. Sweetness of spirit and joyousness of heart are essential to full health. . . . We do not wonder that some people have poor health when we hear them talk for half an hour. They have enough dislikes, prejudices, doubts and fears to exhaust the strongest constitution. Beloved, if you would keep God's life and strength, keep out of the things that kill it.[79]

Likewise, Carrie Judd Montgomery warned against people with negative attitudes and confessions. She cited a practical illustration in which a man went to the Bethshan Healing Home in England to receive prayer for healing:

He talked continually about himself and his symptoms, and this prevented him from getting hold on the Lord for healing. At last those who had charge of the Home told him that he would have to leave the Home unless he stopped talking about himself, and his bad feelings. They said, "You can talk about the Lord Jesus, but you must not say anything more about yourself." So when he would forget, and begin to say something about himself, they would lift a warning finger, and he would manage to change the sentence, before it was finished, into some word of praise or exaltation of the Lord Jesus. Not long after this the man was healed.

Positive Attitudes Can Enhance Health and Healing. Simpson further developed this line of thought in regard to sickness and healing, emphasizing not only the effects of negative attitudes, but the healing power of positive attitudes:

A flash of ill temper, a cloud of despondency, an impure thought or desire can poison your blood, inflame your tissues, disturb your nerves and interrupt the whole process of God's life in your body! On the other hand, the spirit of joy, freedom from anxious care and worry, a generous and loving heart, the sedative of peace, the uplifting influence of hope and confidence—these are better than pills, stimulants and sedatives, and the very nature of things will exercise the most benign influence over your physical functions, making it true in a literal as well as a spiritual sense, that "the joy of the Lord is your strength.[80]

Sarah Lindenberger, who supervised a healing home for more than thirty years, often cited, *"The joy of the Lord is our strength"* (Nehemiah 8:10). She called this verse "a stimulant, and a universal tonic . . . for the nerves, for headache and heartache, the blues and depression and sadness and selfishness, fear, worry and sleeplessness, and it will not fail if properly used for every ailment. It has proved most successful even in making homely people handsome, and disagreeable people really attractive, sweet and companionable. . . . Joy is our heavenly Physician's prescription for our physical strength."[81] She advised that it is a permanent prescription to be taken daily.

Sarah knew by the Spirit more than a century ago what medical doctors now know. In a doctoral class I was teaching on Divine Healing, a medical doctor shared that scientific studies demonstrate that attitude and positive actions such as praise and laughter change the bio-chemistry in the brain. Twentieth-century medicine discovered what Scripture already told us three thousand years ago, that *"A cheerful heart is like a medicine, but a crushed spirit dries up the bones"* (Proverbs 17:22).

Simpson, referring to this same proverb, counseled out of his own experience, "Joy is the great restorer and healer. Gladness of spirit will bring health to the bones and vitality to the nerves when all other tonics fail, and all other sedatives cease to quiet. Sick one, begin to rejoice in the Lord, and your bones will flourish like an herb, and your cheeks will glow with the bloom of health and freshness. . . . Joy is balm and healing; and if you will but rejoice, God will give power."

Biblical Principle 7:
Healing Is Enhanced in an Atmosphere of Faith

"When Jesus came into the official's house, and saw the flute-players
and the crowd in noisy disorder, He said, 'Leave; for the girl
has not died, but is asleep.' And they began laughing at Him.
But when the crowd had been sent out, He entered and took her
by the hand, and the girl got up" (Matthew 9:23-25).

"And He could do no miracle there except that He laid
His hands on a few sick people and healed them.
And He wondered at their unbelief" (Mark 6:5-6).

Even Jesus could do few miracles in an atmosphere of unbelief. Unbelief stifles the supernatural. F.F. Bosworth ponders this: "Think of it. Christ under the full anointing of the Holy Spirit, was hindered by community unbelief."

Before raising the young girl from the dead, he removed all unbelieving people and all negative influences from the room. He brought in only those who had faith—her parents and Jesus' three key disciples (Mark 5:35-42). Drawing upon Biblical Healing Principles 5 and 6, the early healing home ministries recognized that healing is nurtured in an environment of faith. William Boardman, who launched the Higher Life movement and helped with Elizabeth Baxter establish Bethshan Healing Home in London, called the healing home a "nursery of faith."[82]

Church historian Ronald Kydd thus describes such early healing home ministries as an "incubational" model of healing:

> The image of an incubator brings into mind specific associations. One is a nurturing hospitable environment in which a new baby is cared for. Another is progress and improvement over time. This is what the incubational ministries offer. They have grown out of the conviction that God wants to heal people, and they have introduced a unique feature: welcoming the sick into residences they have opened. There, over longer or shorter periods of time they pray for their recovery. Testimonies abound that the incubational approach to healing has been effective.[83]

C&MA leader Frederick William Farr explained this principle at Berachah Healing Home, "In the cure of souls a single treatment of a sermon or a public service, rich and powerful though it may be, may not always be effective. Some infirmities will only yield to patient, faithful treatment in a spiritual sanitarium where the time element can be taken into consideration and where correct habits of living can be formed and strengthening exercises of devotion can be engaged in."[84]

Biblical Principle 8:
Healing Involves the Whole Person— Body, Soul, and Spirit

"May your whole spirit, soul and body be preserved complete."
(1 Thess. 5:23)

On the basis of Biblical Healing Principles 4-7, healing home leaders recognized that healing involves the wholeness for the whole person. A.B. Simpson explains, "God has made us a trinity and there is an interdependence between spirit and soul and body which we cannot ignore. The presence of disease is a hindrance not only to our spiritual usefulness but to our higher experiences, . . . divine healing . . . has a reflex influence on every other part of our nature."[85]

Salvation Is Wholeness and Soundness. The Hebrew and Greek words for salvation encompass the meaning of wholeness for the whole person. Simpson explains, "The beautiful expression, 'your salvation' (Psalm 67:2), includes the idea, not only of salvation, but of healing, too, or, more correctly, of that fullness of blessing which the old word *health* so perfectly expressed. The Saxon *hale* gives us the perfect meaning, and it just describes the wholeness and soundness and wholesomeness which the gospel brings into all our life . . . enabling us to say, 'All is well.'"[86]

Holiness Is Wholeness. Simpson further connected health and holiness: "Healing is intimately connected with the spiritual life. . . . Holiness brings healthiness and helpfulness. Holiness is wholeness. A pure heart, a peaceful conscience, and a spirit of rest in God combine the elements that go to make up soundness. Joy is a stimulant, peace a sedative, righteousness a tonic better than all the drugs."[87] Again, Simpson explains, "Holiness is the best preservative of youthfulness, freshness, sweetness, and joy."[88] Andrew Murray also taught this principle: "The more we give ourselves to experience personally sanctification by faith, the more we shall also experience healing by faith."[89]

Whole Person Healing Principles. Sarah Lindenberger taught whole person healing more than half a century before the concept was popularized by Oral Roberts and others, writing in the Alliance journal in 1890, "Our spirit, soul, and body were included in the atonement of Christ." She taught in embryonic form the concept of inner healing of emotions and memories: "Christ has provided for the redemption and restoration of the human mind. . . . our sicknesses and mental pains."[90] Among her principles of whole person health and healing include the following which have continuing validity and value today:

- It is necessary to keep in a healthy and wholesome condition spiritually, nourished by the Word and fed daily by the Bread of Life. . . . The springing life throws off the devil's blows.

- Fear paralyzes and crushes the spirit and body. The devil can create feelings and symptoms and suggest imaginations to the mind, and hold the thoughts with pictures of some horrible danger impending, and if yielded to it will always wither the life. It is necessary to understand this and refuse to fear. We have known this awful fear to take hold of the mind, and to entirely control the thought of those under its power. It is devilish and must be refused and resisted, or the results are very serious, for it checks the inflow of life and cuts off the true source of help.

- A peaceful spirit is God's remedy, and it can be cultivated as a habit. The choice of the will is all that is needed, thus giving God an opportunity to manifest Himself as the God of peace.

- To rely upon our feelings and emotions and to look at symptoms is disastrous. It is in this way that the devil has tripped up many of God's own. The Word does not teach anything about feeling, but the call is a life of faith.

- Cultivate the habit of listening to God's voice in your soul, but beware of a bondage which the devil tries to throw over the conscientious child of God, and thus confuse the mind, get them under condemnation, and bring a fear of disobeying and later on mental confusion.

- Ask God to put in you a love—His love—for all that He would have you do, so that life will be a delight to you and everything easy.[91]

Resources for Implementing This Biblical Healing Principle.

- Read Chapter 7 of *God's Healing Arsenal* on "Treating the Whole Person: Healing Spirit, Soul, and Body."

- Read Chapter 8 of *God's Healing Arsenal* on "Setting Our Spirits Free and Restoring Our Souls."

Biblical Principle 9:
Discerning Root Causes May Be Key to Healing

"The axe is already laid at the root of the trees;
therefore every tree that does not bear good fruit is
cut down and thrown into the fire" (Matthew 3:10).

"Child, your sins are forgiven you" (Mark 2:5, literal translation).

Higher Life healing leaders understood from Biblical Healing Principle 8 that body, soul, and spirit are interrelated and affect one another. Oftentimes total healing involves bringing healing to spiritual or emotional issues which underlie the presenting physical condition. The axe needs to be laid to the roots of the unfruitful tree in a person's life before healing can be complete.

Before a person can be healed, Murray counsels from his own experience, he must discern the root causes of the illness and God's reason for allowing the illness: "If one is sick and desires healing, it is of prime importance that the true cause of the sickness be discovered. This is always the first step toward recovery. If the particular cause is not recognized, and attention is directed toward subordinate causes, or to supposed but not real causes, healing is out of the question."[92] A.J. Gordon explained further the need for discernment:

> For it is not alone that our poor diseased humanity needs a physician with divine skill to remove our deep-seated sicknesses, but especially one with divine insight to fathom and uncover them. The doctor's eyes are often more at fault than his hand. He cannot cure because he cannot comprehend the secret of our plague. How wonderful is the insight of the Great Physician. His penetrating glance goes to the root of disease when ours can only see the symptoms.[93]

The important feature here is to pray for discernment. It is the Divine Physician who perceives the deepest need. We need to be careful not to presume that we know but to let the Holy Spirit reveal the deeper roots. Some of the root causes may include:

- *Need for Confession and Repentance.* Although we must be careful not to blame all sickness or lack of healing on sin, we also acknowledge that confession and repentance often prepare the way for healing. "Confess your sins to one another that you may be healed (James 5:16). Blumhardt discovered in his pioneering healing home ministry, "Many of the repentant feel a new strength flow through them, which has a physically healing effect. It rejuvenates their whole appearance."

- *Past Unresolved Issues.* In the original Greek text of Mark 2:5, Jesus addresses the adult paralytic as "child," indicating that something occurred in the man's childhood which contributed to the man's paralysis. Commenting on this, A.B. Simpson recognized in this story the need for a deeper emotional and spiritual healing, writing, "In dealing with the sick, we must realize the deeper causes of their physical conditions."[94]

- *Preoccupation with Worldly Things.* Carrie Judd Montgomery observed that preoccupation with worldly things can prevent healing: "If the things of the world are precious to us we will be occupied with them, and will not render unto the Lord according to all that He hath done for us. After a failure of this kind I have often seen it very difficult for people to receive healing again from the hand of the Lord."[95]

- *Does the Person Really Want to Be Healed?* Related to discerning root causes is discerning whether or not a person really wants to be healed. Jesus asked, "What do you want Me to do for you?" He did not assume they wanted to be healed. Carrie would permit people to only stay a week unless special exceptions were made. That way, people would not stay indefinitely to wallow in attention-getting.

- *"Finer Touches."* Simpson also observed that mature Christians often have more problems with sickness than younger believers.

He described how some believers receive healing in their earlier Christian experiences, "but when we meet them a little later in their life, we often find them struggling with sickness, unhealed and unable to understand the reason of their failure."[96] This is not due to overt sin or lack of faith, but rather, "because God is leading them into a deeper spiritual experience. He is teaching them to understand His guidance, and some people cannot be guided any other way than by a touch of pain. . . . God is teaching them His finer touches."[97] In times like this God wants to work a "deeper healing." In such cases Simpson advises, "Our principal aim, therefore, should be to take our minds quite off our physical condition and the struggle for health, and to meet the Lord in His spiritual discipline. Then it will be very easy for Him to heal us, and our outward life will simply spring from inward conditions which must inevitably affect our whole physical being."[98]

Once we know the spiritual roots of sickness, Murray counsels, "One of the chief benefits, then, of divine healing is to teach us that our body ought to be set free from the yoke of our own will to become the Lord's property."[99] He explains, "This life of attention and action, of renouncement and of crucifixion, constitutes a holy life. The Lord first brings it to us in the form of sickness, making us understand what we are lacking. He then shows us by our healing, which calls the soul to a life of continual attention to the voice of God."[100] Murray thus believed that there is a close link between our holiness and receiving healing.

Sanctification and healing also go hand in hand: "The link between Holiness and Healing is a very close and blessed one."[101] Murray lays down this axiom: "The more we give ourselves to experience personally sanctification by faith, the more we shall also experience healing by faith."[102] Likewise, Simpson avowed, "There is a spiritual law of choosing, believing, abiding, and holding steady in our walk with God, which is essential to the working of the Holy Ghost either in our sanctification or healing."[103]

God gets greater glory from a believer's healing than from sickness. Simpson remarked that the "sanctifying influence of divine healing is greater than the sanctifying influence of sickness, and that the spiritual blessings which accompany healing have a greater value than the healing itself."[104]

Biblical Principle 10:
Focusing on the Healer, Not the Healing Is Essential

> ". . . fixing our eyes on Jesus, the author and perfecter of our faith"
> (Hebrews 12:2).

Be a Seeker of God Above All. Sarah Lindenberger emphasized that those who come to the healing homes should be first of "seekers of God," not seeking after healing. Simpson warned of the danger of focusing on trying to claim healing without understanding God's purposes before healing can come: "Some dear ones have been so anxious to get well, and have spent so much time in trying to claim it, that they have lost their spiritual blessing. God sometimes has to teach such souls that there must be a willingness to be sick before they are so thoroughly yielded as to receive His fullest blessing."[105]

Lindenberger shared the importance of this emphasis, especially in the ministry of holiness groups like the C&MA:

Many, very many, have found their Sanctifier here, and have learned the sweet secret that it is not a blessing they want, but the Blesser Himself, not an experience, but Jesus. . . . Often we have entreated our guests on their first arrival to banish all thought of healing, and whether they should live or die, fix all their attention on becoming wholly the Lord's. And then it was not too hard to claim the healing too, and it will come without much thought about it.[106]

We seek the Healer, not the healing. We seek not for our self, but for the glory of Christ. Otto Stockmayer, one of the early pioneers of healing homes, set this standard early on:

> God's children must not seek the healing of the body without taking at the same time by faith, all the new position which Christ's redemption gives us, . . . which amounts to this— Nothing more for self, but all for Christ. Before seeking freedom from sickness we must lay hold of the moral freedom which the Redemption of Christ has obtained for us, and by which we are cut off from any self-seeking: from the seeking of our own will, our own life, our own interests, or our own glory.[107]

Get Your Attention Off Yourself. Andrew Murray also stressed to trust God first and get attention off self: "Divine healing . . . calls us to turn our attention away from the body, abandoning ourselves—soul and body—to the Lord's care, occupying ourselves with Him alone."[108] Murray understood that any preoccupation with one's illness, including preoccupation with doctors and medicine, can be a stumbling block to healing: "Then the first thing to learn is to cease to be anxious about the state of your body. You have trusted it to the Lord, and He has taken responsibility." When we learn to trust the Lord, "Thus we learn to relinquish the care of our health entirely to Him. The smallest indication of the return of the sickness is regarded as a warning not to consider our body, but to be occupied with the Lord only."[109] Allowing our minds to dwell on our pains can hinder the healing process.

Healing Comes in Touching Jesus. Healing only comes by taking the attention off our self and putting it on Jesus. Only then can we receive healing. Simpson explains, "Unless you are in contact with Christ the living Healer, there is no healing. . . . Faith is more than believing; it is a living contact with a living Savior."[110] Simpson encourages us to take the hand of Jesus to receive healing: "We can touch each moment that conquering Hand that never lost a battle, that never relinquished a trust, that never grows weak or weary; and strong in the strength of Christ, we can do all things hand in hand with Him."[111]

Healing Is Not the End Goal. Further, healing is not the end goal; it is a means to the goal. The goal is the Higher Life—reaching for more of Jesus and His life operating in and through us, as A.B. Simpson explains:

> There is a still higher phase of this precious truth [Divine Healing] . . . "Your youth is renewed like the eagle's" (Psalm 103:5). This is the quickening life of Christ in our mortal flesh, giving vitality and spring to the body. . . . This is more than being healed of disease and redeemed from death. It is being quickened in the higher life and filled with the vigor and energy of our Lord.[112]

Likewise, Andrew Murray stressed that healing is not an end in itself, but a means: "Most Christians see nothing more in divine healing than a temporal blessing for the body, while in the promise of our holy God, its end is to make us holy."[113] A.B. Simpson captured this thought poetically with grace in his classic hymn "Himself":

> Once it was the blessing, now it is the Lord;
> Once it was the feeling, now it is His Word;
> Once His gifts I wanted, now the Giver own;
> Once I sought for healing, now HIMSELF alone.

For other resources on Biblical Healing Principles, see Appendix 3.

CHAPTER 4

Practices of Higher Life/Alliance Healing Centers

Biblical Practice 1:
Provide Instruction on Healing

> *"My people are destroyed for lack of knowledge."*—Hosea 4:6.

> *". . . but they did not know I healed them"*—Hosea 11:3.

The early healing homes focused on providing instruction on healing principles. "My people are destroyed for lack of knowledge," God prophesied through Hosea. People are often not healed because of lack of knowledge. They don't know they can be healed or don't know God wants to heal them or don't know how to be healed. In the Gospels, we see that the pattern Jesus practiced was that He taught the people, then He healed them. Instruction usually preceded healing.

The early healing home leaders recognized this biblical practice. A.B. Simpson described Berachah Home as "a Home of Rest, *Instruction* and Healing, in the Name of Jesus" (italics mine). Sarah Lindenberger describes the typical scenario at Berachah: "Most of those who come seeking health are at first very imperfectly prepared to receive it. They need much calm and patient teaching, and so many of them absorb it slowly, so that there is much need for rest and instruction, where their minds and hearts may be gently and fully prepared to take the Lord in deliberate, intelligent, and full committal."

Carrie Judd Montgomery likewise focused on what she called "full gospel" teaching. The purpose of her homes was to teach on healing and to encourage people to act in faith so that they could take hold of what God had already given to them. Because divine healing was not a popular subject in the church at the time, healing homes provided a safe environment for people to come and learn about this rediscovered biblical truth and to receive prayer for healing.

Implementing This Biblical Healing Practice in Your Healing Center. We encourage that the principles and practices presented in this manual be used in instructing people in the healing centers.

- Teach the ten principles in the prior chapter. Encourage seekers to confess these biblical principles. Provide a sheet with these confessions:

  ○ I believe that Jesus Christ is the same yesterday and forever (Hebrews 13:8).

  ○ I believe that God is still working supernaturally today through all the gifts of the Spirit (1 Corinthians 2:4-5; 4:20).

  ○ I believe it is God's nature and will to heal (Exodus 15:26).

  ○ I believe healing is provided in Jesus' atonement on the cross for the healing of my body and soul as well as for forgiveness of my sins (Isaiah 53:4-5).

  ○ I believe that without faith it is impossible to please God and that faith plays a role in healing. Lord, I believe, help my unbelief (Hebrews 11:6).

  ○ I believe my attitude affects my health and healing (Proverbs 23:7). I cast down imaginations and bring every thought captive to the obedience of Christ (2 Corinthians 10:4-5).

  ○ I fill my mind with godly, noble thoughts (Philippians 4:8).

○ I believe my healing is enhanced in an atmosphere of faith (Mark 6:4-6).

○ I believe that healing involves my whole person—body, soul, and spirit (1 Thessalonians 5:23).

○ I believe that my healing involves dealing with root causes (Matthew 3:10).

○ I will focus on the Healer, not the healing. I will fix my eyes on Jesus, not on myself, my symptoms, my concerns (Hebrews 12:2).

- Provide instruction on the biblical healing practices in this chapter, especially

○ To wait on God in stillness (Psalm 6:10).

○ To saturate in the Word of God (Psalm 107:20).

○ To examine yourself in preparation for healing (Psalm 139:23-24).

○ To maintain an environment that nurtures faith.

○ To receive the laying on of hands and anointing with oil (James 5:14-16).

○ To soak in repeated prayer (Matthew 7:7).

○ To exercise your authority as a believer (Luke 10:19; Matthew 16:19).

- Provide books, CDs, DVDs, pamphlets, bookmarks, and other materials on healing, faith, etc., as well as personal testimonies of healing. We hope to provide additional resources.

- Understanding who we are in Christ is key to a healthy attitude and acting and speaking in faith. We recommend giving to each seeker the "Who We Are in Christ" bookmark by Dr. Neil T. Anderson of Freedom in Christ Ministries.

- Use the following practical resources for instruction on living a sound and strong faith:

- ○ Paul L. King, *Moving Mountains: Lessons on Bold Faith from Great Evangelical Leaders* (can be used as a 12 week Bible study on faith).

- ○ Paul L. King, *Only Believe: Examining the Origins and Development of Classic and Contemporary Word of Faith Theologies.* (for an in-depth theological study on what is sound and what is not sound in the modern word of faith movement).

- ○ John A. MacMillan, *The Authority of the Believer.*

- Use the following practical resources for instruction on healing:

- ○ Paul L. King, *God's Healing Arsenal: A Divine Battle Plan for Overcoming Distress and Disease.*

- ○ David Smith, *How Can I Ask God for Physical Healing?* (available through C&MA Pastor David Smith, at the following email address: davidsmith@qcac.org).

Biblical Practice 2:
Wait on God

"Be still, and know that I am God" (Psalm 46:10).

"My soul waits in silence for God alone. My salvation [healing] comes from Him" (Psalm 62:1).

The Healing Power of Waiting on the Lord. The Hebrew word for salvation in Psalm 62:1 also means "healing, wholeness, victory." Waiting before the Lord spawns wholeness and healing and victory. Early healing homes understood this and focused on waiting on God as preparation for healing. Andrew Murray advised, "We need to train our people in their worship more to wait on God, and to make the cultivation of a deeper sense of His presence, of more direct contact with Him, of entire dependence on Him, a definite aim of our ministry."

This was such an important step in the healing process that Sarah Lindenberger writes, "We always urge our guests to wait upon the Lord until they see every stopping of the Word of God—if this is not done, there is always failure."[114] Many Scriptures demonstrate the value of waiting on the Lord:

- *We are clothed with the power of the Spirit.* "You are to stay in the city until you are endued with power from on high" (Luke 24:49).

- *We renew our strength.* "They who wait upon the Lord shall renew their strength. . ." (Isaiah 40:31).

- *We receive an inheritance.* "Wait for the Lord and keep His way, and He will exalt you to inherit the land" (Psalm 37:34).

- *We will have new courage.* "Wait for the Lord; be strong and let your heart take courage; yes, wait for the Lord" (Psalm 27:14).

- *Our vision will be fulfilled.* "For the vision is yet for the appointed time; it hastens toward the goal and it will not fail. Though it tarries, wait for it; for it will certainly come, it will not delay" (Habakkuk 2:3).

God Works His Healing in Stillness. Sarah Lindenberger considered waiting on God in stillness as a practical application of the Sabbath Rest principle for restoration of the body. Many Scriptures demonstrate how God works in us His healing powers as we rest in Him and seek His presence:

- *God De-stresses Us in Stillness.* Literally, Psalm 46:10 can be translated, "Relax—cease striving—and know that I am God."

- *God Molds Us in Stillness.* Martin Luther translated this verse, "Be silent unto God, and let Him mold you!" Ironically, doing nothing in the presence of God actually accomplishes something.

- *God Restores Us in Stillness.* He calls us to the rest that restores us in our weariness:

   "Therefore let us be diligent to enter that rest" (Hebrews 4:11). The Greek word for rest is *katapausis*, from which we get the

English word "pause." God calls us to pause. We could paraphrase the verse, "Be diligent to press the pause button in your life."

- *God Reveals Himself More Fully and Intimately in Stillness.* "Be still and KNOW [intimately] that I am God." The Hebrew word for "know" means to know by acquaintance, by experience—to know intimately.

- *God Speaks in the Stillness.* "The Lord said, 'Go out and stand on the mountain in the presence of the Lord, for the Lord is about to pass by." Then a great & powerful wind tore the mountains apart and shattered the rocks before the Lord, but the Lord was not in the wind. After the wind there was an earthquake, but the Lord was not in the earthquake. After the earthquake came a fire, but the Lord was not in the fire, and after the fire came a gentle whisper [still, small voice]. . . . Then a voice said to him, "What are you doing here, Elijah?" (1 Kings 19:11-13)

- *God Manifests His Presence in Stillness.* "Be still before the LORD, all mankind, because he has roused himself from his holy dwelling" (Zechariah 2:13).

- *God Opens Our Eyes and Activates Angels in Stillness.* "And when he had opened the seventh seal, there was silence in heaven about the space of half an hour. And I saw the seven angels which stood before God" (Revelation 8:1-2).

- *God Reenergizes Our Strength in Stillness.* "Be silent before me, you islands! Let the people renew their strength!" (Isaiah 41:1). Bethany Faith Home in Pittsburgh was described as a place where "there they learn to become acquainted with God, drawing health from God Himself, and deep spiritual drafts of light and truth, that fill with peace and rest, and end in joy."[115]

The Power of Stillness. A.B. Simpson emphasized this power of stillness for healing and wholeness. He quoted Mrs. Brodie from the Healing Home ministry in England: "When we reach the point of stillness in Christ then the blessing will come. If the soul is agitated or troubled there is necessity for getting still before God. If this unrest comes from unanswered prayer perhaps the praying even must be stopped for a time. Above all things, get still. Give Him a chance to talk to you and He will soon begin. Then while you are occupied with Him you will soon find He is being occupied with you, and if your great need is physical healing it has begun in the moment of stillness."[116] He described his personal experience poetically:

Many years ago, a friend placed in my hand a little book
which became one of the turning points of my life.
It was called *True Peace.*
It was an old medieval message,
and it had but one thought, and it was this
—that God was waiting in the depths of my being
to talk to me if I would only get still enough to hear His voice.
I thought this would be a very easy matter, and so I began to get
still.But I had no sooner commenced than
a perfect pandemonium of voices reached my ears,
a thousand clamoring notes from without and within,
until I could hear nothing but their noise and din.
Some of them were my own voice;
some of them were my own questions,
some of them mere my own cares,
some of them were my very prayers.
Others were the suggestions of the tempter
and the voices from the world's turmoil.
Never before did there seem so many things
to be done, to be said, to be thought;
and in every direction I was pushed and pulled,
and greeted with noisy acclamations and unspeakable unrest.
It seemed necessary for me to listen to some of them
and to answer some of them;
but God said, "Be still, and know that I am God."
Then came the conflict of thoughts for tomorrow,
and its duties and sorrows,

but God said, "Be still."
And as I listened, and slowly learned to obey,
and shut my ears to every sound,
I found after a while that when the others voices ceased,
or I ceased to hear them,
there was a still, small voice in the depths of my being
that began to speak with an inexpressible tenderness,
power, and comfort.
As I listened it became to me
the voice of prayer,
and the voice of wisdom
and the voice of duty.
And I did not need to think so hard,
or pray so hard,
or trust so hard,
but that "still, small voice" in my heart
was God's prayer in my secret soul,
was God's answers to all my questions,
was God's life and strength for body and soul,
and became the substance of all knowledge,
and all prayer, and all blessing;
for it was the living God Himself as my life,
and my everything.

Beloved! This is our spirit's deepest need.
It is thus that we learn to know God;
it is thus that we receive spiritual refreshment and nutriment;
it is thus that our heart is nourished and fed;
it is thus that we receive the Living Bread;
it is thus that our very bodies are healed,
and our spirit drinks in the life of our risen Lord,
and we go forth to life's conflicts and duties
like the flower that has drunk in, through the shades of night,
the cool and crystal drops of dew.

But as the dew never falls on a stormy night,
so the dews of His grace never come to the restless soul.
We cannot go through life strong and fresh on constant express trains,
with ten minutes for lunch;
but we must have quiet hours, secret places of the Most High,
times of waiting upon the Lord, when we renew our strength,
and learn to mount up on wings as eagles,
and then come back to run and not be weary,
and to walk and not faint.
The best thing about this stillness is
that it gives God a chance to work.

Implementing This Biblical Healing Practice in Your Healing Center. We encourage you to do the following things in putting this principle into practice:

- Share A.B. Simpson's poetic testimony and other testimonies.

- Share these Scriptures in this section with those who come to your healing center.

- Set aside times of stillness before the Lord for both prayer team partners and those who are receiving prayer.

- Set aside times of stillness for those who are ministering to the sick. As we are still before the Lord, we will receive insight into the person's needs. This will be explored further in the section on having a listening ear.

- Ask those receiving prayer to read Chapter 21 of *God's Healing Arsenal* on "The Overcoming Power of a Lifestyle of Peace."

- Make available and encourage them to read Andrew Murray, *Waiting on God.*

- Encourage seekers to pray this prayer of Andrew Murray:

  Some of us are weary, and the time of waiting appears long. And some of us are feeble, and scarcely know how to wait. And some of us are so entangled in the effort of our prayers and our work, we think that we can find no time to wait continually. Father! teach us all how to wait. Teach us to think of each other, and pray for each other. Teach us to think of You, the God of all waiting ones. Father! Let none that wait on You be ashamed. For Jesus' sake. Amen.

Biblical Practice 3:
Saturate in the Word of God

"He sent His word, and healed them, and delivered them
from their destructions" (Ps. 107:20).

To be fed the Word of God enhances healing. James urges us, "in humility receive the word implanted, which is able to save your souls" (James 1:21). The Greek word for "save" is *sozo*, and can also mean "heal, make whole." To have the Word of God implanted within us, saturating us, brings healing to our souls.

Saturate in God's Word. Andrew Murray had lost his voice for two years due to stress on his vocal chords from frequent speaking. He visited the Bethshan Healing Home in London, staying there for three weeks seeking God and meditating upon the Word of God in an atmosphere of faith and peace. He received counsel and prayer from Pastor Otto Stockmayer, the Swiss pastor who began a ministry of healing homes for the purpose of providing a spiritually therapeutic atmosphere. Murray was gradually but miraculously healed, never to have serious trouble with his voice again. Rather, in his later years, even when his body was frail and weak, his voice boomed out strong.

Out of his own experience, Andrew Murray believed in the creative soaking power of the Scriptures to produce health and strength: "Let the Word create around you, create within you a holy atmosphere, a holy, heavenly light, in which your soul will be refreshed and strengthened for the work of daily life."[117]

Read Much of the Word Daily. Wheaton College president Charles Blanchard, a friend of A.B. Simpson, wrote of the healing power of

Scripture, describing how a physician prescribed to a depressed, nervous, sick woman to read the Bible an hour for thirty days then come back and see him. She eventually obtained an appetite for the Word and came back to the doctor a different woman. He told her, "I saw as soon as you came into the room that what you needed was not medicine nor anything else that man could give or do. What you needed was God. You have now come in touch with Him. Keep in touch with Him and you will be well."

Meditate on the Word Daily. To George Müller, the great apostle of faith, renewing and strengthening a positive attitude of the inner man daily is an essential prerequisite. He accomplished this by establishing a habit of walking and meditating on the Word of God before breakfast each morning. Considering it food as nourishment for the inner man, Müller claimed this practice was also beneficial to his health. His own testimony after forty years of this faith walk was: "I cannot tell you how happy this service makes me. Instead of being the anxious, care-worn man many persons think me to be, I have no anxieties and no cares at all. Faith in God leads me to roll all my burdens upon Him." One of his biographers, Roger Steer, noted, "Müller's longevity (he died when he was ninety-two) surely confirms his insistence that he was not worn out by worry."[118]

Confess the Word Daily. "Faith comes by hearing, and hearing by the word of Christ" (Romans 10:17). A.B. Simpson advocated making confessions of faith from Scripture, declaring, "It is not enough to think it, to feel it, to resolve it; we must say it. . . . We must confess Him in order to be saved; so we must receive and keep our sanctification, our healing, and the answers to our prayers by acknowledging God, even before we see His working."[119]

Charles Spurgeon testified of the power of speaking his faith in his own experience: "I find that if I can lay a promise under my tongue, like a sweet lozenge, and keep it in my mouth or mind all day long, I am happy enough."[120] He taught that we use the shield of faith by quoting the promises of God, speaking the great doctrines of the faith, claiming observations from examples in Scripture, and recalling what God has done in our life in the past.[121]

Oswald Chambers also counsels us to speak our faith according to Romans 10:9-10: "In the Bible confession and testimony are put in a prominent place, and the test of a person's moral character is his 'say so.' I may try and make myself believe a hundred and one things, but it will never be mine until I 'say so.' If I say with myself what I believe and confess it with my mouth, I am lifted into the domain of that thing."[122] We want to make clear that this does not mean that you can confess and possess or name and claim anything that you want to, but only what God wills. God does will our healing, so it is right and proper to confess Scriptures relating to healing.

Another Baptist Higher Life leader, F.B. Meyer, advised that even when we do not feel healing change in our body, we should make faith concrete through repeated confessions: "Dare to repeat it often, though you do not feel it, and though Satan insists that God has left you, 'You are with me.' Mention His name again and again, 'Jesus, Jesus, You are with me.' So you will be conscious that He is there. . . . Say over and over, 'I thank You, O my God, that You have kept Your word with me. I opened my mouth, and You have filled it; though as yet I am not aware of any change.'"[123]

A Personal Testimony of Soaking in the Word. In my book *God's Healing Arsenal.* I share my own experiences of the power of soaking in the Word of God daily:

> After seeing excesses in faith teaching, I had become skeptical of confessing healing by faith, but I had become sick and could not get well even with medicine and prayer. My Christian doctor said he did not know why I was not getting well because the medicine should work. He counseled me to take it to the Lord. So I prayed, and the Lord showed me that I had not only abandoned unsound teaching on faith but also sound teaching on faith. So I began daily to confess healing and to give thanks to God for the healing. Within thirty days, I was healed!

All throughout my ordeal with cancer I daily confessed healing and overcoming Scriptures. It changed my perspective and attitude and instilled me with greater confidence. After my surgery, my mind was in such a fog from both the pain and the medications that I could not pray, or read my Bible, or even think. Yet words of Scripture surfaced through the fog of my muddled mind to give me hope and encouragement.

Implementing This Biblical Healing Practice in Your Healing Center. Here are some practical ways you can encourage this practice among the people who come for ministry in your healing center:

- Encourage people to spend much time in the Scriptures.
- Provide a CD or MP3 with Scriptures for them listen to over and over.
- Concentrate especially on Scriptures dealing with healing (such as those listed in Appendix 2 of this Manual)
- Encourage them to hear the Word over and over, confess the Word over and over, and personalize the Word to themselves.
- Have significant Scriptures relating to healing mounted on posters or plaques on the wall.
- Play worship music with Scriptures in the background.
- Ask those receiving prayer to read Chapter 26 of *God's Healing Arsenal* on "Sword of the Spirit I: The Overcoming Power of the Word of God" and Chapter 27 on "Sword of the Spirit II: The Overcoming Power of Biblical Meditation."

Biblical Practice 4:
Examine Yourself in Preparation for Healing

> *"Search me, O God, and know my heart; try me and know*
> *my thoughts, and see if there be any wicked way of pain in me,*
> *and lead me in the everlasting way" (Psalm 139:23-24).*

"Confess your faults to one another, and pray for one another,
that you may be healed" (James 5:16).

Since healing involves wholeness for the whole person, this means searching our hearts to see if we find any spiritual or emotional impediments to healing. We must be careful on one hand not to assume that some issue in the person's life has caused the person to be sick or is preventing the person from becoming healed, but, on the other hand, we want to encourage the person to seek the Lord to see if He will reveal some issue.

Through Repentance. In the Scripture cited above, James declares that confession and repentance prepare the way for healing. Johannes Blumhardt discovered this in his premier healing home ministry: "Many of the repentant feel a new strength flow through them, which has a physically healing effect. It rejuvenates their whole appearance."

In the early 1890s, Pastor Philpott, a Canadian Baptist, contracted a severe throat condition in which he was told by the doctors he would have to give up preaching. He had gone to an Alliance healing meeting, where John Salmon (founder of the Alliance in Canada) and Dr. R.J. Zimmerman were speaking and anointing people with oil. He recalled "I was so disgusted at what I then thought was the biggest lot of humbug I had ever heard from religious teachers, that I left the service before it was half over."

However, as his condition worsened, the Holy Spirit kept bringing to his mind James 5:14. The only people he knew who anointed with oil for healing were Salmon and Zimmerman, but he was so prejudiced against them that he avoided them for some time. Finally, he relented, went to Bethany Healing Home, confessed his unbelief and prejudice, and asked Salmon and Zimmerman to anoint him with oil and pray for him. He was healed instantly that night. The next Sunday he preached three services, and over the next two weeks preached 2-3 times daily at a camp meeting. Eight years later, he continued to testify that he had preached nearly every day since then without a problem.[124]

Through Harmony with God's Will. A.B. Simpson stressed the need of preparing people for healing by bringing them into harmony with God's will: "We shall often find that God is dealing with men and women through their very sickness and we want to be careful first to get them into harmony with His will and spiritually prepared for the blessing of healing."[125]

Through Yielding in Humility. Carrie Judd Montgomery counseled, "The sick one may say, 'I do not know of anything wrong in my heart or life.' But if there is a delay in healing, if there is difficulty, if faith does not spring up in the heart, there must be a yielding to God in great humility, and brokenness of spirit, for God to search the very inmost being. He alone can show the reason why faith does not spring up and take full possession of the heart."

We do not want to assume that a person has some fault to deal with, but we do want to encourage the seeker be totally honest and open before God. We urge them to pray the prayer of Psalm 139, "Search my heart, O God." When the person is totally surrendered to God, the Holy Spirit may reveal some area that needs to be confessed or changed.

Implementing This Biblical Healing Practice in Your Healing Center. Here is a practical way you can encourage this practice among the people who come for ministry in your healing center:

- Have those coming to receive prayer read *How Can I Ask God for Physical Healing?* by David Smith. This C&MA pastor has provided a wonderful guide based on this biblical practice for people to prepare their hearts for healing. Writing from a pastor's heart, he outlines a process for personal healing. This is not meant to be a formula, but flexible guidelines in seeking the Lord for how you can overcome. I would encourage you to follow this process to help seekers prepare themselves to overcome their distress or disease. Give them a handout with these steps below. Guide them in meditating upon and praying over each step.

Before Praying for Victory or Healing Ask Yourself These Questions:

- *Need:* What is my real need?
- *Want:* What do I want Jesus to do for me?
  - Crystalize your desire.
  - Cultivate what you want.
  - Resist what you don't want.
  - Refine your desires.
- *Lessons:* What is God teaching me through this affliction?
  - God knows what you need.
  - Desire God Himself.
  - Grow deeper in His ways.
  - Dig further into wisdom.
- *Scripture:* What do I believe the Bible says about healing and overcoming?
- *Love:* Does God love me?
- *Faith:* Will God give me victory or heal me, and will He do so at this time?
- *Causes:* What is the underlying cause of my distress or sickness?
- *Barriers:* Am I removing barriers to victory or healing?
- *Deliberation:* Have I thoroughly prepared my inner life through interior rest and through upward praise?
- *Commitment:* Am I ready to give myself totally to God?

While You Are Praying for Victory or Healing Ask Yourself These Questions:

- *Readiness:* Which Scriptures am I claiming for my healing or overcoming my distress?
- *Others:* Have I called others to pray?
- *Ask:* Am I ready to ask God to heal me or to give me the power to overcome my distress?
- *Authority:* Do I need to exercise authoritative faith?

- *Sensations:* Are there further triggers of faith that God gives?
- *Encounter:* Is my authentic faith leading to an encounter with the risen Christ?

After Prayer for Overcoming or Healing Ask These Questions:

- *Do:* Am I believing and acting like I have overcome or God has healed me?
- *Trials:* Am I prepared for trials of faith?
  - Confront temptations.
  - Understand God's timing.
  - Persevere in faith.
- *Abide:* Am I continuing to draw life from the risen Christ?
  - When God says not yet.
  - When God says no.
- *Providence:* Am I trusting Christ even if He has not healed me or I have not received an answer to my prayer?
  - Understand Paul's testimony.
  - Discern God's hand at work.
  - Abandon self to Divine Providence.
  - Experience personal transformation.
  - Gain strength to live with pain.
- *Living:* After my healing or victory over distress, am I a changed life?
  - Drawing life from Christ.
  - Renewed strength.
  - Spiritual breathing.
  - Divine health, freedom, and victory.
  - Living for God's pleasure.
- *Purpose:* Am I using my new strength, health, and victory for God?
  - God heals you or enables you to overcome for a purpose.
  - God did not heal you or give you victory for yourself.

- God's grace compensates when you are not healed or do not receive the answer to prayer.
- God renews your strength.[126]

Recommended Resource

David J. Smith, *How Can I Ask God for Physical Healing?* Grand Rapids: Chosen Books, 2004.

Biblical Practice 5:
Provide an Atmosphere of Faith

"And He did not do many miracles there because of their unbelief"
(Matthew 13:58).

"They began laughing at Him. But putting them all out,
He took along the child's father and mother and
His own companions, and entered the room
where the child was" (Mark 5:40).

Where unbelief reigns, the power of God is extinguished. Where faith abounds, the supernatural power of God is released. It is not that Jesus was powerless, but that the power of God only operates in an environment of faith. James cautions us, "But he must ask in faith without any doubting, for the one who doubts is like the surf of the sea, driven and tossed by the wind. For that man ought not to expect that he will receive anything from the Lord, being a double-minded man, unstable in all his ways" (James 1:6-8).

When people are not feeling well, they are not at the top of their game. Their faith is not going to be at its strongest. They do not need to be berated for lack of faith. They need to be bolstered in their faith. Like Moses, when they are weary in battle, they need Aarons and Hurs to come alongside and lift up their sagging arms. As a community of healing, we need to provide an environment of faith for them. The early healing homes recognized this need and its biblical basis.

When the paralyzed man was let down through the roof to Jesus by his friends, Scripture records, "And Jesus seeing their faith said to the paralytic, 'Son, your sins are forgiven'" (Mark 2:5). And then Jesus healed him. Not on the basis of the paralyzed man's faith, but on the basis of the environment of faith which his friends had provided by their actions.

When the little girl had died, Jesus sent all the mourners and scoffers out of the room. He rid the location of unbelief and doubt. He brought in the hopeful parents and His faithful, believing disciples. In that ambience of faith, He raised the little girl from the dead (Mark 5:35-42).

The disciples followed this model of Jesus. When the faithful disciple Tabitha (also known as Dorcas) died, Peter sent all the mourners out of the room. He then prayed over her, spoke to her, and raised her from the dead (Acts 9:36-42).

The Power of a Faith Filled-Atmosphere. Notice in these Scriptures the power of an environment filled with faith:

- "And these signs shall follow them who believe" (Mark 16:18). "These signs shall follow THEM—the Church, not 'him'—the individual. It was not the faith of a lone solitary evangelist but that of a Spirit-filled Church which brought healing to the streets of Jerusalem after Christ had gone away."—F.F. Bosworth

- "They were continually devoting themselves to the apostles' teaching, and to fellowship and to the breaking of bread and to prayers. Everyone kept feeling a sense of awe; and many wonders and signs were taking place through the apostles" (Acts 2:42-43).

- "They lifted up their voices to God with one accord and said, 'Grant that Your bondservants may speak Your word with all confidence while You extend Your hand to heal, and signs and wonders take place through the name of Your holy servant Jesus.' . . . . And when they had prayed, the place where they had gathered together was shaken, and they were all filled with the Holy Spirit and began to speak the word of God with boldness" (Acts 4:24, 29-31).

- "At the hands of the apostles many signs and wonders were taking place among the people and they were all with one accord in Solomon's portico" (Acts 5:21).

Implementing This Biblical Healing Practice in Your Healing Center. We can provide an environment of faith by dispelling unbelief and through faith-filled words and actions. Here are some practical ways you can encourage this practice and strengthen the faith of the people who come for ministry in your healing center:

- *Provide Testimonies.* Hearing how God has touched other people's lives with His healing power enhances the faith of the sick person. "They overcame by the blood of the Lamb, by the word of their testimony, and they loved not their souls unto death" (Revelation 12:11). Part of the instruction was given through people who had themselves been healed, not only sharing their testimony of healing, but practical instruction on the process through which they obtained their healing. Sarah Lindenberger explains:

  Here the seeker of God . . . is brought into actual contact with those who have passed through the very experiences that he or she is passing through, and these witnesses to God's power and grace, which are constantly met, become an inspiration, an encouragement to hope, and a pattern for imitation, which mere abstract teaching could never affect. And so these things grow real in light of another's victorious life and the timid one is led to step out to follow on in the footsteps that mark the way the Shepherd leads.[127]

- *Create an Expectancy of Healing.* For Simpson, an optimistic attitude, rather than pessimism, can have a positive effect on health. In his pamphlet *How To Receive Divine Healing,* he counseled not to expect sickness: "Don't expect to have a spell of weariness and reaction," but rather "just go calmly forward, . . . expecting Him to give you the necessary strength to carry you through." Again, A.B. Simpson exhorts, "Expect the Lord to prove the reality of His power and to give the signs which He has promised. . . . We may expect this latter rain."

- *Foster a Peaceful Atmosphere.* Montgomery founded "Faith Rest Cottage," explaining, "The peace and quietness which pervade our little Home, and communion with those of like precious faith, will often aid the dear, struggling ones to come into the place of victory."[128]

- *Pray Together as a Church for the Spirit to Move.* F.F. Bosworth avowed, "A Spirit-filled and praying church produces an atmosphere in which it is easy for God to work and hard for the devil to interfere, because this atmosphere is the Holy Spirit Himself, who is more than a match for the devil."

- *Fill the Atmosphere with Praise.* "God inhabits [is enthroned upon] the praises of His people" (Psalm 22:3). Paul Billheimer, in *Destined for the Throne*, describes this environment of faith-filled praise: "God dwells in an aura, an atmosphere, an enswathement of praise. Where there is joyful praise, there He is dynamically and benevolently active. Where there is adoration, reverence and acceptable worship & praise, there He openly manifests His presence. His presence expels Satan. Satan is allergic to praise. Where there is massive triumphant praise, Satan is paralyzed, bound and banished."[129]

- *Provide Respite Care.* Sometimes people just need a break or a change of pace. The healing center provides periodic temporary visits in order to seek physical healing and spiritual refreshment. Carrie Judd Montgomery wrote that "so many sick ones are harassed by family cares at their own home, that they cannot take the necessary time for Bible study in this direction."

- *Provide a SWAT Team.* Read Chapter 12 in my book *God's Healing Arsenal*, on "Gathering Your God Squad—God's Overcoming

SWAT Team." There I describe how when I was going through my ordeal with cancer, God led me to put together a SWAT team, a God Squad, to help provide counsel and fight the battles with me. We can provide those who come to us for prayer a SWAT team to help reinforce their faith.

- *Bind Hindering Spirits.* Sometimes people bring with them the evil spirits that are harassing them in body, mind, emotions, and spirit. This does not necessarily mean the need for casting out demons, but it does mean rebuking evil influences and hindering spirits that would hinder the healing process. Alliance missionary John MacMillan would quietly bind spirits of fear, rebellion, bitterness, dissension, etc., whenever he perceived hindering spirits. As a result, it transformed the atmosphere and people were set free, put at peace, and received wholeness. Jesus gave authority to us as His disciples over such forces: "Whatever you bind on earth shall have been bound in heaven and whatever you loose on earth shall have been loosed in heaven." (Matthew 16:19).

- *Release Healing Power.* We have authority to loose as well as to bind. We bind hindering spirits; we loose or release the power of the Holy Spirit to heal and angels to minister. Jesus declared to the woman with hemorrhage of 18 years, "Woman, you are loosed from your sickness" (Luke 13:12).

- *Encourage the seeker* to read Chapter 15 of *God's Healing Arsenal* on "Worship Before Warfare: The Overcoming Power of Worship."

- *Play Worship Music.* A.W. Tozer declared, "The Presence of God is more important than the program." Provide an atmosphere that manifests the presence of God. "God inhabits the praises of His people" (Psalm 22:3). God often touches a person in body, soul, and spirit in the midst of worship. In your healing center, you could have a live worship team or a CD playing worship music in the background. Songs that focus on the majesty and compassion of God, the presence and power of Jesus, healing, and overcoming can foster that ambience of faith. Here are some suggested worship songs, CDs, DVDs, and MP3 (note that these are by no means all or even the most current songs and media, just some suggestions of what have been especially helpful for me).

○ Marcus and Joni Lamb, *Healing Waters* CD/DVD. Daystar.com Includes songs such as "Rise and Be Healed," "Healing in This House," and healing Scriptures and meditations.

○ Songs "Show Me Your Face," and "In Your Presence, O Lord" on the CD, Paul Wilbur, *Lion of Judah*. Hosanna/Integrity Music.

○ Song "By His Wounds We Are Healed" on the CD *Ancient Words* by Integrity Music.

○ "Show Me Your Face" on the CD *Ancient Words* by Integrity Music.

○ *God's Grace: Integrity Music's Scripture Memory Songs*, Integrity, 1992.

○ *Overcoming Anxiety: Integrity Music's Scripture Memory Songs*, Integrity.

○ *Personal Victory: Integrity Music's Scripture Memory Songs*, Integrity.

○ *Healing: Integrity Music's Scripture Memory Songs*, Integrity.

○ *Power of Thanksgiving: Integrity Music's Scripture Memory Songs*, Integrity.

○ *Renewing Your Mind: Integrity Music's Scripture Memory Songs*, Integrity.

○ *Spiritual Warfare: Integrity Music's Scripture Memory Songs*, Integrity.

○ Charles Wesley, "And Can It Be."

○ "In Christ Alone."

○ "You Are God Alone."

○ The music group Selah's CD *Hiding Place* has healing songs such as "You Raise Me Up", "I Need Thee Every Hour," "You Are My Hiding Place," "Through It All."

- *Encourage a Joyful Spirit.* Charles Spurgeon, who had a strong healing ministry with thousands of people healed through his prayers, advised, "Let your conscious feebleness provoke you to seek the means of strength: and that means of strength is to be found in a pleasant medicine, sweet as it is profitable—the delicious and effectual medicine of 'the joy of the Lord.'"[130]

- *Encourage Seekers to Focus on Jesus.* In our healing rooms we instruct the people being prayed for to focus on Jesus and be in an attitude of receiving from Him, and not be occupied with praying for themselves because we are focusing on that. Just be still before the Lord and receive from Him.

He is the author and perfecter of our faith (Hebrews 12:2). S.D. Gordon wrote, "A right mental attitude exerts enormous influence. . . . this is the process of faith at work, a simple faith in Christ, in-breathed by the Holy Spirit. . . . That mental attitude [thinking on Christ] will vitally and radically affect your body."[131] Hudson Taylor likewise exhorts us to focus our mind on Christ: "How then to have our faith increased? Only by thinking of all that Jesus is and all He is for us: His life, His death, His work, He Himself as revealed to us in the Word to be the subject of our constant thought."[132]

The classic Higher Life faith writers taught that a positive mental attitude *can* affect one's health and outcome of life. However, it is not by our own mental effort, but by letting our thoughts dwell on Jesus and His Word. Higher Life healing pioneer Charles Cullis gives us timeless counsel: "The promises are revealed to those who are 'looking unto Jesus.'. . . If you are constantly 'looking unto Jesus,' you will be kept in perfect peace and safety." Early Methodist leader Hester Ann Rogers testified of such health: "By constantly looking to Jesus, I receive fresh strength in every time of need."

- *Encourage Seekers to Avoid Negative Attitudes of Fear, Doubt, and Anxiety.* Just as a positive mental attitude may result in positive effects such as healing, so negative attitudes may result in negative effects. The 17th century French archbishop Fenelon, precursor of Higher Life thinking, warned about the consequences of a negative mental attitude: "The strivings of the human mind not only impair the health of your body, but also bring dryness to the soul. You can actually consume yourself by too much inner striving. . . . Your peace and inner sweetness can be destroyed by a restless mind."[133]

Charles Spurgeon suffered much pain from his gout and fell into deep depressions, but also found the importance of this principle, testifying, "Worry kills, but confidence in God is like healing medicine."[134] Spurgeon's friend F.B. Meyer avowed that negative thinking can even cause illness: "The healthiest people do not think about their health; the weak induce disease by morbid introspection."[135] Moreover, Simpson warned, "Worry, fear, distrust, care—all are poisonous!"[136]

- *Encourage Seekers to Speak Positively, Not Negatively.* In her healing homes, Carrie Judd Montgomery would not permit negative speaking, stressing Proverbs 18:21, "Death and life are in the power of the tongue." She taught that there is a "connection between a sanctified tongue and divine health in body."[137] Negative speaking reflects an unsanctified tongue and leads to the opposite of divine health.

- *Instruct Seekers to Repeat Scriptures on Faith.* As stated earlier, "Faith come through hearing, and hearing through the word of Christ" (Romans 10:17). The more that we speak and hear the Word of God, the more it is ingrained in our minds and hearts. As Scriptures on faith become internalized within us, our faith is increased and the likelihood of healing increases as well. See Scriptures on faith and healing in the Appendix.

- *Make Available Other Resources to Encourage Faith.*
  - ○ Read Chapters 22 and 23 of *God's Healing Arsenal* on "The Overcoming Power of the Shield of Faith" and "The Overcoming Power of Acting Your Faith."
  - ○ George Muller, *The Autobiography of George Muller.*
  - ○ Charles Price, *The Real Faith.*

Biblical Practice 6:
Lay on Hands and Anoint with Oil with the Prayer of Faith

Laying on of hands and the use of anointing oil are not required in healing centers but are biblical practices that were almost always used in early healing homes as an enhancement of faith. They were called by early Higher Life leaders such as Andrew Murray and A.B. Simpson as "points of contact." The concept of a point of contact as an expression of faith is rooted in two biblical passages, especially in relationship to healing: 1) James 5—anointing with oil and laying on hands, and 2) Mark 5:27-28—the woman touching the hem of Jesus' garment. In these Scriptures, touch or physical contact appears to be an aid or accompaniment to faith.

Andrew Murray seems to be one of the earliest, if not the earliest, leaders to speak of laying on of hands and anointing with oil as points of contact. He explains this concept:

Sometimes a man needs a visible sign, appealing to his senses, which may come to the aid to sustain his faith and enable him to grasp the spiritual meaning. The anointing, therefore, should symbolize to the sick one the action of the Holy Spirit who gives the healing. . . . We also should regard it, not as a remedy, but as a pledge of the mighty virtue of the Holy Spirit, as a means of strengthening faith, a *point of contact* and of communion between the sick one and members of the Church who are called to anoint him with oil.[138]

Points of Contacts Are Stepping Stones to Our Faith. A.B. Simpson expands upon Andrew Murray's teaching, viewing anointing oil as a means of enhancing faith, "Jesus still uses a few outward signs as stepping-stones to our faith. Anointing with oil in the name of the Lord is not a means in a medical sense; it is simply an outward sign to suggest through the senses more vividly the spiritual reality which it signifies. . . . The Lord addresses us through every vehicle which can convey to us His thought and His touch."[139]

A Point of Contact Is Touching Jesus Himself. It is important to understand that anointing oil and our hand have no intrinsic power in themselves. Any point of contact must involve touching Jesus Himself. A.B. Simpson tells us the key: "It involves not only our hand but His personality. Faith must recognize the Lord Jesus Himself and come into immediate contact with Him before it can draw His healing virtue or His comforting love."[140] Andrew Murray counsels us, "Let each contact with the blood be contact with the Lamb, more particularly with His gentleness and meekness. Let your faith touch just the hem of His garment and power will go out from Him."[141]

A Point of Contact Is a Touch of Faith. A.B. Simpson understood that for laying on of hands and anointing oil to be effective, faith must be exercised: "There is a touch of faith as well as a touch of God. . . . The blessings which God has to impart to us through the Lord Jesus Christ . . . are already granted, completed and prepared and simply awaiting the contact of a believing hand to open all the channels of communication."[142]

Points of Contact Have No Inherent Healing Power. A.B. Simpson clarifies, "Hezekiah's sickness was a fatal one. It is foolish to talk about his being healed through a mere poultice of figs of a disease that was declared by God Himself to be unto death. . . . The figs (used by Isaiah on Hezekiah's disease) were merely a sign to help his faith to rise from the natural to the supernatural, just as the oil of anointing is a sign of the touch of the Holy Spirit, but has not in itself any inherent healing power."[143]

Distinguish from Counterfeit Healing Touch Methodologies and Beliefs. Higher Life and Alliance leaders were careful to distance themselves from questionable healing beliefs and practices, such as Christian Science, healing by magnetism, or hypnotism. In addition to these, many other New Age beliefs and practices have infiltrated society and often even the church, such as Reiki, Therapeutic Touch, and psychic healing. Advise seekers to avoid such beliefs, practices, and groups.

Implementing This Biblical Healing Practice in Your Healing Center. Here are some practical ways you can encourage this practice and strengthen the faith of the people who come for ministry in your healing center:

- *Be sure to ask the person permission to lay on hands.* Some people do not like to be touched, especially by someone they do not know and especially if they have been physically abused.

- *When appropriate, lay hands on the part of the body needing healing.* Jesus sometimes touched a particular part of a person's body for healing—putting his fingers in the ears of a deaf mute and touching his tongue with His own saliva (Mark 7:33-34). On other occasions he put saliva or mud on the eyes of the blind (Mark 8:23-25; John 9:6-7).

  If the physical need is not near a private part of the body, ask if it is OK to lay hands (foot, hand, shoulder, head, back, etc.) If close to a private part, then have the person lay hands on their own body. Sometimes the touching of a knee by someone of the opposite sex could be viewed as inappropriate. We would suggest that if a man is praying for a woman's knee (or vice versa) to have the person put his/her hand on the knee and then put your hand on that person's hand.

- *Explain the biblical purpose of anointing with oil (James 5:14-16).*

- *You can anoint with oil by placing oil on your fingers and then laying your hand on the top of the person's head or by anointing the forehead.*

Although it is not necessary, I make the sign of the cross on the person's forehead. In some situations, you may be able to anoint the part of the body affected by sickness or injury.

• *When the power of God is manifested, tell them it is not a magic power.* Sometimes laying hands on a particular part of the body will stir a healing sensation. Power can be transmitted through a physical touch when done in faith and when we make real contact with Christ. A touch in faith may at times result in physical manifestations from the Holy Spirit such as heat, electrical impulse, falling, or swooning, etc., but they are not always to be expected or sought.

At the Berachah Healing Home, when a worker laid her hand on the right leg of a woman's named Mrs. Dean who had problems with her legs due to a spinal condition, Mrs. Dean immediately had a "prickling, tingling sensation." Later she felt a twitch in her back that enabled her to sit upright. When she laid her hands on Mrs. Dean again, Mrs. Dean felt the prickling sensation again. As A.B. Simpson counsels, "This does not mean some kind of magic or magnetic power possessed by some individuals enabling them to remove diseases by a touch."[144] Rather, this is the supernatural power of God.

• *Instruct the person, "You can activate your faith by laying hands on yourself."* You can tell the person, "You may not have someone nearby to lay hands on you, but you can lay hands on yourself in faith—touching and praying over a particular part of your body that is diseased or in pain." As a professor in the Missionary Training Institute at Nyack, New York, John MacMillan shared with his students one of his secrets of receiving healing and maintaining health. He made it his practice daily to lay hands on various parts of his body, praying for divine healing and health in each part. In this way he experienced the divine energizing he talked so much about throughout his writings."[145] He acted out his faith, combining his belief in the believer's authority and exercising this principle of point of contact.

One example that he shared was that just after leaving a building following anointing another missionary, MacMillan slipped on an incline by a spring and painfully twisted his ankle on a stone. Placing his hands on the injured spot, as was his custom in prayer, he prayed for healing. He records that he received an instant answer to prayer—no sprain or swelling, just a bruise, and he gave God the glory![146]

- *Instruct the seeker, "Don't depend upon the touch or feeling—Depend on Jesus."* A.B. Simpson counseled, "Just identify yourself with Jesus, and say, 'Jesus is within; not I, but Christ; He is my righteousness and my faith, and He is my bodily life too.'. . . Be sure that you do not depend upon the anointing, be sure that you do not depend upon the touch—these are like Gehazi's staff. Be sure that you do not depend on any feeling. Be sure that you are not looking for any thrill or any physical sensation. Keep your mind off all these."[147]

- *Pray specifically.* Related to laying hands on the afflicted part of the body is the concept of praying specifically. Speak to the mountain of difficulty. Here are some examples of how to pray specifically:

  - Pray that whatever is blocking lungs from receiving oxygen be removed in Jesus Name!

  - Pray that any fluid buildup in lungs or anywhere else be expelled from the body.

  - Pray for heart to be strengthened.

  - Pray for better blood flow and oxygen to be delivered to every organ with every heart beat beginning immediately.

  - Pray for supernatural strength for and supernatural wisdom for the doctors and nurses assisting them.

  - Pray, "I curse every cancer cell in this person's body. I command every cancer cell to wither and die, never to return. I declare this person is redeemed from the curse of cancer."

○ Pray, "I rebuke formulation of fistulas, stenosis of the bowels, inflammation of the intestines."

○ Pray, "I speak to the spine to come into proper alignment according to the Word of God which says, 'I will make the crooked places straight'" (Isaiah 55:2).

Good resources for how to pray specifically for certain physical conditions or diseases include the following:

- Hunter, Joan. *Healing the Whole Man Handbook: Effective Prayers for Body, Soul, and Spirit.* Kingwood, TX: Joan Hunter Ministries, 2005, 2006.

- *How to Minister to Specific Diseases,* Spokane, WA: Healing Rooms Ministries, revised 2005.

Biblical Practice 7:
Soak in Longer Repeated Persistent Prayer

"Ask and it shall be given to you; seek and you shall find, knock and the door shall be opened unto you" (Matthew 7:7).

"Is anyone among you sick? Then he must call for the elders of the church and they are to pray over him, anointing him with oil in the name of the Lord; and the prayer offered in faith will restore the one who is sick, and the Lord will raise him up, and if he has committed sins, they will be forgiven him. Therefore, confess your sins to one another, and pray for one another so that you may be healed. The effective prayer of a righteous man can accomplish much" (James 5:14-16).

All too often we do not see answers to prayer because we do not persevere in prayer. We live in a microwave society in which everything is instant. God certainly does heal instantly, as I have both witnessed and personally experienced on several occasions.

Nonetheless, it often takes repeated prayer to spark an answer. Daniel prayed 21 days before he received an answer. George Müller wrote that he had prayed for some things 3000 times. Great revivals are born out of hours, months, and even years of prayer. So why shouldn't this apply to healing as well?

Actually, it does. James exhorts ongoing action of confession to one another and prayer for one another. The use of the present tense in in this passage means continual or repeated confession and prayer, not a one-time action. Many times we do not see answers to prayer for healing because we do not persevere in prayer for healing. Two minutes of prayer may sometimes get results, but perhaps more often, it is repeated prayer over time—hours, days, weeks—that yields an effect.

Repeated Prayer Is Like a Battering Ram. Healing home pioneer Johannes Blumhardt believed that repeated prayer was especially effective as spiritual warfare:

> How many attacks does it take before the walls of a well-entrenched city are breached? Our prayers, it might be said, are hammer-strokes against the bulwark of the princes of darkness; they must oft be repeated. Many years can pass by, even a number of generations die away. However, not a single hit is wasted; and if they are continued, then even the most secure wall must finally fall. Then the glory of the Lord will have a clear path upon which to stride forth with healing and blessing for the wasted fields of mankind.[148]

Repeated Prayer Is Like a Sitz Bath—Soaking Prayer. Today this concept is called "soaking prayer." We all know how soothing soaking in a bathtub can be. This is even more so when we need healing. When I had colorectal cancer, during my treatments I was instructed to take sitz baths for about 20 minutes daily due to blisters from radiation. Those baths were soothing and healing. In the same way, soaking in prayer can be like a soothing and healing sitz bath.

Although there is a time in which it is appropriate to pray only once and then praise God from that point forward, more often we need repeated prayer. In Jesus' Sermon on the Mount, when He exhorted, "Ask and it shall be given to you, seek and you will find, knock and the door will be opened to you," literally He was saying, "Ask and keep on asking; seek and keep on seeking; knock and keep on knocking."

In 1909 a man dying of tuberculosis came to see Mary Loud, pastor of the Alliance Faith Mission in East Weymouth, Massachusetts. She anointed him with oil, assisted by her husband, a layman, and after a half hour of prayer, he was healed instantly. If she had just anointed him with oil and expected immediate results, he would have left unhealed. Because she and her husband took time to soak the man in prayer, he was miraculously healed!

Repeated Prayer Is Like a Labor and Delivery Room. Intercessory prayer is often called "travailing prayer." It is like going through the birthing process of labor. Paul likened spiritual formation to pregnancy, "My dear children, for whom I am again in the pains of childbirth until Christ is formed in you" (Galatians 4:19). One of the earliest African-American healing evangelists who operated a healing home was Sarah Mix, through whom Alliance healing home leader Carrie Judd Montgomery was healed. Sarah probably served typically as a midwife in the African-American 19th century tradition, so it was natural for her to be regarded somewhat as a spiritual midwife, birthing healing as she prayed for people over a period of time. One woman named Mrs. G.A. Wilton, who was in despair over being an invalid, described the prayer ministry of Sarah Mix over her: "In less than an hour after she began to labor with me, I got up, dressed, and walked out into the other room as well as anybody, perfectly free from pain and all my lameness gone."[149]

Repeated Prayer Is the Divine Physician's Treatment Plan. Just as a medical doctor might prescribe a repeated treatment for an ailment, or a chiropractor might give repeated adjustments, so the Divine Physician may have a prayer treatment plan over a period of time. Jesus gave the second touch to the blind man who received a partial healing, saying, "I see men as trees walking." Sarah Mix would make repeated visits to a sick person's home like a doctor making house calls. A woman named Mrs. Sarah Burr bedfast with numerous illnesses recounted, "She came full of faith believing the Lord would raise me up and restore me to health, and after the first treatment, I walked out of my bedroom across the sitting-room and back, and from that time there was a change."[150]

Consider this example from one of the early healing homes, which we mentioned earlier, of God as the Divine Chiropractor. In July 1899 Mrs. N. S. Dean, who had been bedfast or wheelchair bound for 17 years due to a spinal condition, was dramatically healed after one of the workers spent about six hours in prayer for her. She testified, "I stood upon my feet twice, which I had not done for 17 years." The worker continued to pray five hours a day for three weeks, resulting in stiff and atrophied muscles being strengthened. One day her ribs creaked "like an old saddle" as they were adjusted into proper place through prayer. Her short leg was lengthened an inch with a grating sound.

Implementing This Biblical Healing Practice in Your Healing Center. Here are some practical ways you can encourage this practice and strengthen the faith of the people who come for ministry in your healing center:

- *Take your time in praying.* Don't be rushed. Spend time waiting on God. Take 20-30 minutes to pray for the person. Some of the early healing room workers would spend hours in prayer over a person.

- *Pray Scriptures over the person.* Use the list of healing and over-coming Scriptures in the Appendix of this manual. Personalize the Scriptures for the person and his or her need.

- *If the person is not healed or is only partially healed, don't give up.* Continue to pray—again and again. In 1897, the young son of a woman in Montana suffered a scrotal hernia from a fall. Because he was so frail, it was too dangerous to have surgery. The mother heard about the Alliance healing prayer meetings, and took her son for prayer, but he was not healed immediately. For three months she continued to take him weekly for prayer, and the hernia disappeared without medication or surgery.

- *Encourage the person to pray or receive prayer daily or weekly, like a daily radiation treatment.* When I was treated for cancer, I received radiation therapy five days a week for several weeks. It would take just a few minutes of zapping me from three different angles. Over time the tumor was reduced in size. In fact, it was reduced much more than they expected it to be through the radiation treatment. That is because I was also receiving daily spiritual radiation treatment through prayer. The radiation did what it could do, and God did the rest!

As another example, when my son Chris had Crohn's Disease, we would gather as a family each evening for about 5-10 minutes soaking him in prayer like daily radiation treatments. Although he was not healed at that time, he did from time to time receive some measure of relief from pain. This is what various studies have shown—that progressive healing takes place over time.

- *Encourage the person receiving prayer to read Chapters 29 and 32 of* God's Healing Arsenal on "More Principles of Overcoming Prayer Power" and "The Overcoming Power of Standing Firm."

Biblical Practice 8:
Exercise the Authority of the Believer

"But as many as received Him, to them He gave the right [authority] to become children of God, even to those who believe in His name" (John 1:12).

"Behold, I have given you authority to tread on serpents and scorpions, and over all the power of the enemy, and nothing will injure you" (Luke 10:19).

John 1:12 proclaims that believers have authority as a child of God. John MacMillan asserts that it is available as the right of every believer: "Such authority is not the property only of a few elect souls. On the contrary, it is the possession of every true child of God. It is one of the 'all things' received in Christ."[151] Even the weakest and most uneducated believer, declares MacMillan, "is able by the cross and its conquest of the powers of hell" to drive away the fiercest foes.[152]

From the very beginning of the Healing Home movement, the doctrine of the authority of the believer was recognized and practiced. Johannes Blumhardt learned to understand and exercise this authority during the two-year deliverance of the demonized woman in his congregation. "Jesus is Victor!" was his cry as the woman was set from the oppression and control of evil powers. This was the very impetus of the healing home movement.

The Higher Life movement, especially through the Christian and Missionary Alliance, was on the forefront of pioneering teaching and practice of the authority of the believer initially through A.B. Simpson, George Watson, and other early Alliance leaders, C&MA missionary John MacMillan wrote the original book *The Authority of the Believer*, beginning with a series of articles in *The Alliance Weekly* in 1932, then compiled with other material and published as a book. These are Higher Life/Fourfold Gospel principles of the authority of the believer.

Believers Have the Authority of Faith. Based on Jesus' words to the seventy disciples in Luke 10:19, A.B. Simpson asserted,

> He did not promise the disciples power first, but the authority first; and as they used the authority, the power would be made manifest, and the results would follow. Faith steps out to act with the authority of God's Word, seeing no sign of the promised power, but believing and acting as if it were real. As it speaks the word of authority and command, and puts its foot without fear upon the head of its conquered foes, lo, their power is disarmed, and all the forces of the heavenly world are there to make the victory complete.[153]

Believers Have Throne Rights Through Throne Union. Expanding upon A.B. Simpson's teaching, John MacMillan taught that believers have the right to assert "in prayer the power of the Ascended Lord, and the believer's throne union with Him. . . . Where in faith the obedient saint claims his throne-rights in Christ, and boldly asserts his authority, the powers of the air will recognize and obey."[154]

Therefore All Things Are Under Our Feet as Christ's Body. Citing the Scripture, "He has put all things under His feet" (Ephesians 1:22), MacMillan comments, "The feet are members of the Body. How wonderful to think that the least and lowest members of the Body of the Lord, those who in a sense are the very soles of the feet, are far above all the mighty forces."[155]

Believers Are God's Law Enforcement Officers. A.B. Simpson again declares, "'I give you authority.' This is the policeman's badge which makes him mightier than a whole crowd of ruffians because, standing upon his rights, the whole power of the state is behind him. . . . Are we using the authority of the name of Jesus and the faith of God?"[156]

We Lack More Power Because We Do Not Claim Our Authority. Simpson stresses the importance of operating in the authority we have been given:

This was the secret of Christ's power that He spoke with authority, prayed with authority, commanded with authority, and the power followed. The reason we do not see more power is because we do not claim the authority Christ has given us. The adversary has no power over us if we do not fear him, but the moment we acknowledge his power, he becomes all that we believe him to be. He is only a braggart if we will dare to defy him, but our unbelief clothes him with an omnipotence he does not rightly possess.

God has given us the right to claim deliverance over all his attacks, but we must step out and put our foot upon his neck as Joshua taught the children of Israel to put their feet upon the necks of the conquered Canaanites, and faith will find our adversaries as weak as we believe them to be. Let us claim the authority and the victory of faith for all that Christ has purchased and promised for our bodies, our spirits, or His work."[157]

Implementing This Biblical Healing Practice in Your Healing Center. Here are some practical ways you can encourage the people who come for ministry in your healing center to exercise their authority as a believer:

- *Teach these principles on the authority of the believer.*

- *Make available to seekers these materials on the authority of the believer and ask them to read them.*

  ○ John A. MacMillan, *The Authority of the Believer.*

  ○ K. Neill Foster and Paul L. King, *Binding and Loosing: Exercising Authority over the Dark Powers.*

  ○ Chapter 30 in *God's Healing Arsenal* on "Praying with Commanding Confidence."

- *Teach seekers to use their authority over sickness to claim health and healing.* Healing is a privilege for the Christian as a provision of the atonement and needs to be affirmed actively and strenuously, as MacMillan asserts, "We should claim this gracious relationship to the fullest degree for our own flesh and bones, and refuse the sicknesses that seek to fasten upon our physical frames."[158]

- *Speak to the mountain with commanding faith.* John MacMillan counsels, "The command of faith is the divine means of removing [mountains] out of the way: 'You shall say to this mountain, Be removed and be cast into the sea; and it shall obey you.' The question involved is not that of an imposing faith, but that of an all-sufficient Name. . . . As he speaks to the mountain in the name of Christ, he puts his hand on the dynamic force that controls the universe. Heavenly energy is released, and his behest is obeyed."[159]

- *Speak to the roots of the disease or to the cause of the symptoms.* MacMillan suggests this practice: "It is a good exercise to 'say' aloud to our difficulties, as we kneel in prayer, 'Be thou removed.' The *saying*, if in faith in the name of the Lord, will cause a stirring at the roots; and as we keep steadfastly holding to God and *saying*, the time will come when the tree which has been opposing, or the mountain which has been hindering, will quietly move into the sea of oblivion."[160]

- *Declare that the person is redeemed from the curse of the disease.* F.F. Bosworth explains, "In Gal. 3:13 we read: 'Christ has redeemed us from the curse of the law, being made a curse for us.'. . . Tell me the name of your disease and I will tell you one from which you have been redeemed and can be healed."[161] A.B. Simpson adds, "Of course we know that it was a far-reaching and eternal curse, but it was also a temporal curse. . . . Therefore, it is perfectly scriptural to say Christ has redeemed us from consumption, fever, inflammation, having been made curse for us."[162]

- *Speak forth a blessing upon the person.* Not only do we rebuke a curse and any fear associated with it, but positively we speak a blessing. A.B. Simpson explains, "The blessing of Moses seems to suggest this danger and to answer this fear. 'Let Reuben live and not die, and let not his men be few' (Exod. 30:6)."[163]

- *Lead the seeker in taking back ground by actively refusing illness, not passively acquiescing to it.* John MacMillan exhorts that we should positively resist the devil and refuse what comes to us from him: "We must also cooperate with Him—against the things and the forces which assail our individual lives with a faithful and firm refusal of their right to control our bodies or our circumstances. Too often the Christian passively accepts whatever comes to him as being the will of the Lord, yielding without resistance at times to the wiles of the enemy himself. . . . That 'God has spoken' is the ground upon which every forward step in the spiritual life must be taken."[164]

- *Teach seekers to rebuke the Enemy themselves.* MacMillan speaks prophetically and forcefully, "God throws upon man the responsibility for the continuation of the conditions we question. . . . We realize they are the working of the enemy. We cry to God to rebuke the enemy and to alter things. Through the teaching of the Word, He replies, 'My children, rebuke the enemy yourselves. The authority over him is yours. Its responsibility I have committed to you.'"[165] Ultimately, we need to be teaching those who are seeking prayer to take authority themselves and maintain their own victory.

- *Exercise the authority of binding and loosing.* Jesus declared to His disciples, "Whatever you bind on earth shall have been bound in heaven; whatever you loose on earth shall have been loosed in heaven" (Matthew 16:19). This concept was taught and practiced by many in the Higher Life movements, including Andrew Murray, A.B. Simpson, Jessie Penn-Lewis, and especially John MacMillan. In his classic book *With Christ in the School of Prayer,* Andrew Murray advocated that we pray, "Grant especially, blessed Lord, that your Church might believe that it is by the power of united prayer that she can bind and loose in heaven, cast out Satan, save souls, remove mountains, and hasten the coming of the kingdom."[166]

  o <u>Bind the Strong Man in the Person's Life</u>. John MacMillan practiced this frequently in real life experience on the mission field: "The way out is blocked—is it not a gracious call to prayer, lest the great adversary block our efforts and shut us up in a small place? We have prayed for the binding of the strongman—we must watch and pray that the strong man does not bind us."[167]

  o <u>Bind Spiritual Forces, Not People</u>. MacMillan cautions misuse of this practice: "The authority committed to the believer is over the powers of the air and never over his fellowmen or their wills. He is called to bind the unseen forces, but to deliver his brethren."[168]

○ Bind and Loose Appropriately. Fred Hartley has compiled an excellent list of things to bind and loose in his book *Church on Fire*:

BIND	LOOSE
Fear	Courage
Poverty	Provision
Violence	Peace
Sickness	Health
Deception	Truth
Darkness	Light
Bondage	Freedom
Confusion	Clarity
Foolishness	Wisdom
Unbelief	Faith
Hate	Love
Unforgiveness	Forgiveness[169]

- *Teach the seeker to exercise authority over depression.* MacMillan writes, "It is this authority of Christ that must be exercised by the believer, or, in case of his absolute inability, by some instructed soul on his behalf. There are few ministries of the church that are becoming more urgent than that of releasing from spiritual bondage the increasing multitude of children of God who suffer from the attacks of deceiving spirits, or perhaps from nervous complaints that result from unrecognized working of the enemy."[170]

Biblical Practice 9:
Train and Authorize Teams of Workers for Healing Ministry

"and He gave them authority and power to heal the sick and cast out demons" —Matthew 10:1.

Jesus trained His disciples through teaching, example, and hands-on-ministry how to pray for the sick and deal with demons. He taught them kingdom principles. He modeled for them how to minister to those who were sick and oppressed. He elicited their assistance in working with Him. After training them, then He sent them forth to minister on their own, authorizing them, "Heal the sick, raise the dead, cleanse the lepers, cast out demons. Freely you have received, freely give" (Matthew 10:6).

Who May Be Authorized? All twelve of the apostles were commissioned by Jesus to anoint with oil (Mark 6:13). James specifies that the sick should call for the elders of the church to anoint them with oil. The elders thus have a special calling and authorization for healing ministry. This indicates that the sick are coming under authority. Does this mean then that only elders and the original apostles can anoint with oil? Not at all. We see also that an additional large group of disciples known as "the Seventy" prayed for the sick (Luke 10:1, 9). Ananias, referred to in Scripture only as a disciple, not a leader, laid hands on Saul for healing. Paul further indicates that every believer is a minister (Ephesians 4:12).

The early Higher Life/Fourfold Gospel/Alliance leaders recognized that not only elders could lay on hands and anoint with oil. A qualified elder may not always be available, or some elders may not believe in God's healing power or may not be able to pray a prayer of faith. It was the view of A.B. Simpson that when a qualified elder was not available that whoever was called to pray for others and was under proper authority could anoint with oil and pray for the sick. In fact, this was the practice of most of the Alliance healing homes. The majority of Alliance-related healing homes were led and operated by women.

Sarah Lindenberger was one of those early women who acted as an elder with Simpson's full approval. She became the deaconess (in effect, the pastor) of the Berachah Healing Home at Nyack, New York. When a qualified male elder was not available (which was the majority of the time), she would anoint and pray over people for healing. When an elder figure was present, she anointed and prayed right alongside him. She was recognized as being in authority because she was under authority. She acted authoritatively in believing for and claiming healing for people.

Therefore, it is quite biblical and acceptable today for pastors or elders to designate and train healing prayer workers. They can authorize non-elders to lay on hands and anoint with oil. Anyone who is anointed by God, trained, and under appropriate spiritual authority may be authorized to participate in the Healing Centers.

Other Qualifications for Praying for the Sick. As with all authority, however, healing power and the authority of the believer can be misused and abused. In the context of appointing leadership, Paul cautions against indiscriminate sanctioning of authority, warning, "Lay hands suddenly on no man" (1 Timothy 5:22). This has broader implications about who should or should not authorized to pray for the sick.

- *The Need for Consecration.* MacMillan cautions that "the authority of His name could never be efficacious in the mouth of an unspiritual disciple."[171] It is only a "consecrated hand" that can direct throne power of Christ.[172]

- *The Need for Moral Purity and Freedom from Addictions.* Those who are laying on hands and anointing with oil should be morally pure and free from addictive habits or behaviors. Pastor Schrenk, who was a friend of A.B. Simpson and worked with healing home leader Otto Stockmayer, cautioned about the results of transmission of unclean spirits:

  About the laying on of hands by those who are not themselves sanctified. I see great danger in this; and in faithfulness to my Lord and to the Church of God, I do not hesitate to warn every Christian to beware, and to not receive anointing from every man or woman whom you may meet with, but only from those who are really sanctified.

  I believe in the transmission of spirits through the laying on of hands, and I believe, from real and sad experience. There is such a thing as the transmission of carnal spirits. I have seen and heard of cases in which the evil spirits, instead of being cast out, have come into the persons on whom hands were laid, and subjected them to their influence. We should be very careful, dear friends, and to whom we choose to lay on hands, and let us be careful how we do it ourselves. Let each ask the Lord 'Am I sanctified, am I the person who is the fit instrument in Thy hands? Am I a channel though whom the Holy Spirit can convey a real, lasting, eternal blessing to others, so that those whom I anoint with oil, and upon whom I lay hands in Thy name, may receive the Holy Spirit?'"[173]

Holiness healing evangelist Maria Woodworth-Etter, a friend of Carrie Judd Montgomery also cautioned: "Some people, when they pray for anyone and lay on hands, throw their slime off. That is spiritualism. . . . Be careful who lays hands on you, for the devil is counterfeiting God's work.[174]

More recent examples of such warnings include Francis Frangipane, who has warned of the danger of transfer of spirits, whereby people have fallen into sexual sin, tobacco addiction, or depression after a person had hands laid on them. He remarked, "I can't explain theologically how such a thing can happen. I know that pure water passing through a rusty pipe will be stained. Regardless, it frightens me that a Christian can lay hands on someone's head and impart evil."[175] Gary Greenwald, has given the same admonition in a *Charisma and Christian Life* article entitled "The Dangerous Transference of Spirits."[176]

Elder-like Qualities in Which to Equip Your Workers. James 5:15-19 presents six qualities of elders that relate to healing ministry. Your workers may not formally be elders of a church, but, if they live out these qualities in their lives, they can have an effective healing ministry:

- *To become healing prayer partners held in high esteem who have the respect of the people.* James writes, "Is anyone among you sick?

Let him call for the elders of the church. . ." If your workers are respected, people will call on them for prayer.

- *To become workers who can pray and pray effectively.* ". . . and let them pray over him, anointing him with oil in the name of the Lord." A person who has a passion for intercessory prayer will have an effective healing ministry.

- *To model compassion.* The word "effective" in Greek means "energetic." Effective healing prayer partners pray energetically with passion from their heart. They are not half-hearted in their prayers. They pray fervently with genuine concern for the well-being of others. Healing energy is imparted by those who have the energy of the Spirit within themselves. Just as Jesus extended His compassion through touch, so healing prayer partners extend compassion through the laying on of hands and praying earnestly.

- *To be prayer partners of faith, who can pray a prayer of faith.* ". . . and the prayer offered in faith will restore the one who is sick, and the Lord will raise him up." I have known "elders" who cannot pray a prayer of faith believing that God wants to heal. I have also known people who do not have the title or office of elder who can pray a prayer of faith. Those are the people I want praying for me when I have a serious illness.

- *To demonstrate wisdom, maturity, and discernment sensitivity to the Holy Spirit and supernatural insight for revealing root causes, inner emotional issues, or sin hindering wholeness, victory, or recovery.* ". . . and if he has committed sins, they will be forgiven him." God may reveal deeper root issues through spiritual discernment and supernatural gifts of the Spirit such as words of knowledge, words of wisdom, prophetic insight, dreams, visions, or discernment of spirits.

- *To persevere in prayer and faith.* "Elijah . . . prayed earnestly that it might not rain, and it did not rain on the earth for three years and six months. And he prayed again, and the sky poured rain, and the earth produced its fruit."[177] Effective healing prayer partners continue and continue and continue to pray even when the answers do not come, and they press through and pray expectantly until the answer does come.

Implementing This Biblical Healing Practice in Your Healing Center. Here are some practical ways you can encourage this practice among your healing prayer partners and strengthen the faith of the people who come for ministry in your healing center:

- *Provide regular or periodic training sessions.*

- *Equip Healing Prayer Partners through Jesus' Training Model.*

  - <u>Jesus ministers, the disciples observe.</u>— "Come and you will see. . . . Follow me." (John 1:39, 43). Have them observe you and learn as you minister.

  - <u>Jesus ministers, the disciples assist.</u>—"He did not allow anyone to enter with Him, except Peter and John and James, and the girl's father and mother" (Luke 8:51). Jesus took His three best disciples to assist Him in raising the dead child to life. Train your workers to assist you.

  - <u>Disciples minister, Jesus observes.</u> With the 5000 hungry people, Jesus told His disciples, "You give them something to eat" (Mark 6:37). He involved His disciples in the miracle. Jesus did not feed the 5000; the disciples did. Jesus only prayed; the miracle of multiplication of the loaves and fishes took place in the disciples' hands. When your workers have observed, assisted, and been trained, have them take the lead and then observe them.

  - <u>Disciples are sent out to minister, then report back to Jesus.</u>— "The Lord appointed seventy others, and sent them in pairs ahead of Him. . . The seventy returned with joy, saying, 'Lord, even the demons are subject to us in Your name'" (Luke 10:1, 17). When your workers are ready, have them minister on their own.

- *Train Healing Prayer Partners through Jesus' Techniques.*

  ○ Create an environment of faith. Jesus took those who lacked faith out of the room. Peter likewise sent the mourners out of the room.

  ○ Speak healing words of faith to the afflicted person. Jesus spoke to the dead girl, "Talitha cum," meaning, "Little girl, rise." And then He took her by the hand and lifted her up. Peter spoke to the dead woman, "Tabitha, rise." Then he took her by the hand and lifted her up.

  ○ When possible, lay hands on the affected area of the body. Jesus put his hands on a blind man's eyes, a deaf man's ears, a mute man's lips.

  ○ Use verbal rebukes, not prayer and laying on hands when confronting demons. When Jesus was dealing with demons, He did not lay on hands; He only spoke a word of command against them.

  ○ Most important of all, like Jesus, show compassion.

- *Train Healing Prayer Partners to Prepare Their Hearts.*

  ○ To search their hearts and confess every sin the Lord brings to mind.

  ○ To pray in faith.

  ○ To pray with pure motives.

  ○ To developing a hearing ear. To listen to the voice of God and open the eyes of their heart—dreams, visions, prophecies, word of knowledge.

- *Train Healing Prayer Partners to Work Together as a Team.* It is vital to put together a prayer team ministry of two or more people. Three are preferable. Two can minister to the person and the third can observe and pray, and perhaps give additional insight. Why are more than one preferable to act as a team?

○ Because it was modeled by Jesus and His disciples. He sent the disciples out two-by-two (Matthew 10:1-6). The early apostles and disciples continued the pattern. The apostle Paul always traveled with at least one other person in his ministry. The only time recorded that he did not, in the city of Athens where he ministered alone, he was unsuccessful.

○ Because He declared His manifest presence to be powerful with two or three. "Where two or three are gathered in My name, I am in their midst" (Matthew 18:19).

○ Because of the power of a three-fold cord. "Two are better than one because they have a good return for their labor. For if either of them falls, the one will lift up his companion. But woe to the one who falls when there is not another to lift him up. Furthermore, if two lie down together they keep warm, but how can one be warm alone? And if one can overpower him who is alone, two can resist him. A cord of three strands is not quickly torn apart" (Ecclesiastes 4:9-12).

○ For accountability and protection. The biblical principle, reinforced repeated times in different contexts in Scripture, is that in the words of two or three witnesses a thing shall be established (2 Corinthians 13:1; Matthew 18:16, 20; 1 Timothy 5:19; Deuter-onomy 17:7; 19:15).This is especially crucial when working with the opposite sex. To avoid all temptation or appearance of evil, a woman should never pray alone privately with a man and a man should never pray privately alone with a woman.

○ For prayer support. We need the Aarons and Hurs to hold up our hands in spiritual battle.

○ For insights from the Lord. It is in body ministry that God speaks and acts. As a team is praying, the gifts of each are considered. One person may receive one insight, another person second insight, still another person a different insight, like different pieces of a puzzle when put together showing the whole picture. Sharing insights confirms what a person is sensing from God.

- *Instruct healing prayer partners in each of the principles and practices mentioned in this manual.* Be sure that they understand them, believe them, and implement them in their personal lives as well as their ministries.

- *Ask the all of the healing prayer partners to come a half-hour ahead of the healing ministry time to soak in worship and praise music, pray, dedicate the time to God, and listen for insights from the Holy Spirit.* You might also take Communion together. This is also a time that teams can be assigned together and encourage unity as they prepare to pray for the sick.

- *Have the healing prayer partners minister to each other,* praying for each other, listening to the Holy Spirit for each other.

- *Impart to the workers that they need to be committed and have a heart for prayer.* This kind of ministry takes time, patience, and perseverance.

- *Give the following instructions for healing center prayer partners:*
  - Prepare yourself spiritually—search your heart for anything that would hinder your ministry.
  - Spend time in stillness before the Lord.
  - Saturate in the Word and meditate on the Word.
  - Put on the full armor of God daily.
  - Confess the truths of the Word of God.
  - Confess who you are in Christ.

- *Train the workers in prayer.* Here are some powerful Higher Life/Fourfold Gospel/ Alliance prayer resources:
  - Fred Hartley (President of College of Prayer), *Prayer on Fire* and *Church on Fire.*
  - David Chotka, *Power Praying.*

○ Jonathan Graf, *The Power of Personal Praying.*

○ Andrew Murray, *With Christ in the School of Prayer.*

○ A.B. Simpson, *The Life of Prayer.*

○ Paul Billheimer, *Destined for the Throne.*

- *Train workers in exercising their authority as a believer.* Here are some powerful Higher Life/Fourfold Gospel/Alliance resources:

   ○ John A. MacMillan, *The Authority of the Believer* (C&MA missionary).

   ○ Paul L. King, *A Believer with Authority: The Life and Message of John A. MacMillan.*

   ○ K. Neill Foster and Paul L. King, *Binding and Loosing: Exercising Authority over the Dark Powers.*

- *Train workers in spiritual warfare.*

   ○ See Chapter 11 for an introduction to spiritual warfare in the Higher Life/Fourfold Gospel heritage.

   ○ Have workers read Chapter 16 of *God's Healing Arsenal* on "Praying on the Armor of God" and prepare themselves daily by praying on the armor to protect themselves and their family.

   ○ For a comprehensive guide on the theology and practice of spiritual warfare, see missiologist/professor Ed Murphy's book *The Handbook on Spiritual Warfare.*

- *Train Workers to Receive and Give Words from the Lord* (prophecy, words of knowledge, words of wisdom, dreams, visions and revelations).

   ○ Through impartation of spiritual gifts (Romans 1:11).

   ○ Through stirring up spiritual gifts (2 Timothy 1:6).

   ○ Through teaching workers to listen for the voice of God and see into the heavenlies. Sarah Lindenberger counseled those coming to the Berachah Healing Home, "Cultivate the habit of listening to God's voice in your soul." How do we teach people to do this?

✔ By learning to listen to your spirit.

✔ By being still and waiting on the Lord.

✔ By nourishing your spirit.

✔ By releasing your spirit.

✔ By seeing in the spirit.

See Chapter 7 on "Using Gifts of the Spirit in Healing Ministry" for a more detailed explanation of how to listen for the voice of God.

- *Train workers to be aware of manifestations of God's power and presence.* See Chapter 8 on "Understanding and Discerning Manifestations of God's Presence and Power" for more specific information on this.

- *Train workers to minister with humility.* In all exercise of authority and faith in healing ministry, we have great need for humility. John MacMillan reminds us: "So Jesus says, when you as servants have done all those things which are commanded you; when you have uprooted trees, removed mountains, healed the sick, led multitudes to salvation—remember that you are still servants of God. What you have done is simply what He has endued you with power to do, and what you have engaged to do for Him. You have not done anything of yourselves—all has been of His working."[178]

Biblical Practice 10:
Provide Ongoing Pastoral Care Support

"Neither do I condemn you; go and sin no more" (John 8:11)

Because divine healing was not a popular subject in the church, healing homes provided a safe place for people to come and learn about this "new" truth and also pray for and receive healing. Carrie Judd Montgomery, Sarah Lindenberger, and Johannes Blumhardt all demonstrated a "pastoral" model of healing. Rev. Blumhardt spent two years of pastoral care with his first healing patient until she was delivered. Carrie Montgomery and Sarah Lindenberger would circulate through the homes daily, checking in on each guest. One of the main differences between healing crusades or services and the healing center concept is that healing centers can provide ongoing pastoral care.

Healing is not maintained in isolation from the healing community as a whole. Continued health and healing are nurtured through the church community. The deeper root issues of inner healing and sanctification that have arisen are dealt with in ongoing discipleship through the local church.

Five Types of Ongoing Pastoral Care. In Chapter 7 of my book *God's Healing Arsenal*, I mention five sources of emotional and physical distress based on *Hope When You're Hurting* by Larry Crabb and Dan Allender. These represent five types of ongoing pastoral care or referral that may be needed.

- *Spiritual Warfare*—The cause is demonic harassment. Pastoral care is given through exercising spiritual authority over the harassing spirits and teaching seekers how to exercise that authority themselves and walk in victory.

- *Dysfunctional Background*—The cause is psychological in nature. Pastoral care is given through counseling, inner healing, or referring to others who can provide such specialized care.

- *Biochemical Disorder*—The cause is medical. Pastoral care is given through continued soaking prayer for healing and referral for medical treatment.

- *Undisciplined Living*—The cause is personality weakness. Pastoral care is given through discipleship in sanctification and especially in the fruit of the Spirit of self-control or self-discipline.

- *Deficient Spirituality*—The cause is distance from God. Pastoral care is given in instructing the person to seek God Himself and providing an environment that draws people to the Manifest Presence of God.[179]

Implementing This Biblical Healing Practice in Your Healing Center. Here are some practical ways you can encourage this practice and provide ongoing pastoral care of the people who come for ministry in your healing center:

- *Provide a safe place*—not pushing or artificially forcing.

- *Encourage and challenge faith and expectancy.*

- *Don't blame or condemn for lack of faith or sin.* Be uplifting and encouraging.

- *Don't coddle.* Carrie Montgomery would normally only allow people to stay a week, so that they would not get complacent and just settle in, and not deal earnestly with the issues in their lives that might impede healing.

- *Manifest love, peace, and presence of Jesus even when healing does not occur immediately.* People should always sense the presence and love of Jesus through caring, sensitive people.

- *Provide continued healing prayer opportunities.* If they still need a healing touch from God or other issues have arisen, encourage them to come back to receive more healing prayer.

- *Encourage them to spend time in the Word, time in worship, and in confession of the Word and truths of God.*

- *If the person is not involved in a local church, encourage the person to find a church home.*

- *Sometimes a lifestyle change is needed in order to be healed or maintain health.* Encourage the seeker to read and apply Chapter 9 of *God's Healing Arsenal* on "A Wholeness Lifestyle—The Overcoming Power of Holy, Healthy Living." Discuss with them the "For Reflection" questions at the end of the chapter.

- *Stir faith.* Sometimes people will come to your Healing Center who are part of a church that does not believe in the healing power of God or that, in some way, compromises or waters down the healing message. They will need encouragement to keep their faith strong and stand in faith.

- *Provide a SWAT team*, or Aarons and Hurs, to help encourage and strengthen their faith and fight their battles.

- *Minister to the families of those who come for prayer.* They may need healing in some way as well.

- *Provide further instruction.* Instruct the person receiving prayer to read Chapter 8 of *God's Healing Arsenal* on "Setting Our Sprits Free and Restoring Our Souls." Ask the person to reflect on the questions at the end of the chapter and see what areas of spiritual bondage need to be dealt with and in what ways his or her minds needs to be renewed.

- *Develop a healing community.* Read Chapter 40 of *God's Healing Arsenal* on "Developing a Community of Healing: How to Implement a Healing Ministry in Your Church" for more information to provide ongoing pastoral care support.

CHAPTER 5

How to Develop a Healing Center

Types of Healing Center Ministries

Healing Centers are flexible and can be established in a variety of ways and settings. They can be short-term or long-term; they can be operated in a designated room or time of ministry in a church, a house or building set aside for ministry, a campground or retreat center, even in a tent or a booth at a community festival.

Short Term Healing Prayer Ministry (20-30 minutes). This is often the easiest, quickest, and best way to start. You can designate time and space for soaking prayer ministry to take about 20-30 minutes to pray for a person. Some people call this "consecrated space" or "sacred space." As in the chorus "We are standing on holy ground," we set apart ourselves and a location to be used specially by God for Him to manifest His presence in love and peace and healing power.

- *A dedicated prayer ministry room in the church.* If your church is open most of the time, you can set aside a Healing Prayer Room where a person can come just about any time to pray and meditate. You can dedicate certain times in which people will be available to pray. Pray over the location and anoint the doors and furnishings with oil, much like was done over the furnishings of the Tabernacle in the Old Testament (Exodus 30:26-29). Speak words of faith, declarations of faith and healing, peace and wholeness over the space that you have set apart.

- *A ministry prayer time in a neutral location.* Some people are reluctant to come to a church. Sometimes a center in a non-religious location—a shopping center, office complex, booth at a community fair. Don't limit how and where the Holy Spirit might desire to manifest His healing power. Even your local Walmart or K-Mart can become a Healing Center.

- *A certain night of the week or month.* Often times, a good way to start is to designate a monthly healing prayer night, such as the first Thursday of each month. If interest grows, you can add additional healing prayer nights (the first and third Thursday of the month). As interest continues to grow, it may become a weekly ministry.

- *Turning one of your existing meetings into a weekly healing prayer night.* If you have a Sunday or Wednesday night Bible study, prayer meeting, or service, you might consider refashioning it as a weekly healing ministry night.

- *If the person is too sick to come to a healing prayer ministry time,* take the healing prayer to that person. Make an appointment for the healing prayer teams to visit the person in at home or in the hospital.

- *Ask the healing prayer partners to come a half-hour ahead of the healing ministry time to pray together as a team, dedicate the time to God, and corporately listen for insights from the Holy Spirit.*

- *Train and schedule sufficient healing prayer team members to handle the amount of people coming for prayer.* It is best to have a three-member prayer team and at least two teams available. Sometimes you may have only one person come for prayer, another time you may have a dozen. If you have three prayer teams spending a half hour with each person individually, it would take three hours to pray for a dozen people one-on-one.

- *Have someone act as a greeter to take information* (see Seeker Information Sheet in Appendix 4) *and talk with the person until a prayer team is available.*

Extended Healing Prayer Care (for several hours or days). This requires setting aside more time and people who have more time available. You may find someone who has a calling to this extended care ministry. Prayer intercessors who have a vision or burden to pray will often spend hours praying. Find them in your church or community and utilize their passion for prayer.

- *A Healing Prayer Room.* This could be open during all the time the church building is open for people to come and soak in prayer for hours on their own. Leave some literature, worship music, CDs and DVDs on faith and healing in the room as resources for seekers.

- *Longer prayer ministry by appointment.* Some ministry may take an hour or even several hours. Time can be set aside to pray unhurriedly to deal with the deeper roots of spiritual and emotional issues that come to the surface in the course of prayer.

- *Healing Retreats.* These can be scheduled periodically on a Friday night and Saturday for several hours of ministry both individually and corporately.

Residential Healing Prayer Care (days or weeks). This is the original healing home model, in which a person can come and stay for days or weeks as a spiritual retreat. Because of the cost and time involved, this type of healing center is likely to be less common, but some may have a vision for this.

- Purchase or rent a house for this purpose.
- Set aside a cottage or cabin at a Christian campground.
- Develop a healing/retreat center out of a farm.

For information about retreat centers, here are some websites:

http://www.ehow.com/how_8563694_start-christian-retreat-center.html.

https://www.masterplans.com/business-plan-articles/Business-plans-for-christian-retreat-centers.

http://www.christhaven.net/ (this is a Christian retreat center in Colorado where I have stayed a couple of times).

http://www.fairhavenministries.net/ (founded by C&MA pastor/counselor Charles Shepson).

Remote/Distance Intercessory Healing Prayer. God can heal over long distances as well as through an atmosphere of faith in healing centers. This is illustrated in Scripture when the centurion came to Jesus and told him he was not worthy for Jesus to come to his home, but "Just say the word, and my servant will be healed" (Matthew 8:8). Jesus marveled at the faith of the centurion and declared, "Go, it shall be done for you as you have believed," and his servant was healed the very same hour (Matthew 8:13). Healing from a distance was no issue for Jesus. Nor was it an issue for the centurion. If we take hold of the same kind of faith as the centurion, He will heal as we pray, believe, and declare healing through the Holy Spirit.

Carrie Judd herself was healed through the long distance prayers of the first African-American healing evangelist, Sarah Mix. Carrie followed the example of her healing mentor.

Not only did she pray for people who attended her meetings and healing home, but she also prayed for people at a distance when they sent letters requesting prayer for healing. Carrie's biographer Jennifer Miskov relates:

Modeled to her by Sarah Mix, many were healed through Carrie's ministry of long distance praying. An example of this can be seen in 1882 when at one of her meetings, Carrie and the others prayed for a specific request sent in by Mrs. C. M. Dutcher who "had been severely ill for nineteen years with disease of the spine." A few days after the prayer meeting,

Dutcher was strengthened enough to walk a quarter of a mile to her church.

Another example of this model comes from a local newspaper article about Richard Huffman. He was told by physicians that his sickness of a paralyzed nervous system and hardening in his spinal column was incurable. Not too long after that, he got a hold of Carrie's *Prayer of Faith*. A reporter notes that "he was so much struck by its contents that he wrote to her and proposed that she should pray for him at her weekly prayer meetings." She agreed and organized a time when she would pray "at the same time" as him. Shortly after prayer was given, he began to grow stronger and could walk up the stairs for the first time in three years. Ever since his healing, he claimed that he had been "leaping and walking and praising..."[180]

Organizing Your Healing Center

Register Your Healing Center. While we do not franchise the Higher Life/Fourfold Gospel/Alliance Healing Centers or require a registration fee, we accept contributions and request that you notify us of your intent to establish a healing center and work in association with Dr. Paul King and the Higher Life/Alliance Heritage Renewal Network. You can contact Paul King at paul@paulkingministries.com. As funds are available, we hope to establish a website dedicated to the Higher Life/Alliance Heritage Renewal Network and Healing Centers. We will list your healing center in our newsletters, websites, etc.

Determine What to Call Your Healing Center. You could call it a name related to the name of your church. It could be the historic and biblical theme in this manual—Higher Life Healing Center. It could be a name related to your vision or some aspect of healing. If your healing center is the only one in your location, you could name it after your town. If your Healing Center is part of the Christian and Missionary Alliance, you might want to call it an Alliance Healing Center. You could call it a Healing Home, House of Healing, Healing Room, Prayer Room, Healing Prayer, Healing Community, Community of Healing, Prayer Retreat. Some examples of healing homes or centers include the following:

- *Shalom Center* (peace, well-being, wholeness)
- *Berachah House* (A.B. Simpson's name for his healing home—meaning "House of Blessing")
- *Rapha Center* (Hebrew word for healing)
- *Sozo Center* (Greek word for salvation, wholeness, healing) (Note: Pandita Ramabai, a Higher Life leader in India, named her ministry "Mukti Mission," "mukti" being an Indian word for salvation.)
- *House of Peace* (Carrie Judd Montgomery's healing home in Oakland, California)
- *Higher Life Healing Community/Alliance Healing Community*
- *Wholistic Healing Center* (instead of the commonly used term "holistic," thus signifying the idea of whole person healing without New Age beliefs or practices)

Designate Healing Center Directors. Someone who has a vision for this ministry should be trained and authorized to be a Healing Center Director, under the authority of the pastors and elders of the church. Someone is needed with organizational skills for planning, organizing, implementing, managing, and overseeing. If the Director does not have those skills, then perhaps someone who does have those skills could become a co-director or assistant director. Often it is good for a couple to work together as a team as co-directors. It is also of value to train Assistant Directors to lead when the directors are not able to be present.

If the Healing Center is not part of a local church (such as in a neutral location or a campground), the Healing Center Directors should work cooperatively with local churches and pastors. They should encourage seekers to become involved in a church that believes in healing if they are not already.

Prepare Your Healing Center Location. Create an ambience of faith and peacefulness. God tells Habakkuk to "Write the vision, make it plain." People absorb more of what they both see and hear. Here are a few ideas:

- *Prepare the room visually.*
  - ○ Soft warm colors, not bright flashy colors.
  - ○ Posters or pictures on the wall relating to healing.
    - ✔ Healing Scriptures.
    - ✔ Painting of Jesus laying on hands.
    - ✔ Painting of Jesus hands extended.
    - ✔ Painting of the Lord's Supper elements of bread and wine.
    - ✔ Painting of Jesus walking on the water.
    - ✔ Painting of Jesus comforting or showing compassion.
    - ✔ Logo. If your church is affiliated with the Christian and Missionary Alliance, you may want to have the C&MA Fourfold Gospel Logo of Jesus Christ as Savior, Sanctifier, Healer, and Coming King displayed prominently. Or perhaps a banner with the pitcher logo, representing Christ as Healer and the laver logo of representing Christ as Sanctifier.

- *Prepare the location comfortably.*
  - ○ Provide soft worship music.
  - ○ Provide comfortable seating.
  - ○ Make provision for those with disabilities. Sometimes someone will come to your healing center in a wheelchair. Be sure your healing center is handicapped accessible. Some may need a cot or a sofa or a mat on which to lie.

- *Stock the location with supplies.*

- ○ Provide literature on faith, healing, and overcoming.

- ○ Have tissue available for tears, which often flow in abundance in healing center ministry.

- ○ Have bottles of anointing oil for each prayer team.

- ○ If you want to offer communion as part of your healing ministry, keep a stock of communion elements. You can do this in several ways.

  - ✔ Keep Matzos like those used in Jewish Passover services and a bottle of juice in the refrigerator.

  - ✔ Make available Gluten-free Matzos for those who have a gluten allergy.

  - ✔ Christian supply stores have packaged communion cups with a sealed wafer. Although this is more expensive, they may be fresher (be sure to check expiration dates).

- *Prepare the location spiritually.*

  - ○ Pray over the room and anoint the room with oil, similar to the Old Testament practice of anointing objects and the doorposts of the building.

  - ○ Ask the healing prayer partners to come a half-hour ahead of the healing ministry time to pray together as a team, dedicate the time to God, and corporately listen for insights from the Holy Spirit.

Launch and Promote Your Healing Center. Your Healing Center can be promoted in many different ways. These are just a few suggestions:

- *Launch by hosting a Healing Seminar led by Dr. Paul King.* He can explain, train, and help you and your healing prayer partners put these principles into practice.

- *Register your healing center* with the Higher Life/Alliance Heritage Renewal Network. We will promote it in newsletters, websites, etc.

- *Put a sign outside your building near the street or on your marquis.* Something like: Healing Prayer, Thursday, 7 pm. Sometimes people will just walk in off the street.

- *Post flyers, brochures in Christian bookstore, grocery store, Walmart, or Kmart.* We have had people call or walk in asking for prayer from a simple flyer.

- *Promote on social media*—Website, Facebook, Twitter.

- *Publish testimonies*—in Sunday morning service, online.

- *Have messages on healing.*

- *Hold a healing seminar or conference.*

- *Have the pastor promote the Healing Center from the pulpit. This is one of the most effective ways to promote.*

- *Ultimately, the greatest means is to pray for God to draw people.* People will be supernaturally drawn like a magnet through a prophetic word, through an urge to come to your building, such as the angel's word to Cornelius: "Now dispatch some men to Joppa and send for a man named Simon, who is also called Peter; he is staying with a tanner named Simon, whose house is by the sea" (Acts 10:5-6).

In 1892, 37 year-old businessman John Woodberry, after a series of financial reverses, surrendered to the call to ministry God had place on his life in his early twenties. He and his wife were soon introduced to the C&MA through a prophetic word from a stranger to go to a certain address—the address of the Alliance Home in Grand Rapids, Michigan, "and there learn the Way more perfectly." They initially scoffed at the idea, but by the next morning they were convicted by the Holy Spirit to go. When they arrived at the location, they were again surprised at the greeting: "Are you Mr. and Mrs. Woodberry? Captain _____ said you were coming!" They recounted of the experience, "In that Alliance Home truths were unfolded, such as we had never dreamed of, as Mrs. Dora Dudley, open Bible upon her knee, led us on from salvation to the deeper knowledge of sanctification, divine healing, and the glorious return of Christ."[181]

There they were filled with the Spirit and introduced to the C&MA. They determined to go to the Nyack Missionary Training Institute, miraculously sold their home within two hours, and moved their four children to New York. They eventually became long-term missionaries to China. Such are the kinds of experiences the Holy Spirit may engineer if we are sensitive to the Holy Spirit.

Use Your Healing Center as a Means of Evangelism. Early on in the healing home ministry of Berachah Home, A.B. Simpson reported more than 100 people converted through the ministry of the home. Simpson emphasized, "The first great aim of the work is to lead the sufferer to know Christ, and to receive Him fully. Then the healing has not been seriously difficult."[182] The Beulah Home in Grand Rapids was advertised as a place with "'Jesus in the midst' where the weary, sick, tired, *unsaved* may come for a time and learn more perfectly the way of faith."[183] Sarah Lindenberger explained how this ministry emerged at Berachah:

> It has proved at many times to be a source of salvation and the birthplace of souls. Many longing and seeking for healing here have found they must first be saved, and have given Christ their souls and then their bodies. Many have come with Christian friends, although not themselves Christian and have been so touched with the reality of the lives they have seen day by day that they could no longer hold back their hearts from the Blessed One."[184]

This can be a model for Healing Center ministries today. Inviting unbelievers who have a physical or emotional need to receive prayer in a non-threatening environment, can open doors for them to be receptive to receiving Jesus as Savior as well as Healer. Here are some ways you can use the Healing Center as an evangelistic tool:

- *Put up a sign inviting people to walk in for prayer.* It has been our experience that with just a sign, "Healing Prayer—Thursday, 7 p.m.," people will walk in off the street and ask for prayer, some of them unbelievers who are seeking.

- *Set up a booth at a community festival.* David and Jayne Ann Harder, the Oklahoma state directors of IAHR served as missionaries in Cyprus found this effective both in their missions work in Cyprus and in their evangelistic outreach in the United States. Some people are seeking counsel from psychics and astrologers. What better way to lead them on the right path by providing a Christian alternative.

- *Be aware of the "Kairos" times in which people are especially open and prepared to be receptive to the Gospel. Kairos* is the Greek word meaning quality time, or due season. These are times of crisis or change in a person's life.

- *Use the Treasure Hunt approach.* Kevin Dedmon, in his book *The Ultimate Treasure Hunt,* describes the practice of a group of believers seeking the Lord for those whom He is preparing to receive the Gospel. God gives supernatural words of knowledge. We have a biblical example of this when Ananias received a vision of the Lord telling him, "Get up and go to the street called Straight, and inquire at the house of Judas for a man from Tarsus named Saul, for he is praying, and he has seen in a vision a man named Ananias come in and lay his hands on him, so that he might regain his sight" (Acts 9:11-12).

Connect Your Healing Center with the Local Church. If your healing center is not a part of a local church (such as at a neutral location, a para-church ministry, or a campground), connect your healing center with a local church ministry (or ministries). Build good relationships and accountability with the pastors and leaders of local churches. Ask them to serve on your Advisory Board. Encourage them to go through the training in this manual and then to serve as ministry prayer partners. Refer people to a local church that believes in healing.

Brainstorm Other Ways of Becoming a Healing Community. Becoming a community of healing can involve much more than described in this manual. We are called to be ministers of reconciliation wherever we go. Here are some additional ideas:

- *Impart a Healing Ministry Vision to Every Believer.* Every believer has a call to a healing ministry in some way. Wherever a believer is, there is a healing ministry—on the job, in the supermarket, at school, on the Little League baseball field, in your neighborhood.

- *Preach a series of messages on healing and put them into practice.*

- *After instruction in a church service, have the congregation break into groups of 3-4 to listen to the Holy Spirit and pray for one another's needs.* Dr. Ron Walborn, Dean of Alliance Theological Seminary, did this at the Communion and Healing service at a General Council of the C&MA. Some people received instant healing, and others received partial healing on the spot. We did this in our local church, and a 19 year old prayed for his older brother, who had one leg shorter than the other, and no arch in his foot from birth. Immediately, the leg grew out and his foot formed an arch.

- *Hold seminars on healing.* Include practical hands-on clinic ministry time.

- *Make available prayer for healing at every service.* I never let a service go by without some sort of opportunity or invitation for prayer for healing. As A.W. Tozer stresses, "The Presence of God is more important than the program." Manifesting God's presence through prayer for needs is more vital than anything else on our agenda.

- *Keep anointing oil handy.* We keep a bottle of anointing oil on the Communion table. I sometimes carry a bottle of anointing oil with me.

- *Give opportunities for testimonies of healing in Sunday services.*

- *Hold special meetings for healing monthly.*

- *Take the Healing Center to others.* Advertise that the elders or the Healing Prayer Team are available to make appointments to come and pray with people if they cannot come to the healing center.

- *Establish marketplace healing ministry.* Anywhere can be a healing center—even a Walmart. Study the book *The Ultimate Treasure Hunt* by Kevin Dedmon* and train people to listen to the Holy Spirit. Then go out into the marketplace and look for the clues the Holy Spirit gives for people in need.

- *Hold nutrition and health seminars.* If we believe in whole person health and healing, promoting healthy living is a part being a community of healing.

- *Host a free medical clinic.* Bring in doctors or nurses who will volunteer their time for those who cannot afford medical care.

- *Host a Whole Person Health Fair.* Whole person health includes physical, mental, emotional, social, financial, marital and spiritual health. Possible features of such fairs could include free health and fitness screenings and assessments (blood pressure, cholesterol, diabetes, etc.), community health resources, Communion, freebies and giveaways, certified financial counseling, and tons of great information!

- *Take a whole person missions team to another country.* People who have been trained in whole person healing principles can go on a short-term mission trip to minister to the whole person in body, soul, and spirit in another country or culture.

- *Stir your entire community to become a community of healing.* Partner with other churches to capture the spirit of healing and create an entire community environment conducive to healing.

---

* This is a good practical biblical-based resource, but it does not imply endorsement of all Dedmon's teachings.

CHAPTER 6

Using Jesus' Prayer Ministry Model

"Come and you will see. . . . Follow me" (John 1:39, 43).

Jesus declared that He did what He saw the Father doing. Then He told His disciples to follow Him, observe Him, and do what they saw Him do. This chapter provides a six-stage prayer model, adapted from and similar to the five-step prayer model described by John Wimber in his book *Power Healing* but is based on the actual practices of Jesus. This is not a formula but a suggested process for ministering effectively. You don't have to use all of these steps all of the time, but they have been very helpful and effective and are biblically based.

Step 1: Interview

Jesus frequently interviewed people before ministering to them. He asked the blind man, "What do you want Me to do for you?" (Matthew 20:32; Mark 10:51). He asked the father of the epileptic boy, "How long has this been happening to him?" (Mark 9:21).

So while this is not a medical interview or case history, our first step is to ask questions. Find out about the condition or the situation. While listening horizontally to the person, be attuned vertically to the

Holy Spirit for insight into the root of the problem (what they are telling you may not be the real or major problem). Discern whether hurt, resentment, etc., might have impacted the illness or might hinder healing. Ask questions like:

- What do you want us to pray for?
- Where does it hurt?
- How have you dealt with this problem in the past?
- What started this?
- How long have you had this condition?
- When did it first happen?

Step 2: Diagnosis

God is the Divine Physician. He knows the correct diagnosis and the best prescription. Discern from the Spirit the real issue, the ultimate cause – whether physical, spiritual, social, emotional, or a combination. Review Biblical Principles for Healing #8 and #9 to identify what might apply in this person's life. Here are some of the diagnoses of Jesus:

- **Root Causes from the Past.** When the paralytic was brought to Jesus, He discerned some trauma or issue from the man's childhood as well as a need to feel forgiven. "Jesus said to the paralytic, 'Take courage, son; your sins are forgiven'" (Matthew 9:2).

- **Inner Motivation or Hindrances.** Jesus recognized that some people don't really want to be healed; they want attention, and He probed to see the person's intentions. "When Jesus saw him lying there, and knew that he had already been a long time in that condition, He said to him, 'Do you wish to get well?'" (John 5:6).

- **Identifying the Beginning Point or Source.** Jesus asked the father of the epileptic boy, "How long has this been happening to him?" (Mark 9:25). He was pinpointing the time when the illness started. The father responded, "From childhood," or literally, from infancy, in the preverbal stage before a child learns to talk. Something involving an evil spirit occurred at that time to keep the boy from developing normally.

If you don't have enough information, pray for illumination and discernment from the Holy Spirit. If prompted by the Holy Spirit, delicately and sensitively ask probing questions that could be related to the problem, such as, "Is there bitterness in your life toward. . .?" "Have you ever been abused, molested. . . ?" (The Lord may give you a word of wisdom or knowledge or discernment of spirits.) Then focus in on that particular problem.

- Why does this person have this condition?
- What is the root cause?
  - Natural
  - Spiritual
  - Emotional
  - Relational
  - Traumatic experience
  - Demonic
- What is the scope and significance of the problem?
- What words of knowledge or wisdom or mental pictures are you receiving from God?

Step 3: Prayer Selection (type of prayer)

Paul exhorts us to "pray at all times in the Spirit" (Ephesians 6:18). To be in the Spirit is, first of all, to be in the spiritual realm, that is, to be in the heavenlies. So, to pray in the Spirit means that we are praying in the spiritual realm of the heavenly places.

Second, to pray in the Spirit means to pray in a manner guided by the Holy Spirit, prayer from heaven, from the throne of God. Throne prayer is not praying out of ourselves, but through the Holy Spirit.

Third, one type of praying in the Spirit is praying *with* the spirit, that is, supernaturally with our human spirit initiated by the Holy Spirit. This is praying in the language of the Holy Spirit—praying in tongues (1 Corinthians 14:15). Chapter 7 on "Using Gifts of the Spirit in Healing Ministry" describes this kind of praying further.

Types of prayer can be categorized as Prayers to God and Prayer from God.

Prayers to God. These are humanly initiated prayers of our own accord. They can include the following.

- *Invocation* (invoking the Lord's presence) – "Come Holy Spirit. . ."

- *Petition*—asking the person to pray for him or herself.

- *Intercession*—praying in behalf of the person before praying over the person. You might pray something like, "Lord, show Your love for this person," or "I bind any hindering spirits in Jesus' name."

- *Praying in tongues*— "I will pray with my spirit and I will pray with my mind also." (1 Corinthians 14:15). As you pray in tongues, look for an interpretation, direction, insight, or revelation.

- *Prayers of agreement*—Matthew 18:18-20

Prayers from God. These are not prayers initiated on our own but prayers inspired or stirred up by God. They include:

- *Spirit-led Prayer.* Prayers initiated by the Holy Spirit (examples of gift of faith – unction anointing)—Matthew 8:8.

- *Interpretation of Tongues.* "I will pray with the spirit, and I will pray with the understanding." Sometimes as a person is praying in tongues in intercession, the Holy Spirit will reveal what He has been praying through that person. The tongues are interpreted then as a Spirit-inspired and directed prayer.

- *Words of Command.* Jesus frequently commanded directly, rather than praying to God. He may inspire us to do the same—to speak authoritatively a word of declaration or command: "I speak life, healing. . ." An example from one of the early healing rooms was that the healing prayer partner was led to command a woman's spine to be straightened, even though the worker did not know of the curvature of the spine. She continued to command the spine to be straightened, and after about six hours, the woman was healed.

- *Words of Pronouncement.* Sometimes Jesus did not pray or command; sometimes He just declared that it was done. "Go, your child is healed; you are made whole." (Matthew 8:13). If the Lord gives you a clear word to declare, then don't be afraid to speak it. However, do not tell people to claim they are healed if the Spirit has not clearly impressed it upon you.

- *Prayer of Revelatory or Prophetic Nature*—prophetic prayer. As you are praying, the Holy Spirit may supernaturally reveal something to you, or you may pray a prophecy.

Step 4: <u>Prayer Engagement</u>

This is the actual process of the prayer itself. It is not praying a perfunctory prayer; it is engaging the presence and power of God to be active in the process.

Lay on hands. As discussed earlier, this is one of the most frequent biblical practices used by Jesus, His apostles, disciples, elders, and just about everyone. Be sure to ask the person if it is okay for you to lay hands on them. In most cases, they will say yes, but do not just assume. Also check with the Lord. Upon occasion, He may put a check in your spirit or lead you in a different direction.

At times the Spirit has clearly and strongly warned me, "Do not lay hands on that person." Usually it is because of one of three things: 1) the person is not ready to receive; 2) something demonic is going on in the person's life; 3) something physical or sexual is involved in the person's life (such as, they have been physically or sexually abused or they are sexually attracted to you).

Anoint with Oil. Again, seek the leading of the Holy Spirit in the use of oil. I usually place the oil on the person's forehead, but sometimes it may be appropriate to anoint the part of the body in need of prayer. Or sometimes God wants to impart an anointing to someone else through the anointing.

Continue to pray, "Holy Spirit, come and minister." As we continue to soak the person in prayer, asking the Holy Spirit to come upon them, minister to them, and fill them, He may reveal more insights into their needs and may pray them through us.

Pray for specific results. If we pray vague prayers, we get vague results. Sometimes we play it safe by praying generically. When we pray specifically, we are putting our faith to the test. Pray specifically for something that can be noticed, sensed, observed, felt, etc. Lord, reduce this person's pain level."

Pray with eyes open. Jesus frequently prayed with His eyes open, looking to heaven, gazing upon the Father to see what He is doing. As we open our eyes, we look to see what Jesus and the Father are doing. We also look to see the response upon the person for whom we are praying.

Observe what manifestations may occur. We do not seek or try to induce or promote manifestations, but recognize that manifestations do sometimes occur. These may include tears, weeping, flushed face, shaking, trembling, sensations of heat or cold, laughing, falling over, and even upon occasion screaming or convulsing. Such manifestations may be the power of God overwhelming a person, a human emotional response, or it may be demonically inspired. This calls for spiritual discernment.

Step 5: <u>Assess the Prayer Results</u>

We see that Jesus assessed the results of His prayer ministry upon people. Jesus asked the blind man upon whom He laid His hands,

"Do you see anything?" (Mark 8:23). The man received a partial healing, declaring, "I see men as trees walking." Jesus did not tell him, "Well, you just don't have enough faith." Rather, He laid his hands on him again.

Ask Further Questions. So, following Jesus' lead, we ask questions as we have prayed for the person. Some of those questions might be:

- What's happening as we pray?
- Do you sense the power of God?
- Do you feel anything different?
- Is there a change?
- Is there something you can do that you could not do before?
- Is the pain less than it was?
- Is God showing you anything?

Depending on the answers, you might interview the person further and/or re-diagnose and go back through these steps.

Check with after you have prayed and see if, or how, the Lord is touching the person. Take his or her exact words (for example, "there is only a little pain left") then pray, "little pain that is left, leave in Jesus name."

Pray for More Insight from the Holy Spirit. Perhaps the Lord will give further words of knowledge or wisdom, prophecy, or discernment of spirits.

Be Aware of the Process of Healing. Results may be immediate, partial, or more gradual and progressive. Read Chapter 10 of *God's Healing Arsenal* on "Understanding Healing as a Process." Share this process with the person who has received prayer.

Extend Pastoral Care and Sensitivity. If no change occurs, be honest and open about it. Make sure the person does not feel condemned or discouraged. Continue to pray through soaking prayer or schedule another time to meet and pray again, perhaps for an extended time. Follow the suggestions in Chapter 10 on "Pastoral Care for Those Who Are Not Healed."

Step 6: <u>Post-Ministry Directions</u>

Jesus frequently gave post-ministry directions to those for whom He prayed or with whom He interacted.

- To the woman caught in adultery, He commanded, "Go, and sin no more" (John 8:11).

- To the man born blind whom Jesus healed, He followed up by asking him, "Do you believe in the Son of Man?" Then He gave him the opportunity to affirm his faith in Jesus not only as his Healer but as his Messiah (John 9:35-38).

- For the young girl He raised from the dead, He instructed with practical awareness of a child's needs that food be given her for nourishment (Luke 8:58).

- To the woman with a hemorrhage who touched the hem of His garment, He affirmed, "Daughter, your faith has made you well," then bade her, "Go in peace" (Luke 8:48). He dealt with the whole person—the woman's spiritual life (her faith), her self-esteem and acceptance ("Daughter"), and her emotional state ("peace" in place of her fears, anxieties, and emotional scars).

Similarly, as we are led by the Holy Spirit, we can give appropriate follow-up directions and counsel. Some possibilities to consider include:

- *What should this person do to remain healed?* A.B. Simpson would give counsel following healing to: "Use your new strength and health for God; and be careful to obey the will of the Master."[185] Other instructions might include:
  - ○ Ask those who are not believers to put their faith in Christ as Savior as well as Healer.

- ○ Become involved in a kinship or fellowship group in order to remain strong.
- ○ Read, study, and memorize Scripture.
- ○ Maintain positive mental attitude and confession.
- ○ Give an assignment—something more for the person to do.
- ○ Give testimony of your healing—Luke 8:39.
- ○ Report back on progress.
- ○ Pray for the filling of Spirit—Matthew 12:43-45.

- *What should this person do if he or she was not healed or the healing was partial?* Any or all of the above instructions could appropriately be applied in this scenario. In addition to the above, other directions might be:
  - ○ Do more soaking prayer.
  - ○ Provide counseling or refer to a counselor.
  - ○ Take steps of obedience to God.
    - ✔ Repentance – "Go and sin no more."
    - ✔ Restitution.
    - ✔ Change in lifestyle.
    - ✔ Change in thought patterns.

Again, these steps are not a straight-jacket or formula, but they provide biblical guidelines for knowing how to approach healing prayer ministry. These are biblical tools to use as led by the Holy Spirit.

CHAPTER 7

Using Gifts of the Spirit in Healing Ministry

The gifts of healing are not the only gifts used by God in healing prayer. Almost any gift of the Spirit can be used in tandem with gifts of healing and even in the absence of a clear gift of healing. One of my doctoral students did her doctoral thesis on the activation of spiritual gifts in healing. She found that gifts sometimes occur in clusters, and that especially the gifts of prophecy, word of knowledge or word of wisdom frequently accompany or help to foster healing.

As mentioned in Biblical Principle 2 in Chapter 3, all the gifts are needed because oftentimes various gifts or manifestations of the Spirit operate in conjunction with one another. A gift of faith enhances healing power to be manifest. A prophecy, word of wisdom, or word of knowledge often provides illumination and revelation into a person's needs for healing, hindrances and obstacles, and what is needed to prepare for healing. Discernment of spirits can reveal any demonic influences causing sickness or preventing healing. Praying supernaturally in tongues when we don't know how to pray empowers and guides our prayers through the Holy Spirit. Interpretation of tongues provides to our understanding the sense of what was prayed through the Holy Spirit. Dreams and visions provide supernatural illumination and vision.

How to Flow in the Gifts of the Spirit

Know That God Wants to Use you to Minister to Others through the Gifts. A.B. Simpson encourages every believer to flow in the gifts of the Spirit for the edifying of believers, especially the vocal or prophetic gifts: "Every Christian worker and minister should have in a very real way a prophetic message, a message not obtained from books and scribes, but warm from the mouth of God, and fresh from the Holy Spirit."[186]

Be Available. A.B. Simpson was used powerfully by God through many spiritual gifts by his attitude of receptivity, affirming, "At all times my spirit has been open to God for anything He might be pleased to reveal or bestow." Similar to Simpson, you can simply pray, "Lord, make me an instrument, a channel of Your life and love and power. I am open to You for anything You desire to reveal or bestow."

Be Filled with the Holy Spirit. A.B. Simpson would pray for "deeper and fuller baptisms." Pray for God to fill you afresh with His Spirit continually so that His power and illumination flow continually through you.

Receive Impartation of Spiritual Gifts. Paul told the Roman church, "For I long to see you so that I may impart some spiritual gift to you, that you may be established" (Romans 1:11). He also urged Timothy, "Do not neglect the spiritual gift within you, which was bestowed on you through prophetic utterance with the laying on of hands by the presbytery" (1 Timothy 4:14). Ask mature gifted Christian leaders to pray over you for impartation of spiritual gifts.

Stir Up the Gifts within You. Paul reinforces his words to Timothy in his second letter to him, "For this reason I remind you to kindle afresh the gift of God which is in you through the laying on of my hands" (2 Timothy 1:6). Sometimes we have let our giftings lie idle, and we need to be encouraged to pick them up and activate them once again.

Take All That God Promises. Some people think that because gifts are given as the Holy Spirit desires they should not desire spiritual gifts, and so they are passive and do not receive. However, when we understand that Spirit is not stingy and desires to give His gifts, we can take hold of His gifts confidently. A.B. Simpson received this revelation and recorded in his diary that he actively desired all that God had for him: "I had been timid at times about dictating to the Holy Spirit who is sovereign in the bestowal of His gifts, but now *I fully take all that is promised* in His Name."

Listen for the Voice of God. As mentioned in Biblical Healing Practice 8, Sarah Lindenberger counseled those coming to the Berachah Healing Home, "Cultivate the habit of listening to God's voice in your soul." How do we do this?

- *By learning to listen to your spirit.* Your soul is your inner being. Your spirit is your innermost being. The Holy Spirit dwells in your spirit. So listening to your spirit is listening to the Holy Spirit within you. Jesus declared that "out of your innermost being flow rivers of living water" (John 7:38). As we listen to the Holy Spirit in our human spirit, the rivers of living water flow from our spirit through our soul—our mind, will, emotions, attitudes, personality.

- *By being still and waiting on the Lord*—Ps. 46:10. The Hebrew verb for "be still" means to "cease striving, relax." Only when we are still can we hear the still, small voice of God. Jesus said, "My sheep know My voice" (John 10:27). Identify that inner knowing, that strong sense that "You know that you know . . ." It is like a gut feeling, as Jesus declared, "out of your belly [innermost being] shall flow rivers of living water. . ." (John 7:38, KJV).

- *By nourishing your spirit.* Our spirit is nourished by feeding on the Word of God. Jesus proclaimed, "It is the Spirit who gives life; the flesh profits nothing; the words that I have spoken to you are spirit and are life" (John 6:63). James exhorts us, "Receive the word implanted, which is able to save your soul" (James 1:21). As His Word pours into us, it flows out through our soul, not only for our own benefit but for the healing of the minds, will, emotions, attitudes, personalities, and bodies of others.

- *By releasing your spirit.* "Where the Spirit of the Lord is there is liberty" (2 Corinthians 3:18); therefore, we want to become free in the Spirit. Watchman Nee likens this to breaking out of a shell, writing, "The more you are broken, the more your spirit is released." This includes uncovering anything in your life that is binding you, holding you back, and then unleashing the Holy Spirit in and through your life.

- *By enlarging your spirit capacity.* A.B. Simpson, in his book *The Larger Christian Life,* spurs us on to more of the Higher Life in the Spirit: "We need a larger baptism of the Holy Spirit. . . . There are capacities in the human spirit none of us has ever yet begun to realize! . . . New baptisms awaken the dormant powers that we did not know we possessed."

Ask for the Holy Spirit to Teach You How to Hear. Our Higher Life Healing Rooms Director, Jerry Fidler, shared about when he first started praying for the sick as a Baptist pastor how he wanted to learn how to hear God speak when praying for others:

I was pastoring in Dayton, Oregon, and going over to a fellow pastor and friends conference on healing in a nearby town. I prayed, "Lord, would you tell me before the person is prayed for what the issue/need is. I want to learn how to hear your voice and know how to pray for others." Later that night after a wonderful praise and worship time one of the guest speakers asked the crowd of 300 if anyone was in pain and hurting right now, to raise your hand. Eight people raised their hands, and then he asked them to stand. He then pointed to two of them and asked them to come forward. As they started to walk to the front I heard the Lord whisper in my spirit "it's her neck." The pastor asked the first lady where she was hurting and she said, "I was in a car accident, and it's my neck." He went on to pray for her and she was healed. James said, "you have not because you ask not" (James 4:2). We need to ask, and ask with the right motive.[187]

Open Your Eyes to See in the Spirit. I encourage people to paraphrase and personalize Paul's prayer in Ephesians 1:

Father of Glory, I pray that you will impart to me the Spirit of
  wisdom and revelation
to open the eyes of my heart—
that I may more fully, deeply, intimately, know Christ,
that I may more fully, deeply, intimately, know the hope of
  Your calling,
that I may more fully, deeply, intimately, know the riches of
  my inheritance,
that I may more fully, deeply, intimately, know the exceeding
  greatness of
Your power and energy in my life.

Exercise the Gifts According to Your Faith. Based on Paul's exhortation in Romans 12:4-6, A.B. Simpson likewise exhorts us, "Let us be willing to speak as the oracles of God and prophesy according to the proportion of our faith."[188] Even if you feel your faith is small, exercise the faith you have to flow in the gifts, and He will give you more faith. Be expectant that God is going to minister through you supernaturally to minister to the needs of others.

Do Not Be Afraid to Speak Out. Sometimes we doubt we are hearing from God, or have strong impressions come to us that do not make sense to us. A.B. Simpson stirs us, "Fear not to speak the message which the Holy Spirit has burned into your soul for the quickening and the rousing of your brethren. It will be a word in season for some weary soul."[189] Jerry Fidler shares his own experience of questioning whether he was really hearing from God:

As part of the healing room ministry a few years ago our prayer team was praying for a lady in her late 30s and I heard in my spirit the Lord say, "Put your thumbs on her wrists and tell her

I love her." It was a gentle and faint voice, and for some reason I thought that somehow it had come from me, and I ignored it. A minute later the same thing happened again, and so I had an internal debate with myself if this had come from me, or could it possibly be from the Lord. A few minutes later it came back a third time so I took a risk and said, "Okay Lord, I will."

She was sitting in a chair and wearing a long sleeve sweater. As I knelt down I reached out for her wrists and she instantly recoiled and pulled her arms back. I said to her, "Let me tell you what has been happening. For the last several minutes the Lord has been telling me to put my thumbs on your wrists, and to tell you He loves you, and I wasn't sure if that was from Him, but it has come back a number of times, and I think it is from Him." With that she let me have her wrists, and unbeknownst to us there were two vertical scars, one on each wrist where she had tried to take her life. She dissolved into tears as the Lord brought about a wonderful inner healing, and renewed her in His love![190]

Using Revelational Gifts in Healing Prayer

The Gift of Prophecy. A.B. Simpson defines prophecy simply as "the power to receive and give forth special messages of the Holy Spirit for edification, exhortation and comfort of His people, . . . the 'word in season to him that is weary.'"[191] It could be a direct message from the Holy Spirit, or a "quickening touch" of a word of Scripture especially addressing the condition or need of the person to whom the word is spoken.

This gift was manifested both in the healing home ministry itself and in God's supernatural leading people to the healing homes. For Mrs. Hester, who had a tumor, heard an audible voice on May 12, 1897, prophesying, "Go to that Home on the Hudson [Berachah] and stay a few weeks." She obeyed the prophetic word of the Lord and was subsequently healed.[192]

In 1892, Clay Anderson had a spinal injury that contorted his body. One night he heard an audible voice prophesying to him, "Take your brother, go to the Alliance healing home in Detroit, for you will be healed."[193] He followed the supernatural divine direction, received prayer at the Beulah home and was healed.

Word of Knowledge. Although they did not use the current terminology of "word of knowledge," healing home workers did at times receive supernatural knowledge from God about a situation or a person's condition. For example, at Berachah Home, while praying with a woman, one of the workers received a prophetic impression from the Lord from Isaiah 55:2, "I will make the crooked places straight." What she did not know when she gave that supernatural word of knowledge was that the woman had curvature of the spine. This stirred the woman's faith, as through soaking prayer, the woman was healed.[194]

A.B. Simpson operated in this gift from time to time in his healing meetings. Early on in his weekly Friday healing meeting, he received a supernatural word of knowledge that someone was resisting coming to be anointed for healing. A woman named Mrs. Williams came forward and admitted she was the one. Simpson anointed her, and she became unconscious in another world for half an hour. When she came back to consciousness, she was singing and praising the Lord, without pain or weariness for the first time in 23 years.

William Christie, a C&MA missionary to Tibet, operated in the supernatural word of knowledge. A former Tibetan priest had become severely ill and had tried to find relief for seven years through sorcery and witchcraft. He was lying on a bed when Christie was summoned by the man's wife to pray for him. Christie "was swept by a strong impression that if this man would forsake heathenish ways, and put his trust in Jesus Christ, the power of God would be manifested, and he would be healed." As a result the man confessed Jesus as his Savior and the family burned all of the occult paraphernalia. Then Christie "rebuked the disease in the name of Jesus" and "suddenly the former priest felt a touch of life, and he arose," and was totally healed.[195]

How do you know if you are receiving a supernatural word of knowledge? In all these cases, they had a very strong impression—a conviction. This is not a general impression but something that is more specific and clear. If you are sensing this, but you are not sure, you can phrase it in the form of a question. "This comes to my mind _____. Does this mean anything to you? For some people, it comes as a clear mental image or even an actual visual image.

Word of Wisdom. A word of wisdom is not a natural wisdom that can be gained through the experiences, observations, or study by non-Christians as well as Christians. A word of wisdom is a supernatural wisdom of God beyond one's own capabilities endowed by the Holy Spirit for a need of the moment. An Old Testament example was the supernatural wisdom God gave Solomon for justice and counsel (1 Kings 3:16-28), yet he lacked human wisdom in personal living. Jesus exercised supernatural words of wisdom when the Pharisees tried to trip Him up with trick questions.

I find oftentimes when I am writing to give counsel to someone, or when I am praying for someone, but don't know how to pray or what to pray, the Holy Spirit will write through me or pray through in the moment a special word of wisdom. It is not something that I had already known or had pondered on but wise counsel that came to me in an instant. Many people will say to me, "You prayed exactly what I needed, even though I did not tell you." This comes from listening to the Spirit in our soul.

Using Internal and External Visions and Dreams in Healing Prayer

The Holy Spirit may give us an external vision we see with our eyes, an internal vision we see vividly in our mind (either with our eyes open or closed), or a dream (which in the Bible is sometimes called a night vision). A.B. Simpson affirms, "The Lord Jesus still gives His people hours of vision and revelation when they are elevated above the clouds and shadows of the present and permitted to come into closer touch with eternal things."[196]

Personally, I receive very few visions with my eyes open. Most of the visions I see are clear mental images. However, once while driving one day, I had a clear vision of the letters IL letters in a searing reddish-white fiery light like a red-hot brand. I thought maybe the letters IL were the initials of someone's name, but I never found such a person. Then about a month later, the Spirit said, "Now is the time." I shared it in a church where I was speaking. The Spirit revealed to me at that time that the letters IL meant the Roman numerals for 49. Several people responded that the number 49 was especially significant in their lives at that time.

One couple was celebrating their 49th anniversary, and the Lord was saying to them that their marriage was just as red-hot as when they got married. A woman approaching her 50th birthday was assured by the Holy Spirit that He had her number, that she was not getting too old, and that Lord was firing her up once again. The Spirit gave me a word for another 49 year-old man that he was going through a change in his life in which the Lord was branding him for a purpose.

More often, such revelation comes as an internal vision, that is, a mental picture, image, word, or thought or a symbolic image vividly in our mind. These are often ways in which words of knowledge, words of wisdom, or prophetic words are conveyed. Dreams and visions often involve symbols or images that have spiritual meaning. Such images, pictures, or thoughts are often symbolic—objects, people, animals, numbers, actions—not necessarily a real happening, but symbolic of something real. The Bible is full of symbols with spiritual meaning. A good book on hermeneutics or biblical interpretation provides a sound guide. These are just a few samples:

- <u>water themes</u>—rivers/streams/ocean/rain/clouds—Holy Spirit, revival, refreshing

- <u>paths/road, traveling, transporting</u>—spiritual direction and purpose, or lack of

- <u>plants/trees</u>—spiritual growth

- <u>rocks/stones/bricks</u>—foundations, building (or, negatively, stumbling blocks)

- <u>food/eating, drinking</u>—spiritual nourishment and health, or lack of

- <u>colors</u>—variety of meanings in Scripture, or of personal meaning to the person

- <u>numbers</u>—variety of meanings in Scripture, or of personal meaning to the person

- <u>shapes/patterns</u>—examples, types, repetition

- <u>buildings</u>—often of our own person or of the church. After I had surgery for colorectal cancer to remove parts of my colorectal tract, no cancer was found, and I was healed. However, I did not feel healed with parts of my insides removed and the pain and trauma of the surgery. During this time, I had a vivid dream of walking through the shell of a cluttered broken down house in shambles that was being stripped and renovated. The frame was still intact, but the rest of the house was going through an extreme makeover. The Lord showed me that He was renovating me from the inside out.

- <u>ladders, stairs, escalators</u>—ascending or descending in spiritual growth and progress, entering heavenly realm

- <u>sun/moon/stars</u>—often symbolic of persons or groups of persons

- <u>spiritual warfare imagery</u>—soldiers, armies, or military action, angels or demonic forces

- <u>Fire or smoke</u> in the Bible often symbolizes the fire of God—cleansing, refining, consuming, or providing light and heat.

When praying for people for inner healing, I sometimes receive from the Lord a mental image of fire cleansing or cauterizing wounds, or burning away all that is painful in the past. Twice I saw a vivid vision with my eyes of flaming letters or numbers. On one occasion, the Lord was showing me it was a like a branding iron in people's lives—branding them for Jesus.

Writing on sanctification of the mind, Simpson illustrated his teaching by citing a woman who received a vision of an empty skull filled with fire, as symbolic of the Holy Spirit filling the mind with the thoughts and feelings of God.[197]

- <u>authority figures</u>—kings, rulers, princes, officials, policemen, soldiers—being under authority or having spiritual authority

- <u>clothes</u>—may symbolize putting on the new or taking off the old.

Sometimes we will receive more than one dream, vision, or mental image, or more than one person will receive similar, but related, insights. A principle mentioned several times in Scripture is that something is confirmed or established by two or three witnesses (Deuteronomy 17:6; 19:15; Matthew 18:16; 2 Corinthians 13:1; 1 Timothy 5:19). These multiple images will confirm their reality and reinforce their importance to the one who is receiving prayer.

In one of our monthly Higher Life Healing Rooms, a couple came in off the street, whom we had never met before. They had seen our sign for healing prayer and came into the church for prayer about a particular need. However, when our prayer team was seeking the Lord about what He would reveal, I received a word of knowledge through two separate but related mental images that had nothing to do with their prayer request. The first was a zigzag pattern like on a sewing machine or on a graph chart; the second was a crooked stream meandering back and forth. The Lord revealed to me that they felt a purposelessness in their lives, that they were going back and forth, up and down, but going nowhere. Both husband and wife suddenly began weeping. It was exactly what they had felt. They had moved to a new town and had not been able to find work or a church or new friends. They felt all alone with no purpose in their lives. As a result, God ministered to them in a powerful way and they found purpose and hope—and a new church and friends!

Jerry Fidler shares how his wife Kelly began to see mental visions from the Lord in what she thought was a strange and silly impression:

My wife Kelly and I were at a conference in Branson, Missouri, about learning how to hear the voice of God as you pray, and she was in a group praying for the lady who was leading the worship at this conference. Each group would then take a few minutes of silent prayer asking the Lord how they should pray for this person, and then share what the Lord had put on their heart.

Kelly said she had a picture flash in her mind of a girl twirling a hula-hoop around her waist, and she thought that that was nutty and she wasn't going to share it. However it persisted, and she thought, "Alright, Lord, I'll risk it. She then said to the worship leader, "I know this sounds strange, but I keep seeing a picture of a girl with a hula-hoop, and I don't know what that means."

The worship leader said, "That requires balance, and my life is so out of balance now." From that seemingly silly picture the Lord clearly identified her need, and directed the group in how to pray for her.[198]

Sometimes the Lord may give you a dream, vision, or mental image, but you will not know what it means or whom it is for at the time. Later, God reveals to you the meaning and the person to whom it applies as in the vision I mentioned above with the white/red-hot brand IL. It is good and scriptural to write down these visions, dreams, and mental images. God told Habakkuk, "Record the vision, and inscribe it on tablets, that the one who reads it may run. For the vision is yet for the appointed time . . ." (Habakkuk 2:2).

Using the Miracle-Enhancing Gift of Faith in Healing Prayer

The great prayer warrior E.M. Bounds describes the gift of faith as mountain-moving faith in God, not as ordinary, everyday faith but as the summit of a peak: "When a Christian believer attains to faith of such magnificent proportions as these, he steps into the realm of implicit trust. He stands without a tremor on the apex of his spiritual outreaching. He has attained faith's veritable top stone which is unswerving, unalterable, unalienable trust in the power of the living God."[199] Higher Life devotional writer, Mrs. Charles Cowman, echoes this teaching: "The faith of God is in-wrought within our hearts by the Holy Ghost. And that is the faith that will say to the mountains, 'Be removed!' And they will melt like wax at His spoken word through us."[200]

This is what biblical commentators consider a supernatural degree of faith, a "Spirit-imparted faith," or as the great early church father Chrysostom called it, "the mother of miracles." This is the kind of faith, A.B. Simpson declared that is needed in the most difficult situations, the kind of faith that will pull down strongholds and "uproot sycamore trees of evil."

Sometimes the gift of faith will rise up within you as you pray for a person and you will speak with such faith that you know beyond the shadow of a doubt that the person is being healed. It is that inner knowing—you know that you know that you know that you know. . . ! This is the kind of faith that stirs prayers to be answered and heightens healing to be manifested.

It is the kind of faith A.B. Simpson calls "the faith of God," the God-kind of faith needed for the emergencies and crises of life. Once after talking with a depressed teenage girl and unable to dissuade her, faith rose up in me to bind the suicidal spirit and declare her free and whole. On the day she had determined to commit suicide, she received Jesus Christ as her Savior and was freed from her depression.

Using the Gift of Discernment of Spirits in Healing Prayer

Discernment of spirits is a special gift of the Holy Spirit to be able to identify if a manifestation is of the flesh, the Spirit, demonic, or a mixture, and to be able to identify particular spirits. C&MA missionary statesman Robert Jaffray calls it a "God-given supernatural instinct." A.B. Simpson experienced it as a "quickening in the soul."

When dealing with sickness, discernment of spirits is especially needed. Some illnesses have direct demonic roots, and others are purely biological. Still others involve emotional or spiritual issues. It is vital not to call something demonic when it is not. It is also vital to find out if something demonic is involved and to deal with it, otherwise healing will not occur.

Discerning the Presence of a Spirit to Be Cast Out. Sometimes we will sense strongly the presence of evil and know we are dealing with a demon in someone's physical or emotional illness. A.B. Simpson's associate William T. MacArthur recounted of one of his experiences of discernment of spirits: "The conviction seized me that there was no disease present, but simply an evil spirit," which was then cast out of an eight-year-old boy.[201]

Discerning When Casting Out Demons Is of No Value. A. B. Simpson, for example, discerned a woman was demonized, but could not get free or be healed because she ultimately did not want to get rid of her demon companion.[202] John MacMillan would similarly discern that a person would get partially free but did not want to give up a sin or demonic presence in order to become fully free.

Discerning a Spirit of Bondage Bringing Condemnation. Sometimes we will discern that no evil spirit needs to be cast out, but yet an evil spirit is binding, oppressing, or harassing a person. A.B. Simpson recalled "the case of a person who came to me for spiritual counsel and relief. He began by several humbling confessions which were given most sincerely and we have no doubt accepted by the Lord in His abundant mercy and grace. But we discerned a spirit of bondage and a severity and harshness in dealing with himself which deprived him of the comfort which the Lord mean for him in His forgiving grace and love."[203] He discerned this was not a demon to be cast out, but to be bound and rebuked, loosing the man from this inner emotional bondage.

Distinguishing the Human from the Spirit. A.B. Simpson had the gift to discern the Spirit from the flesh, or what he called the "human element": "I noted first a quiet but real quickening in my own soul, . . . so that I saw not only the working of the Spirit, but also a very distinct human element, not always edifying or profitable. And God led me to discern . . ."[204]

Discerning the Flesh from the Demonic. At other times, we will discern that no demon is present. Sometimes we may even discover by the Spirit that the person is operating in the flesh, even though it may appear to be demonic. I have seen cases in which a person appeared to be manifesting demonically, but the Holy Spirit revealed that the person just wanted to get attention and so was feigning a demonic attack.

Discerning Specific Spirits. Sometimes you will know instinctively what evil spirits are harassing a person. You will clearly know the type of spirit (infirmity, deception, fear, etc.) or even the name of a particular spirit. Some people who operate in discernment of spirits can actually see the evil entities or can smell or taste the presence of an evil spirit.

Discerning a Combination of Factors. Sometimes we will discern a combination of factors, which might include spiritual, emotional, physical, and demonic. We will need to sort out when to deal with a demon, and when to deal with the flesh. As someone with discernment has quipped, "You can't cast out the flesh and you can't crucify a demon."

Discerning When Something Is Not Demonic. It is most important that you do not call something a demon when it is not. That can bring great devastation, guilt, and condemnation upon a person. Discernment of spirits is not having a critical spirit. Discernment of spirit operates with humility, compassionate pastoral care, and great sensitivity both toward the Holy Spirit and toward the person.

Learning to Discern. Again, the gift of discernment of spirits depends a great deal upon hearing and recognizing the voice of the Holy Spirit as well as having a deep understanding of Scripture. The more we listen to the voice of the Spirit and abide in the Word of God, the more discerning we will become. Discernment grows through exercise and practice (Hebrews 5:14). Discernment of spirits is also corporate, meaning that others will bear witness of the truth of the discernment.

Use of Praying in Tongues in Healing Prayer

Higher Life/Fourfold Gospel/Alliance ministries have always believed that all of the gifts of the Spirit are operative today, including the gifts of tongues. In the early healing homes, before the Azusa Street Pentecostal revival, tongues were uncommon though not totally unheard of. When the Pentecostal movement arose, the C&MA, Fourfold Gospel, and most Higher Life leaders accepted the reality of speaking in tongues. While some Higher Life leaders became Pentecostal, the Alliance and most Fourfold Gospel leaders objected to the view that tongues was the initial or primary evidence of the baptism in the Spirit.

Many C&MA and Fourfold Gospel leaders experienced and valued speaking in tongues even though not accepting that it must be the initial evidence. Others, like Carrie Judd Montgomery, circulated in both camps. Many Alliance, Fourfold Gospel, and Higher Life leaders experienced tongues, and even those who did not saw in those who did both a great godliness and the benefits of tongues. They spoke highly of the value of praying in tongues both for personal edification and also as valuable ministry and intercessory tool. C&MA leader William T. MacArthur called praying in tongues "the double equipment."

The Use of Tongues in Healing Prayer Intercession. Praying in tongues can be of great value in intercession when praying for a person needing a touch from God. Paul explains, "In the same way the Spirit also helps our weakness; for we do not know how to pray as we should, but the Spirit Himself intercedes for us with groanings too deep for words; and He who searches the hearts knows what the mind of the Spirit is, because He intercedes for the saints according to the will of God" (Romans 8:26-27). Just as the Holy Spirit intercedes *for* us, He intercedes *through* us. Here are a number of ways praying in tongues can be of great benefit in healing prayer intercession:

- *Expressing the Holy Spirit's Burden in Intercession.* A.B. Simpson understood tongues to be an expression of the unutterable groanings of the Holy Spirit from this passage in Romans 8, explaining that God sometimes gives "a new tongue to adequately express the burdens of the Holy Spirit's prayer. . . knowing 'that He who searches the hearts knows the mind of the Spirit, because He makes intercession for the saints according to the will of God.'" So often when I have not known how to pray for a person, when I pray in tongues my mind is illumined, and I am able to know how to pray and what to pray. Sometimes I am actually groaning and weeping in tongues, expressing the depth of the hurts and wounds a person is experiencing. It is the Holy Spirit's expression of weeping with those who weep.

- *Greater Awareness of Spiritual Warfare.* Robert Jaffray, a Presbyterian who became a missionary with the C&MA, testified of his own experience of praying in tongues that he received "a clearer understanding of the mighty works of the Holy Spirit and of evil spirits, in these last days of the Present Age." When we are praying supernaturally in the spirit realm, it attunes us to the presence and work of both the unseen heavenly spirits and the unseen evil spirits. It is an aid to discernment of spirits and often goes hand-in-hand with it.

- *Supernatural Intercession.* William MacArthur, another associate of A.B. Simpson, found great value in intercession at the throne through praying in tongues, writing of "the blessedness of this experience—the heavenly intoxication of the supernatural song, or the blissful agony of supernatural intercession; yet these are among the blessings indicated in our Apostle's description of the Spirit-filled life—to quote him further, he says: 'Praying with all prayer and supplication in the spirit.'"

I too have found great power in interceding for others in tongues. Once I was driving by my church, and the Holy Spirit led me to stop, go inside, and kneel at the altar. He brought to my mind a teenage girl and gave me a burden to pray for her for half an hour in tongues. The girl had been set free from demonic bondage after being involved in a coven of witches. I found out later that at the very time I was praying, the girl had come under intense temptation to return to the occult coven. She was able to overcome the temptation and retain her victory.

- *Supernatural Understanding.* "I will pray with the spirit and I will pray with the mind also" (1 Corinthians 14:15). As we pray in tongues, many times (though not always) we may receive a kind of interpretation of what we have been praying. It is not a word-for-word translation, but rather an awareness or sense of what we have been praying. Just as above, I did not know exactly what I was praying in tongues, but I had a general but definite awareness that this girl was in trouble.

This was a vital source of prayer power and wisdom from God for Carrie Judd Montgomery at her Home of Peace in Oakland, California. Dr. Jennifer Miskov, who wrote her doctoral dissertation on Carrie's life and ministry, related the following story of Carrie's boldness and faith through praying in tongues to bring physical and emotional healing to a distraught and burnt-out missionary:

> Mrs. Norton came to the Home of Peace straight from India and was a "nervous wreck." He said that Carrie [n]ever waited for people to ask her for prayer, she just always would go over and lay hands upon them and pray for them. And she went over to Sister Norton and laid her hands upon her and began praying, praying in tongues. And Sister Norton had just come back from India and she said, "You're praying in

Hindustandi," you're saying "Take, my little one, take, take, take, take, take." So Mary believed and began to take and in a few days she was absolutely restored, she said "I've just been taking, taking, I've been taking. . . ."[205]

It may occasionally occur, as it did with Carrie on this and other occasions, that the tongues in which you are praying may be recognized as an actual language. Always be open for the Holy Spirit to use you in any way He may choose.

- *A Trigger for Other Gifts to Be Manifested.* I have found that sometimes when I pray in tongues, I will then pray for the person in English and the prayer will express exactly what was on the person's mind or what his or her unexpressed need was. This could be an interpretation, a word of wisdom or knowledge, a prophetic prayer, or discernment of spirits.

The Use of Tongues by the Person Needing a Touch from God. If those who come receiving prayer have received the gift of tongues as a personal prayer language, encourage them to pray in tongues even if they do not understand what they are saying. Paul declares that praying in tongues speaks mysteries and edifies, or builds up, the person spiritually. Since our spirit affects our mind and emotions and body, when we pray in tongues, we can be built up mentally, emotionally, and physically as well. Here are some examples of the personal therapeutic value of praying in tongues:

- *Expressing Our Burdens through the Holy Spirit.* Just as praying in tongues for intercession, as A.B. Simpson noted, can be an expression of the unutterable groanings of the Holy Spirit in intercession, so it can be for the person receiving prayer: "we cannot always expect to fully understand our own prayers, but must often pour out our hearts before Him in wordless agony and unutterable desire."

- *Strengthening the Inner Man.* William T. MacArthur, close associate of A.B. Simpson and father-in-law of actress Helen Hayes, testified of a divine inner strength: "It is being strengthened with might by His Spirit in the inner man. . . ." I found that inner strength and relief by praying in tongues while in pain after cancer surgery. I could not think or pray or read the Scripture because I was in so much pain even though doped up by the medications. When I would pray in tongues, the pain lessened and a Scripture or a song would come to my mind.

- *Rejuvenation of Body and Mind.* Mattie Perry had been an evangelist, pioneering district superintendent, and church planter with the Christian and Missionary Alliance. She had also founded Elhanan Bible Institute and Children's Home. However, she became weak and disabled. When she experienced praying in tongues, she recalled, "The old, tired feeling went like the dropping of an old garment. My memory was quickened and my nerves steadied instantly." She was healed and then ministered with a greater evangelistic and healing ministry. She found praying in tongues to be therapeutic, healing to her body and soul.

- *Healing from Blood Poisoning While Praying in Tongues.* David Wesley Myland was a pastor and state superintendent for the Christian and Missionary Alliance. While preparing for a C&MA conference at his church, his furnace exploded, and he was severely burned and nearly died. A few weeks later he saw a vision of a choir of angels singing, and he began singing along with them in a new language of heaven. He was healed as he sang in tongues. He explains how he began to write the interpretation: "I took out a piece of blank paper and began to write with my left hand, tried to write with my pencil between the first and second finger. I could not get along very fast and involuntarily took it over into my right hand, the hand that had been so badly swollen, and I found I was healed; the sores were there but I was healed. There wasn't a particle of pain or stiffness, and I wrote the words of the Latter Rain Song, word for word, as fast as I could write."

- *Healing from Breast Cancer Through Praying in Tongues and Interpretation.* The *Alliance Weekly* in 1913 recorded this testimony:

"I was awakened with the power of the Lord upon me and as I began praising Him in the unknown tongue, He gave me the interpretation, 'This thing I will cast off from thy being.'. . . I got up that morning and ate my breakfast, but soon realized that God was working in that cancer, and it seemed to be literally pushing out of my breast." Five days later she saw a vision of Christ and His presence filled the room. She was lifted up off her bed on her feet with no effort of her own. The pain was gone and a week later the cancer dropped off her chest "like a hard, heavy stone."[206]

Implementing This Biblical Healing Practice in Your Healing Center. Here are some practical ways you can encourage this practice and strengthen the faith of the people who come for ministry in your healing center:

- *Be Sensitive to the Spirit and Non-Offensive When Praying in Tongues.* If you are ministering in a context outside of a Pentecostal or charismatic church ministry, praying in tongues is often very controversial and sometimes taboo. Because the Apostle Paul limits speaking in tongues in a public worship service, stipulating that it must be followed by an interpretation, many people mistakenly think that a person must never speak in tongues without an interpretation. They do not understand the difference between the public use of tongues in a worship service and the use of tongues in prayer intercession, or else they think it makes no difference.

  Rather than making it a source of contention, praying in tongues should bring healing and reconciliation. Therefore, we recommend that if you do have the gift of praying in tongues and use it in intercession for other people, that you either pray in tongues quietly under your breath or else ask the person if it is okay for you to pray in tongues out loud.

- *If you pray in tongues, oftentimes, the Holy Spirit may then pray through you with your understanding, so that you will know how to pray specifically.* Or the Holy Spirit may through interpretation give you a revelation of how to proceed or pray or to give a word of wisdom or a supernatural word of knowledge.

- *Instruct the person to read Chapter 31 in God's Healing Arsenal on "The Overcoming Power of Praying in a Supernatural Language."*

- *Make available Jack Hayford's book The Beauty of Spiritual Language.* Jack Hayford introduces people to the value of praying in tongues in a gentle pastoral manner.

- *Do not tell a person, "You need to speak in tongues."* Rather, say, "Praying in tongues could be of great benefit to you—physically, emotionally, mentally, and spiritually."

- *Do not tell a person, "You are not filled with the Spirit if you don't speak in tongues."*

- *Do not try to get a person to speak in tongues by telling them to move their mouth around and babble or repeat certain words over and over again fast.*

- *Encourage the person to follow A.B. Simpson's suggestion: "Often pour out our hearts before Him in wordless agony and unutterable desire."* As they just cry out and pray out their agonies and desires before God, it may flow into another language of the Spirit.

- *Tongues may also be an expression of overflowing praise.* When people receive a touch from God, they may become so over-whelmed with the love or joy of God that they naturally over-flow into another language of the Spirit. In the words of Charles Wesley's great hymn, "Oh for a thousand tongues to sing my great Redeemer's praise, the glories of my God and King, the triumphs of His grace." Encourage them to follow A.B. Simpson's counsel to speak out the inexpressible in their heart: "If you have, in some simple form, the old gift of tongues welling up in your heart, some Hallelujah which you could not put into articulate speech, some unutterable cry of love or joy, out with it!"

CHAPTER 8

Understanding and Discerning Manifestations of God's Presence and Power

Sometimes nothing will happen as you are praying for people for healing; at other times unusual physical manifestations of God's presence and power may occur. Manifestations are not necessary, but they do happen. While we don't need to see manifestations to know that God is at work, they are often signs of God's working. Don't go seeking such manifestations, but don't be surprised or dismayed if they happen.

Such manifestations did occur frequently through the ministry of A.B. Simpson and his associates, although they were careful not to draw attention to them. Simpson testified of the manifestations through his own healing anointing: "Dear friends, I never feel so near to the Lord . . . as when I stand with the Living Christ, to manifest His personal touch and resurrection power in the anointing of the sick."[207]

While the historic healing home ministries were usually private and low key, dramatic charismatic manifestations occurred from time-to-time in the healing homes and other public healing meetings, occasionally being reported in periodicals such as Carrie Judd Montgomery's *Triumphs of Faith* and the *Alliance Weekly*. Supernatural manifestations were not the focus of the healing homes and were not sought after, but from time to time, testimony would be given of unusual supernatural manifestations of the presence and power of God. Most of these were long before the Azusa Street Pentecostal revival. Modern day Pentecostal and charismatic healing ministries do not have a monopoly on unusual manifestations. God's healing power was sometimes manifested dramatically in these pre-Pentecostal (or might we say, proto-Pentecostal) healing homes. Here are just a few illustrations.

Supernatural Manifestations in the Environment

A Powerful Experience of the Manifest Presence of God. A.W. Tozer declared, "The Presence of God is more important than the program." By that He meant the manifest presence of God, not His omnipresent. The Manifest Presence of God is tangibly perceived, sometimes in physical or visible ways. Sometimes the very atmosphere seems electric with the power of God. People described such experiences of the tangible presence of God at Berachah Healing Home as "days of heaven on earth."[208] One woman testified, "At the very threshold of this House Beautiful I was impressed with the presence of the Holy Spirit."[209]

Manifestations of the Glory of God. Upon occasion, but rarely, both in the Bible and in experience, a glory cloud appears. This may take the form of a white or golden cloud or fog or bright light. Or audible sounds may occur such as a voice or singing, or sounds of a wind or roaring. In 1898 Lizzie Elledges testified in the *Alliance Weekly* that she heard an audible voice prophesying to her, "The Lord hath given the healing faith." The voice also sounded like an unknown tongue and a cloud of glory filled the room.[210]

Manifestations of the Ground or Building Shaking. When the disciples prayed for God's healing power and signs and wonders to be manifested, Luke records, "And when they prayed, the place where they had gathered together was shaken, and they were all filled with the Holy Spirit" (Acts 4:31). I have experienced this on several occasions as God manifested His presence in a powerful way while I was in prayer. Each time, I have checked online to see if an earthquake had been recorded, and in vast majority of the cases, no earthquake had occurred. This was a supernatural quaking of the Spirit.

Supernatural Manifestations of Anointing Through Prayer Partners

After the early church gathered together and prayed that God would "extend Your hand to heal, and signs and wonders take place through the name of Your holy Servant Jesus," they were all filled with the Holy Spirit and "the place where they gathered together was shaken" (Acts 4:30-31). In some cases, supernatural anointing was accompanied by shaking. In others, people were healed through a shadow cast upon them or with cloths that had been anointed. We cannot force a pattern or practice, but we can be aware that God will sometimes work in unusual supernatural ways. Here are some examples:

Trembling. Sometimes while praying for a person, you may sense the power of God come upon you in such a way that your hands or body begin to tremble. This is usually an indication that God is moving in a powerful way.

Heat through your hands. Frequently when I pray for people, they will tell me that they feel heat or fire coming through my hands even though I seldom feel it myself. God often manifests His presence through fire in Scripture. One of the frequent metaphors to describe God or the Holy Spirit is fire. God is an all-consuming fire (Hebrews 12:29). John the Baptist declared that Jesus would baptize with the Holy Spirit *and fire* (Luke 3:16). Such fire is often associated with cleansing, purifying, refining.

An electrical charge through your hands. Similar to heat, sometimes it will feel like electricity or static. These manifestations usually indicate that God is imparting healing or a touch of empowering and strengthening, a divine energizing. A.B. Simpson describes this in his own healing ministry: "The effect of prayer and anointing is sometimes like an electrical shock in a mild form. . . . Many members of my congregation have experienced this aid in some form, often by a direct cure of some ailment, physical as well as spiritual."[211]

Dr. T.J. McCrossan, a Greek professor, C&MA pastor, and president of Simpson Bible Institute, experienced this while praying for the sick as well. In one particular instance, along with healing evangelist Charles Price, he laid hands on a Chinese pastor's wife who was dying from tuberculosis. He described what happened: "The result was that God sent a mighty power (somewhat like bolts of electricity) down our arms into her body. Personally, we could hardly endure it, but we knew well it was God answering prayer, for we saw that she had fallen into a peaceful sleep." For about half an hour she lay still on the platform, though "her dress was constantly twitching and moving just over her lungs. Suddenly she leaped to her feet perfectly well."[212]

Oil supernaturally dripping from your fingers. This is rarer, but occasionally someone has a special anointing for healing manifested through oil supernaturally dripping from his or her hands. I witnessed this occurring on one occasion through the hands of an Alliance pastor' wife.

Overwhelming power flowing through you causing the person you are praying for to tremble or fall or become weak or faint. This is not a power of our own making but a manifestation of the power of God flowing through us. We have read in church history about this happening through the ministries of people like Jonathan Edwards, Charles Finney, Peter Cartwright, Kathryn Kuhlman, and other healing ministers, but it also occurred frequently through the ministries of Higher Life leaders like A.B. Simpson, F.F. Bosworth, and T.J. McCrossan, as well as frequently today.

Early in A.B. Simpson's ministry, he anointed a woman with oil who had come for prayer. She fell under the power of the Spirit, unconscious for about half an hour, then she got up healed, without pain for the first time in nearly 20 years.

It is even possible that as you are praying for people, you may be overcome by the power of Spirit as well. C&MA Field evangelist Wilbur F. Meminger describes a time when the anointing was so heavy that those who were praying for the sick fell under the power of the Spirit themselves: "At the time of prayer for the sick, wave after wave of holy emotion rolled over us, and shouts of victory arose as the sick were healed. Some who were assisting were prostrated by the power of God."[213]

Manifestations Upon People Receiving Prayer

Sensations of electricity or shaking. Trembling or shaking seems to be a response to the overwhelming presence of the Lord and the moving of the Holy Spirit, sometimes in fear, sometimes in joy, sometimes connected with a sense of humbling, sometimes just with a sense of the awesomeness of God. These manifestations occurred fairly frequently in early healing ministries. For example, at Berachah Healing Home in March 1891 Julie Boyd was healed as she described, "a divine electricity coursing through my whole body" caused the whole bed to shake.[214]

E.D. Whiteside, known as "the praying man of Pittsburgh," was the superintendent of the Alliance work in Pennsylvania and founded the Alliance Home in Pittsburgh as a place of rest and healing. A woman by the name of Zolla McCauley, who had double curvature of the spine and partial paralysis in her body, went to the home in Pittsburgh for prayer. When she was prayed over a thrill like an electrical shock went through her body and she was healed.[215]

What is fascinating is that several years before Whiteside himself had been healed by similar experience of electrical shocks going through his body: "Like a flash of electricity, I was instantly thrilled. Every point of my body and nerves was controlled by a strange sensation that increased in volume, until I bowed lower and lower to the floor. I was filled with the ecstatic thrill. My physical frame was unable to stand the strain."[216]

Feeling of heat. Just as sometimes heat flows through our hands when we pray for people, so that heat or fire flows through people. However, it is not just through the laying on of hands, but sometimes people experience this manifestation of God without anyone touching them. John Wesley reported that his heart was "strangely warmed." A.B. Simpson experienced this himself, recording it in his personal diary in 1907: "A distinct sense of warmth—at times a penetrating fire—filled my whole body. . . . God showed me plainly that it was the Holy Spirit. . . . It continued for more than 6 hours. . . I got alone with God and on my face opened all my being to Him to fill."

It should not be surprising then to understand that God sometimes manifests His presence and healing power through a feeling of heat in the bodies of the people receiving prayer. It is kind of like a "Holy Spirit hot flash." Sometimes healing comes to the part of the body feeling heat. Sometimes the heat goes from head to toe. At times the heat indicates that God is burning something away—cleansing or purifying by fire.

Feeling of Water Flowing. A woman had been suffering from several diseases for 18 years from the age of 9 to 27. These afflictions, which included ingrown toenails, corns, spinal problems causing severe back pain and headaches, mental incapacity, and inability to absorb nourishment, had almost totally debilitated her. She had endured several surgeries, and was told she would have to go to a sanitarium. On September 10, 1895, she was taken to an Alliance healing meeting, where they laid hands on her. She shared what happened next: "It seemed as though I felt water flowing over my body and instantly every pain and ache left."[217] Similar to the soothing power of a whirlpool bath, she experienced the healing waters of the touch of Jesus upon her body.

Feeling an Invisible Hand. Sometimes people will feel a hand touching them, even when no person is physically doing so. Josephus

Pulis had been delivered from alcoholism and was used by God in Alliance healing ministry, with many people healed. However, he experienced a physical and mental breakdown. A.B. Simpson prayed for him, and nothing happened at the moment. However, Pulis recalled, "I remember that he asked Jesus to visit me that night after I had retired, and no sooner had my poor head touched the pillow than I felt a touch like a hand on the inside of my head and going all over my brain. This lasted about four hours, and oh, such glory as filled my soul I can never describe. It was unspeakable."[218] It was like a spiritual and emotional massage of his brain by Jesus. He did not receive total healing at that time, but it started the healing process over time.

Feeling a Breeze or a Breath. Some people will sense a breeze blowing upon them or a breath breathing into them. The Hebrew and Greek words for "Spirit" can also be translated as breath or wind. So it is not surprising that people might experience the holy, healing breath of Jesus through the Holy Spirit. On the evening of Jesus' resurrection in the Upper Room, Jesus breathed upon (literally, "breathed into) the disciples, and said, "Receive the Holy Spirit" (John 20:22). On two other occasions, Josephus Pulis, experienced this breath of God when he was suddenly stricken down almost to the point of death: "I offered the mighty prayer of silence as I lay there before Him, my hope and trust, and He breathed upon and into me His own divine life, which alone is healing, and in less than a half an hour, I was better than ever." He testified, "All these glorious manifestations began like a spark in the smoking flax."[219]

Leg-lengthening. One woman was prayed over at a healing home for several days for several hours a day. One day her ribs creaked "like an old saddle" as they were adjusted into proper place through prayer. Her short leg was lengthened an inch with a grating sound.[220]

Another woman suffered from a hip joint disease stemming from an accident. Out of joint, one leg had grown three inches longer than the other and left her in constant severe pain. She claimed the healing promises of Scripture and prayed that the Alliance pastor would come an anoint her with oil. An hour later, he showed up at her door. After he spent some time in prayer for her, the pain subsided, and she was able to walk without crutches. Over time, her leg shortened three inches to its normal length. Her eyesight was also healed and she never had to wear glasses again.[221]

Falling under the Power of the Spirit. As mentioned above, sometimes people are so overwhelmed by the power of the Holy Spirit when someone prays for them under an anointing that they become weak and cannot remain on their feet. At other times, it occurs even when no one is touching them.

Some people call this "resting in the Spirit." A.B. Simpson himself described in his personal diary this kind of an experience happening to him: "A very mighty and continued resting of the Spirit down upon my body until it was almost overpowering and continued during much of the night."

T.J. McCrossan explains the benefit of this manifestation in relationship to healing, "It is the prayer of faith that heals. Going under this power seems, however, to bring an extra spiritual blessing."[222] Some biblical examples of people falling under the power of the Spirit include the following:

- *Balaam Fell Down with Vision and Prophecy.* Balaam, in his poetic prophecy, says he was falling down as he received a vision (Numbers 24:16): "The oracle of him who hears the words of God, and knows the knowledge of the Most High, who sees the vision of the Almighty, *falling down*, yet having his eyes uncovered."

- *Queen of Sheba Fainted with Awe* (1 Kings 10:5; 2 Chronicles 9:4)— "there was no spirit left in her." Some commentators like Jonathan Edwards view the fainting of the Queen of Sheba as an expression of this phenomenon.

- *Priests Unable to Stand to Minister Because of the Glory of the Lord* (2 Chronicles 5:13-14).

- *Ezekiel Fell on Face from Awe of God* (Ezekiel 1:28; 3:23; 44:4)— three occasions of falling on his face at the manifestation of the glory of God. Many commentaries indicate this was not a voluntary falling, but a supernatural result of the awesomeness of God's presence.

- *Daniel Fell on Face from Fear* (Daniel 8:17).

- *Daniel Fell from Vision and Voice from God* (Daniel 10:8-10). Daniel had three manifestations of this phenomenon when he saw a vision and heard a voice. First, his strength was sapped. Then he fell forward into a deep sleep or unconsciousness. Then, a hand touched him, and he was set trembling on his hands and knees.

- *Peter, James and John Fell on Their Faces in Fear* (Matthew 17:16-18).

- *Soldiers Fell When Jesus Says, "I Am!"* In the Garden of Gethsemane, when the soldiers approached Jesus, and He said, "I am [He] ["He" is not found in the Greek], they all fell backward at the awesomeness of the statement of Jesus that He is the "I am" (John 18:5-6).

- *Paul Fell from Flash of Light from Heaven.* Paul at his conversion on the Damascus road fell when he saw the light from heaven flashing about him (Acts 9:3-4).

- *Peter Fell into a Trance* (Acts 10:9-11).

- *Philippian Jailer Trembled and Fell at Paul's Feet* (Act 16:29). Jonathan Edwards cites this as an example of the phenomenon.

- *John Fell at a Vision of Jesus.* John writes, "And when I saw Him, I fell at His feet as a dead man" (Revelation 1:17).

These all appear to be a response to the overwhelming power and glory of God in fear, conviction, revelation, or blessing.

Other Body Movements. Mrs. E. L. McLaine had dislocated her shoulder so that it sagged two inches and caused her arm to be lifeless. After several Bible readings and anointing at the C&MA Beulah Healing Home in Detroit, on January 25, 1892, the power of Lord came into her arm and shoulder and it began moving up and down on its own for half an hour, then she was healed.[223] In 1896, an elderly lady had fallen and fractured several bones. She went to the Beulah Healing

Home where Dora Dudley anointed and prayed for her and felt the bones moving back into place.[224]

Sometimes strange body manifestations may occur as a blessing to the person even if sickness and healing are not involved. Once my wife and I were leading a woman to Christ as Savior. As she prayed a prayer to receive Christ, she felt her stomach move as if a baby was moving and kicking her in her womb, but she was not pregnant. I pointed out to her the Scripture, "out of your belly shall flow rivers of living water." All of the sudden, she shouted out excitedly, "That's it! The Bible has my experience! That is exactly what I feel!" She realized it was the Holy Spirit was showing her that He was birthing new life in her—new life in Christ.

Dreams and Visions. Just as we may receive dreams and visions in ministering to people, so they too may receive dreams and visions that are catalysts for healing. Mrs. Hester, who had a tumor, heard an audible voice on May 12, 1897, prophesying, "Go to that Home on the Hudson and stay a few weeks." She went to the home and received prayer for several weeks from Dr. Peck and Miss Lindenberger. She had a dream "which was more than a dream" of heaven and the coming of Christ and then she was healed of her tumor.[225]l

Sometimes they will not understand the meaning of the dream or vision they have received. As you pray for them, the Holy Spirit may give you a word of knowledge or wisdom, a prophetic word, or tongues and interpretation to provide supernatural insight into what they have seen.

Several Manifestations at the Same Time. Lizzy Elledges was mentioned above as hearing a voice and seeing a glory cloud. As part of the same experience, she fell to the floor and could not speak or move, then her body was "shaken by the power of God." A fire went through her body and she recounted that she "felt a new life coursing through my veins." Even as she was writing this testimony, she wrote, power like an electrical shock was coming upon her.[226]

The Healing Power of Holy Laughter. Reader's Digest quips, "Laughter is the best medicine," based on Solomon's proverb: "A joyful heart is good medicine, but a broken spirit dries up the bones" (Proverbs 17:22). This Scripture attests to the healing power of laughter. Scripture is filled with expressions of joy and laughter:

- "You greatly rejoice with joy inexpressible and full of glory" (1 Peter 1:8).
- "The disciples were filled with joy and with the Holy Spirit" (Acts 13:52).
- "Jesus rejoiced in Spirit" (lit., "leaped or danced with much joy") (Luke 10:21).
- "God will fill your mouth with laughter" (Job 8:21).
- "Our mouth was filled with laughter" when the Lord set the Israelites free (Psalm 126:2, 5, 6).
- In the distress of her infertility, Sarah said of God's prophetic word that she would bear a child, "God has made me laugh" (Genesis 21:6).

The "holy laughter" movements have turned many people off because of perceptions of emotional excess. Certainly, excesses have occurred and some of the laughter movement appears to be of the flesh rather than the Spirit, but we must be careful not to dismiss all such manifestations as being of the flesh. The Higher Life movements and the Christian and Missionary Alliance have a long and rich heritage of the healing and overcoming power of genuine holy laughter.

Very early in Simpson's ministry, before he even knew about or believed in divine healing, he personally witnessed "the power of divine joy to heal disease." He recalled that in the earliest years of his ministry he visited a dying man not expected to live through the night. He led him to salvation and through what he called a "baptism of glory" and a "baptism of holy gladness" he was miraculously healed:

But as I visited him, as I supposed for the last time, and tenderly led him to the Saviour, and as he accepted the gospel and became filled with the peace of God and the joy of salvation, there came upon him such a baptism of glory and such an inspiration of the very rapture of heaven, that he kept us for hours beside his bed as he shouted and sung, what we all believed to be the beginning of the songs of heaven, and we bade him farewell long after midnight, fully expecting that our next meeting would be above.

But so mighty was the uplift in that soul that his body, unconsciously to himself, threw off the power of disease, and the next morning he was convalescent, to the amazement of his physicians, and in a few days entirely well. I knew nothing, at that time, of divine healing, but simply witnessed with astonishment and delight, the power of divine joy to heal disease.

Simpson writes that, "Many a time since have I seen the healing and the gladness of Jesus come together to the soul and body, and the night of weeping turned into a morning of joy. Many a time have I seen the darkly clouded and diseased brain lighted up with the joy of the Lord, and saved from insanity by a baptism of holy gladness."

Dallas Willard writes, "Holy delight and joy is the great antidote to despair and is a wellspring of genuine gratitude—the kind that starts at our toes and blasts off at our loins and diaphragm to the top of our head, flinging our arms and our eyes and our voice upward toward our good God."[227] As we are praying for people diseased in body, depressed in mind, dying spiritually or burnt-out on life, the healing power of laughter can turn their lives around and turn their mourning into dancing. So don't be surprised if someone breaks out hilariously as the healing power of God comes upon them.

Wailing, Groaning, Yelling. Sometimes just the opposite of holy laughter may occur. A person may groan, or wail, or even scream. We should not be frightened when this happens. It is most of the time the Holy Spirit moving upon a person. It may occur for several reasons:

- The person may be under the conviction of the Holy Spirit.
- This is often due to deep inner pain.

- It may be a release of bondage or a deep burden.

- Paul speaks of the Holy Spirit groaning within us (Romans 8:26).

- We see many times in the Psalms people crying out to the Lord.

- Occasionally it could be a demonic manifestation, but there is still no need to fear. God is greater than any demonic presence. Don't assume it is demonic unless you have ruled out emotional or physical distress. If you are certain it is a demonic spirit, just bind the spirit and command it to be quiet. Once when my wife and I were ministering at a church in England, when we laid hands on a woman, she screamed, fell to the floor, and then was silent. She was released from a demonic oppression instantly. If a demon is manifesting, even like a roaring lion, by your authority in Christ, you can silence the spirit.

Discernment and Manifestations

Some people are afraid of the manifestations of the Spirit because they have perceived excesses, misuse, or counterfeits. Paul told Timothy, "God has not given us a spirit of fear, but a spirit of love and power and sound mind" (2 Timothy 1:7, KJV). Fear of manifestations is not from God. A.B. Simpson cautioned that fear of the devil comes from the devil himself. Fear or despising manifestations can quench the Holy Spirit (1 Thessalonians 5:18-21).

Higher Life/Alliance Counsel Regarding Manifestations. For those who may have fear or skepticism about unusual manifestations, Higher Life and Alliance leaders gave wise, discerning counsel:

- *Don't Be Scared of Satan's Scarecrows.* A.B. Simpson assures us, "Many of God's dear children have been hindered in waiting upon Him by fear of certain manifestations and spiritual movements which may not always be wholly scriptural in their methods and results. The enemy loves to use these things as scarecrows to keep away God's children from genuine blessing. Let us . . . simply wait upon God without fear."[228]

- *Don't Let Fear Cheat You Out of the Spirit's Blessings.* Robert Jaffray admonished, "There is a great danger of fear of the works of the devil to such an extent that we shall lose all courage to seek earnestly for the true and full endowment of the Spirit for which our souls hunger. I have met some who are so prejudiced on account of why that have seen that they say they have no desire to ever speak in tongues, forgetting that tongues is one of the gifts of the Spirit. Let us not allow the enemy so to drive us away from, and cheat us out of, the real blessings of the Spirit because he has counterfeited in some cases the gift of tongues. We have no business to be afraid of evil spirits, for His has given us 'power over all the power of the enemy,' and He can give supernatural discernment of spirits."[229]

- *Trust God to Keep You from a Counterfeit.* Citing Matthew 7:9-11, A.B. Simpson encourages to trust God, not our doubts and fears: "Can we not trust our heavenly Father to keep His promise to us, "if a son shall ask bread of any of you which is a father, will He give him a stone him, a stone? Or if he ask a fish, will he for a fish give him a serpent? Or if he ask an egg will He offer him a scorpion? If ye then, being evil, know how to give good gifts to your children, how much more shall the heavenly Father give the Spirit to them that ask Him."[230]

- *Overcome Fanaticism with Truth, Not Criticism or Opposition.* Simpson urges balance and acceptance of what is genuine: "The way to meet and overcome fanaticism is not to oppose all unusual spiritual manifestations, but to accept that which is truly of the Lord and then from the standpoint of a friend gently and wisely correct the spirit of extravagance which you can never do if you take your place among the critics and the enemies of 'spiritual gifts.' The only way to meet error is to go all the way with truth."[231]

- *Claim the Protection of the Blood of Jesus.* Carrie Judd Montgomery recognized the power of overcoming the Evil One by the blood of the Lamb (Revelation 12:11): "I had seen a few manifestations which I knew were of God, but I had seen so many things which were not. . . . I said, 'Father, I believe You are doing a mighty work, but I believe also that the Enemy is there and at work to counterfeit and hinder. . . . Father, if You have anything more for me, I want it.' I had to ask Him to take away all fear. One day Jesus said to me, 'My precious blood will keep you away from every evil, from everything that is not of God.'"[232]

- *Put Up with Mixture of Flesh and Spirit, Trusting God to Guard.* Following the lead of A.B. Simpson, C&MA pastor N.N. Harriman counseled, "To prevent wild-fire we do not think that preventives should be invented. We believe that 'mixture' is inevitable where God moves in power, and think that is safer to let God guard the door to danger, and put up with some mixture, rather than teach that God can and cannot do this and that, as a means of guarding against danger. God is larger than our human theories, and it is both highly unbecoming and dangerous to be too extravagantly positives in asserting what He is or is not able to do."[233]

Tests for Discerning Manifestations. Higher Life/Alliance leaders used several biblical tests to discern whether a manifestation was from the Holy Spirit, the flesh, a demonic source, or a mixture:

- *Fruit.* Does it bring a person closer to God and encourage Christlikeness? Jesus said, "You will know them by their fruit." (Matthew 7:16-20).

- *Gift of Discernment of Spirits* (1 Corinthians 12:10).

- *Peace of God vs. a Check in One's Spirit* (similar to discernment of spirits). Professor T.J. McCrossan testified, "You will feel at once that it is not of God, . . . your spiritual nature will revolt."[234]

- *Tests of the Word of God.* What does Scripture say about this seemingly supernatural manifestation? Is this consistent with sound doctrine and the ways in which God works? The Higher Life/Alliance leaders recognized this as a primary tool of discerning the genuineness of manifestations: "Never did a soul drift into fanaticism or wildfire who did not, at first, either accept a strained or a perverted interpretation of scripture, or read into certain passages a meaning made impossible by an intelligent comparison with other passages."[235]

- *Christo-centric Tests.* That is, is Jesus continually confessed as Lord in word and deed in the person's life (1 Corinthians 12:1)? Does the spirit behind the manifestation confess the deity and humanity of Jesus Christ?—that Jesus Christ came in the flesh (1 John 4:1-3)?

- *Transmission of Unclean Spirits.* Has the person experienced pain, or fallen into depression, a bad habit, temptation, or sin after having hands laid on him or her?

- *Occult Exposure.* Has the person been involved in or exposed to psychic or occult practices, cults, or Eastern religions, or is there the possibility of other demonic activity or influence existing in the person's life? Carrie Judd Montgomery observed:

> I have noticed that when people who have touched occult things are in a meeting, the devil will bring forth strange manifestations from them, and the people who have no discernment come in and say, "If that is Pentecostal power, I do not want it." Beloved, it is not the power of the Holy Spirit, but it is the evil one trying to counterfeit and seeking to turn people away from the blessed baptism of the Holy Spirit. If people desire to be filled with the Spirit of God, they must first confess their sins and be cleansed by the blood of Jesus. They must confess to other Christians if they have touched any of these abominations which God has forbidden, and they must ask believing ones to set them free before they can invite the Holy Spirit to possess the temple.[236]

- *Harsh or Forced?* Has this manifestation been manipulated or seem harsh or strained?

- *Depression or Confusion?* During or after the manifestation, does the person have a feeling of depression, confusion, or negative attitude?

- *Impure Motives.* Were the person's motives impure for wanting to receive a supernatural manifestation? Was the person seeking a manifestation rather than or more than God Himself?

- *Is the manifestation uncontrollable* (1 Cor. 14:32-33) or is there any unusual display such as barking, roaring, slithering like a snake, etc.?[237]

For more on discernment of manifestations, read Chapter 11 of *Nuggets of Genuine Gold* on "Discernment in the Spirit-Empowered Life."

Additional Tips Regarding Manifestations

- *Don't be afraid of them.* They are usually either direct supernatural manifestations of the power of God or natural human responses when overwhelmed by the power of God.

- *Don't seek them.* God can work just as well without the manifestations. Leave the manifestations up to Him.

- *Prepare people for manifestations.* You can say something like, "Sometimes people feel something strange happening to them, but don't let that bother you or make you afraid. That is the result of the power of God coming upon you."

  ○ If you sense that someone is feeling faint and may fall as you are praying for them, just have your prayer partner pull up a chair behind them and let them sink into it. That way, they are not embarrassed and no big deal is made about the manifestation.

○ If a person does fall, be sure to have your prayer partner help to catch them and let them down easily.

○ Provide a cloth or blanket to put over women with dresses to protect their modesty.

- *Continue to pray over them, soaking them in prayer* as the Holy Spirit ministers love and peace to them. The Holy Spirit may give you further words of knowledge or wisdom or prophetic words.

- *Let them rest in the Spirit.* If they are in that state for a period of time, you might provide a pillow.

- *If they are trembling violently or convulsing, pray over them.* Pray for discernment from the Holy Spirit as to whether anything demonic might be involved, and quietly under your breath rebuke any spirit contrary to the Holy Spirit.

Additional Resources

Deere, Jack. *Surprised by the Power of the Spirit.* Grand Rapids: Zondervan, 1993.

Deere, Jack. *Surprised by the Voice of God.* Grand Rapids: Zondervan, 1996.

Paul L. King, *Nuggets of Genuine Gold*—Chapter 8 on "Understanding Other Spiritual Gifts and Manifestations" and Chapter 11 on "Discernment in the Spirit-Empowered Life."

CHAPTER 9

Other Tools for Healing Ministry: Communion and Holy Spirit Baptism

The Role of Communion in Healing

We encourage the ministry of the Lord's Supper as part of the Healing Center ministry in the Higher Life/Fourfold Gospel/Alliance heritage. A combined Communion and Healing Service is a standard part of the program at the General Council and District Conferences of the C&MA. Many people do not realize why, but historically in the C&MA, the Lord's Supper has been viewed as a means by which God often heals. A.B. Simpson regarded Communion as receiving the very life of Christ: "The Lord's Supper is very intimately connected with our physical life, and it brings us to the actual bodily strength of the Lord Jesus Christ, if we rightly partake. . . . [It] is deeper than mere healing; it is the actual participation in the physical strength, vitality and energy of our risen Lord."[238]

Speaking at an ordination service which included the Lord's Supper, R.D. Kilgour, a C&MA pastor in the early part of the 20th century and a teacher of the Higher Life and Throne Life message, declared, "Many a flagging spirit, fainting under a host of temptations, has had a fresh touch of God and a restoration of soul at our Lord's table. Eating worthily and discerning with contrition anew the Lord's body has brought healing to the physical life."[239]

F.F. Bosworth, an Alliance pastor and healing evangelist and author of the classic book, *Christ the Healer*, wrote of the need of discerning the body of the Lord in Communion: "The wine is an emblem of the blood of Jesus for the remission of sins, and the bread is an emblem of His body broken for the healing of every man's body. . . . Discerning His broken body will bring deliverance from our diseases, and appropriating His shed blood will cleanse us from our sins." Throughout church history Communion has been viewed as a tool of healing, even as "God's medicine."

A Heavenly Transfusion—Raised Up to More Than You Can Be. Puritan Thomas Watson illustrated the healing power of the Lord's Supper: "Christ's blood has an elevating power, it puts vivacity into us, making us quick and lively in our motions." In a similar manner, Paul Brand, M.D., pictures partaking of the Table of the Lord as a heavenly transfusion: "When we come to the table we come with light breath, a weakened pulse. . . . We muddle along with our weaknesses, our repeated failings, our unconquerable sins, our aches and pains. In that condition, bruised and pale, we are beckoned by Christ to His table to celebrate life. We experience the gracious flow of His forgiveness and love and healing—a murmur to us that we are accepted and made alive, transfused."[241]

Brand envisions that when we drink of the Communion cup, it is as if Jesus is saying to us, "This is My blood, which has been strengthened and prepared for you. This was My life which was lived for you and can now be shared by you. I was tired, frustrated, tempted, abandoned; tomorrow you may feel tired, frustrated, tempted, or abandoned. When you do, you may use My strength and share My Spirit. I have overcome the world for you."[242]

Brand compares ingesting of the Communion juice to receiving a blood transfusion that infuses with fresh life and cleans toxins out of our bodies, involving "furious intercellular warfare . . . and the climactic effect of a serum injection on that struggle."[243]

What a powerful message this conveys for understanding the healing power of the atonement—there is power in the blood of the Lamb! Understanding Communion as an act of spiritual warfare was valuable to me as I partook of the Lord's Supper each night during my treatment for cancer.

Testimonies of Healing Through the Lord's Supper.

- *Healing of Jaundice and Eczema through Communion.* Bosworth shared the story of his associate pastor: "Brother Birdsall . . . was all run down in health, having jaundice and weeping eczema. . . . When we had the Lord's Supper, he put the bread in his mouth, really appropriating the Lord's body for the first time in his life. What was the result? God's lightning struck his body and made him whole, and he gained twenty pounds the next thirty days. The weeping eczema left his body and he has been well ever since."[244]

- *Healing of Optic Nerve through Communion.* Bosworth writes of the healing power of Communion: "Mrs. Rosa McEvoy had paralysis of the optic nerve for fifteen years. . . . She ate the Lord's Supper, discerned the Lord's body with faith, and was healed. She does not even have to wear glasses."[245]

- *Heavenly Medicine from the Throne for Cancer.* When I was taking radiation and chemotherapy for third stage rectal cancer in 2007, I discovered from the early church fathers that the Communion elements of bread and juice were considered "God's medicine for the soul." Bernard of Clairvaux declared, "The body of Christ is medicine to the sick." A.B. Simpson counsels that we can receive renewed energy and healing: "The Lord's very strength is given to you in this blessed communion. . . . get from Him His literal strength, physical quickening which fills our material being with new strength and sends us forth refreshed and enabled for the burdens and pressures and even the infirmities of life."[246]

So each night before I went to bed, I took the medicine prescribed by my Heavenly Physician. It was a little bit of heaven in the midst of the hell I was experiencing. As I record in my book *God's Healing Arsenal*, Communion was a part of the weaponry God led me to use for the healing of my body.

Thomas Watson encourages us to partake of the Lord's Supper as often as we can, because "The more we take of the Bread of Life, the healthier we are." A.B. Simpson encourages us: "You can enter into covenant with Him as your Physician for the days before you . . . and this blessed communion service may be to you an impartation of all that the body of Christ stands for—life, strength, health, fullness of supply for every need of spirit, soul and body."[247]

Making Communion available in your Healing Center will enhance the atmosphere for healing.

Implementing Communion as Part of Your Healing Community

- *Include prayer for healing in your church Communion services.*
- *Teach on Communion and Healing.*
- *Read Chapter 19 in God's Healing Arsenal on "Breastplate of Righteousness II: The Overcoming Power of Baptism and Communion."*
- *Offer Communion weekly in your church services, along with inviting people to receive prayer for healing.*
- *Have Communion elements available at your Healing Center for people to partake if they so choose.*
- *Play Communion-related worship music such as John Michael Talbot's The Lord's Supper, and Robert Stamps, "God and Man at Table Are Sat Down."*
- *For more on Communion and the Higher Christian Life, read Chapter 7 in Come Up Higher on "Throne Banquet—Feasting at the Royal Table."*
- *See also: Perry Stone, Jr. The Meal That Heals: Receiving Your Healing Through Daily Communion. Cleveland, TN: Voice of Evangelism, Inc., 2002.*

Healing and the Baptism with the Spirit

Healing sometimes occurs in conjunction with the baptism in the Spirit. When Ananias laid hands on Saul, he was both healed and filled with the Holy Spirit at the same time (Acts 9:17-18). Many people have had similar experiences. I record several illustrations of these combined encounters of healing and the baptism in the Spirit in my book *Genuine Gold*. I mentioned above the story A.B. Simpson told of a man being filled with a "baptism of holy gladness" on his deathbed, and he was miraculously healed.

It is not surprising that one of the results that may occur as a result of being overwhelmed with the Holy Spirit is physical, emotional, or spiritual healing. When we are filled with the Holy Spirit, we receive power to be a witness of Christ (Acts 1:8). That power includes the power to overcome disease and testify to the healing and saving power of Christ. As the Spirit fills us, the diseased cells are pushed out or transformed. A.B. Simpson understood this connection between the baptism with the Spirit and healing, declaring, "Filled with the Spirit we repel the elements of disease that float in the air as the red-hot iron repels the water that touches it."[248]

Some people do not receive the baptism/filling with the Spirit for some of the same reasons people are not healed.

- Just as in healing, sometimes a gap of time occurs between the prayer and the receiving—as in the experience of Dwight L. Moody when he received his baptism in the Spirit days after receiving prayer.

- Just as in healing, some people have had a bad experience of someone praying over them. They may need inner healing from the pain of that experience.

- Some are afraid that they might speak in tongues or fall on the floor or in some way embarrass themselves. Paul Rader, president of the C&MA after founder A.B. Simpson, urged people not to let this scare them away from receiving the baptism in the

Spirit, "Get alone in your room and wait on the Lord until you are filled. You say, 'I might speak in tongues.' Well, if you do, Hallelujah. I am afraid of you if you are afraid of something the Holy Spirit gives from above. . . . Why not be willing, if the Lord sends it, to speak in tongues? . . . Paul tells us how to regulate the gifts, not to eliminate them."[249]

Implementing this Biblical Principle in Your Healing Prayer Ministry

- Ask the person if he or she is willing to surrender to the Lord and be filled with the Spirit if the person has never been filled with the Spirit since conversion.

- Ask the person receiving prayer to read Chapter 13 of *God's Healing Arsenal* on "Releasing the Overcoming Power of Life in the Spirit."

- Encourage releasing and activating gifts of the Spirit, but don't push someone into an experience like speaking in tongues.

- Recommend other resources on the Baptism/Filling of the Spirit from the Higher Life perspective such as the following:

  o Paul L. King, *Nuggets of Genuine Gold*—Chapter 3 on "The Baptism in the Spirit" and Chapter 4 on "The Baptism in the Spirit and Sanctification"

  o A.W. Tozer, *How to Be Filled with the Holy Spirit*

  o Andrew Murray, *Absolute Surrender*

  o D. Martyn Lloyd-Jones, *Joy Unspeakable*

  o David Schroeder, *Walk in Your Anointing* (Dr. David Schroeder is the former president of Nyack College.)

  o Rob Reimer, *River Dwellers* (Dr. Rob Reimer is a C&MA pastor and adjunct professor at Alliance Theological Seminary.)

  o Randall Harrison, *Overwhelmed with the Spirit* (Dr. Randy Harrison is a C&MA missionary and teaches at the Alliance Seminary in Abijan, Cote Voire.)

CHAPTER 10

Healing the Whole Person— Additional Ministry for Inner Healing or Deliverance

As indicated in earlier chapters physical healing will many times also involve healing of the whole person—soul and spirit as well as body. Sometimes God wants to probe the past of those desiring healing prayer in order to find the root cause, demonic or otherwise, of distress or disease in the person's life. Many current problems find their origin in traumas, wounds, and rejections of years past.

Discovering and dealing with inner root causes can enhance physical healing and in some cases may be more important than physical healing. These next two chapters are introductions to inner healing and deliverance ministries in the Higher Life/Alliance context and perspective. A manual could be devoted to each of these in the future. This manual will provide an overview of these vital companion healing ministries.

Wholeness for the Whole Person— Identifying Root Causes for Physical Illnesses

Inner healing is the healing of the inner person, the psyche, which involves healing of damaged emotions, healing of memories, healing of trauma, inner wounds, rejection, bitter experiences, and release from past bondages, especially through healing prayer techniques.

Late nineteenth century Higher Life and Keswick movement leaders such as C&MA founder A.B. Simpson and Dutch Reformed pastor Andrew Murray began to broaden the idea of a whole person concept in what they called the "gospel of full salvation." Andrew Murray related outer health to inner health, seeing a connection between healing and sanctification, or renewal of the mind. "Health of the soul" and "the presence of Jesus in the soul," Murray wrote, has "a blessed influence on the health of the body."[250] They viewed holiness as wholeness of spirit, soul, and body (1 Thessalonians 5:23).

Inner Healing Is Sanctification. In the wise words of Dr. Shelli Haynes, one of my doctoral students, "Inner healing means that a person dies to self and takes on a new mind, character, and actions that are obedient to God. In the process, thoughts, emotions, desires, and will become increasingly conformed to God's intended design of wholeness for humans, and to His will."

The Bible on Need for Inner Healing

The Bible through and through declares the need for our soul, our psyche, our inner being to be healed and transformed. Paul exhorts, "Be not conformed to the world, but be transformed by the renewing of your mind" (Romans 12:2). Foundational to Christian growth and maturity is renewing our mind. This includes our emotions, attitudes, and memories. Scripture shows us we may need to receive inner healing in the following ways:

Darkness within the Inner Person. Solomon declares, "The spirit of man is the candle of the Lord, searching all the inward parts of the belly" (Proverbs 20:27). The Holy Spirit within our human spirit sheds light on the dark recesses of our soul—our mind, will, emotions, attitudes, and personality that need healing and restoration—which is sanctification.

Wounding Words. The words of a talebearer are as wounds, and they go down into the innermost parts of the belly (Proverbs 18:8; 26:22). Lies that have been spoken to us or about us cause wounds in our inner being.

Hidden Inner Pain. Sometimes painful things happen to us which we try to block out of our memory. The Lord wants to bring them to light. Joseph was a strong leader, yet "He entered into his chamber and wept" from the inner pain of seeing his brothers who had betrayed him and sold him into slavery many years earlier (Genesis 43:30). He needed to be healed of that pain.

Thoughts and Intentions of the Heart. In the Old Testament, the prophet Micaiah revealed the deceptive hidden inner motives of the false prophet Zedekiah, declaring, "Behold, you will see in the day in which you enter your inner chamber to hide yourself" (1 Kings 22:25). In the New Testament, the author of Hebrews proclaims power of Scripture to discern interior thoughts and motives and to distinguish between that which is of the soul and the spirit: "For the word of God is living and active and sharper than any two-edged sword, and piercing as far as the division of soul and spirit, of both joints and marrow, and able to judge the thoughts and intentions of the heart" (Hebrews 4:12).

Renewal of the Childhood Mind. Paul writes of the need for renewal of the childhood mind: "When I was a child, I used to speak as a child, think as a child, reason as a child; when I became a man, I did away with childish things (1 Corinthians 13:11). Much of Jesus' healing, counseling, and deliverance ministry involved children or adults with problems from childhood.[251]

Pain from Your Inner Child of the Past. Jesus warns against causing a child to stumble (Matthew 18:1-6). The Greek word for "stumble" is *skandalion*—causing a scandal. He recognized that the inner child of the past may need to be healed from offenses and traumas in childhood. Jesus addressed the adult paralytic as "child" (Mark 2:5). Jesus had the spiritual discernment to recognize that the man's physical condition had spiritual and emotional roots. In this case, evidently a childhood trauma occurred that caused paralysis. Jesus dealt with the inner child of the past before healing his body.

Feelings of Inferiority and Rejection. We see this in the story of Jabez: "And Jabez was more honorable than his brothers, and his mother named him Jabez saying, 'Because I bore him with pain.' Now Jabez called on the God of Israel, saying, 'O that You would bless me indeed, and enlarge my border, and that Your hand might be with me, and that You would keep me from harm, that it may not pain me!' And God granted him what he requested" (1 Chronicles 4:9-10).

Do you realize that the Prayer of Jabez is a prayer for inner healing? Jabez was born in the midst of his mother's intense labor pains, so she named her son "Jabez," meaning "Pain." How would you like to be named "Pain"? You would feel kind of like Johnny Cash's song "A Boy Named Sue." Every time your mother speaks your name, it conjures up thoughts of inferiority and rejection, "You are such a pain!" When people call your name, they say "Hey, Pain!"

So no wonder Jabez feels hemmed in, stifled. No wonder he prays, "Lord, enlarge me and take away my pain." So many years of being called a pain broke down his God-intended self-image and beat down his self-esteem. He prayed for his inner pain to be healed, to restore him to the image of himself God desired him to have.

Bondage through Soul Ties. Paul warns of wrong soul ties through illicit sexual unions: "Or do you not know that the one who joins himself to a harlot is one body with her? For He says, 'The two will become one flesh'" (1 Corinthians 6:16). Sexual or emotional relationships outside of marriage create soul ties—bondage to that person. Such soul ties need to be confessed and broken.

Painful Memories and Guilt. After Jesus rose from the dead, he met Peter by a charcoal fire—just like the one by which Peter denied Jesus three times. That fire triggered painful memories and guilt in Peter for his failure. Jesus gave him opportunity to reaffirm his faith and commitment to Jesus by asking him three times, "Simon, do you love

Me?" (John 21:9-17). Jesus brings painful memories to the surface of our lives so that He can heal them and express His grace, forgiveness, and love.

Demonic Attack, Especially in Childhood. When a man brought to Jesus his deaf mute son afflicted with seizures from a demon, Jesus asked him, "How long has this been happening to him?" The man replied, "From childhood" (literally, "from infancy") (Mark 9:17-27, esp. v. 21). Jesus brought to the surface that the problem with the evil spirit began in infancy—at the preverbal stage in his life, preventing normal development of speech and health.

On another occasion, Jesus encountered a woman who had been afflicted for eighteen years with a sickness caused by an evil spirit and bound by Satan (Luke 13:11-16). This was not a case of a demon needing to be cast out, but rather freedom from an oppressing or harassing spirit. He pronounced to her, "Woman (literally, "daughter"), you are freed from your sickness." In addressing the woman as "daughter," by going back to her childhood, He was loosing her from the root of the bondage eighteen years earlier as well as affirming God's acceptance of her as a child of God.

"En Utero" Encounters. Medical research has confirmed the reality of "en utero" (in the womb) encounters—that a child senses and remembers in its mother's womb—pleasure and distress, which can be shaped for good or bad. Music, stress, habits, diet—all can play a part. This was revealed in Scripture, thousands of years earlier, indicating that prenatal influences of an emotional or spiritual nature may occur within the womb, both positively and negatively. Positively, when Mary, pregnant with Jesus, greeted her relative Elizabeth, who was also pregnant (with the child that would become John the Baptist), the baby leaped (literally "skirted" or "danced") in Elizabeth's womb (Luke 1:41, 44).

Negatively, we see this in the pain of Jabez and also in the story of Jacob and Esau as twins struggling in their mother's womb, indicative of their future conflict in life (Genesis 25:21-26). Jabez appears to have had fetal distress connected with his mother's abnormal pain, which left psychological marks healed only by prayer in adulthood (1 Chronicles 4:9-10). These "en utero" encounters demonstrate that human activity of a psychological nature does take place in the womb, contrary to those who claim human life only begins at birth.

Childhood Traumas. The Bible also seems to place great importance on the first few years of life following birth. The preschool years in the Bible are a crucial developmental period. Jesus warns against causing a child to be scandalized: Whoever receives one such child in My name receives Me; but whoever causes one of these little ones who believe in Me to stumble [Gr.—*skandalion*], it is better for him that a heavy millstone be hung around his neck, and that he be drowned in the depth of the sea (Matt. 18:5-6). Understanding the nature of a child's development, He warns against harmful nurturing influences especially in the preschool years (*paidion*, diminutive of *pais*). Therefore, painful childhood memories, feelings of rejection, and traumas can have long-lasting impact upon the inner being of a person into their adult years. Here are a few biblical examples:

- *The epileptic boy afflicted with a deaf and dumb spirit*—a crucial early childhood trauma in which a demon attacked him at the preverbal stage in his infancy, causing trauma and preventing the child from hearing properly, learning to speak, and gaining sensorimotor control.

- *The adult paralytic* Jesus addresses by saying, "Child, your sins are forgiven," indicating that the man's paralysis occurred in connection with some childhood trauma in which he needed forgiveness.

- *The adult woman suffering from a hemorrhage*, saying, "Daughter, take courage, your faith has made you well," indicating that her illness probably began in her teenage years, possibly from the onset of menses.

Paralyzing Fears. A.B. Simpson notes that fear often is used by the devil to keep people from being set free and healed: "We must not give place to the devil. Nothing encourages him so much as fear, and nothing dwarfs him and drives him away so quickly as audacity. If you for a moment acknowledge his power, you give him that power. If you for a moment recognized that he is in you, you will find that he is in you. If you let the thought or consciousness of evil into your spirit, you have lost your purity."[252]

Bitterness and Unforgiveness. Additionally, emotional distress in adult experiences may need inner healing as well. Jesus warns of torment that results from bitterness and unforgiveness (Matt. 18:21-35; see also Heb. 12:15).

Lingering Guilt. By a charcoal fire, Jesus took Peter through a three-fold inner healing process due to his lingering guilt for denying Jesus three times by a charcoal fire. The fire apparently triggered in Peter deep remorse, and Jesus gave him a three-fold opportunity to reaffirm both his love for Jesus and reaffirmation from Jesus of his call to feed Jesus' sheep (compare John 15:15-18, 22-27 with John 21:9, 15-17).

Limitations of Healing Centers

Healing Centers Are Not Counseling Centers. It is important to understand that healing centers are not counseling centers. Workers, though trained in biblical healing principles and practices, are not trained as counselors. Further, it is not legal in many states to use the term "counselor" unless the person has been state-certified.

Short-term Healing Centers May Not Be Able to Deal with Deeper Needs. Many times God works miraculously in a 20-30 minute prayer session. However, more frequently much more time and repeated prayer ministry is needed. If you are not able to have a setting that provides prayer ministry over days, or weeks, or months, you may need to refer the person to a ministry that can do so.

Refer for Counseling. Unless you are equipped and trained for counseling, it is best to refer someone to a counselor or to a retreat center for counseling needs. One such center in the Higher Life/ Alliance heritage is Fairhaven, founded by C&MA pastor/counselor Charles Shepson (see website: http://www.fairhavenministries.net/.

The Truth Encounter Approach for Inner Healing

One sanctification/inner healing approach which is rooted in Higher Life/Alliance teaching is Dr. Neil T. Anderson's "truth encounter" methodology, based on John 8:32, "You shall know the truth and the truth shall make you free." Anderson emphasizes "the power of believing the truth."[253] Anderson affirms, "Without exception, all the people I have counseled have had some unscriptural belief the enemy has used to keep them in bondage. It is important to recognize faulty beliefs from the past, to renounce them as lies, and to reprogram and renew our minds with truth."[254] Some Christian licensed clinical psychologists use the Steps to Freedom as part of their practice.

Dr. Anderson's truth encounter approach has roots in Higher Life/Alliance teaching on our identity in Christ and the authority of the believer, especially from the teaching of Alliance missionary and professor John MacMillan. Anderson writes, "John MacMillan's published work on the authority of the believer greatly influenced the development of my own thinking."

This is just a summary of Anderson's truth encounter principles and application from an Alliance/ Higher Life perspective. This is not the only approach, but it is a fairly comprehensive approach that can be used in tandem with other approaches. We encourage the use of Anderson's Freedom in Christ materials as part of an inner healing/deliverance ministry.

Seven Key Areas of Discipleship Sanctification—Freedom in Christ. Anderson identifies seven areas of our life in which we need to have an encounter of truth. These seven steps to freedom in Christ provide an outline for dealing with issues of inner healing.

- *counterfeit vs. real*—renouncing past or current involvement with occult practices and false religions. Higher Life and Alliance leaders recognized oppression of spirit, mind, and body resulting from occult involvement. The very first healing home was launched out of the deliverance of one of Blumhardt's church members being set free from occult bondage.

- *deception vs. truth*—affirming the truth of Scripture and confessing self-deception and self-defense. Many times we have listened to the lies of the devil and negative words which have been spoken to us, so we live in a state of self-condemnation, contrary to the Scripture which affirms, "There is therefore no condemnation to those who are in Christ Jesus (Romans 8:1). Higher Life leaders emphasized knowing and confessing who we are and what we have in Christ.

- *bitterness vs. forgiveness*—choosing intentionally to forgive others who have hurt us (Matt. 18:21-35; see also Heb. 12:15).

- *rebellion vs. submission*—confessing rebellion and insubordination and developing a submissive servant spirit.

- *pride vs. humility*—confessing pride and humbling oneself.

- *bondage vs. freedom*—confessing habitual sin or sins of the flesh (sexual, homosexual, abortion, suicidal, self-abuse such as eating disorders, cutting, substance abuse) and becoming free from bondage to them.

- *acquiescence vs. renunciation*—confessing and renouncing passive acceptance of sins from ancestors (generational bondage) and any curses placed upon you.

A 23-page booklet entitled *The Steps to Freedom in Christ* provides a detailed series of steps, Scriptures, prayers, and statements of confession for each of these seven steps. As you work through each of these seven areas in extended ministry time with the person needing healing prayer and countering the negatives with the truth of the Word of God, His truth will set the afflicted free. Again, this is not panacea for all issues, but it is one of the most biblical, valuable, and comprehensive tools I have found.

The Three "R's" of Truth Encounter. Dr. John Ellenberger, former professor at Alliance Theological Seminary, and his wife Helen, both missionaries with The Christian and Missionary Alliance, have been extensively involved in truth encounter and power encounter ministries, as well as other inner healing approaches such as Theophostic. They recommend the following process of the three "R's" of truth encounter:

- Remember
  - ○ Write down past happenings or issues that Satan might have used as a gateway, foothold, or "grounds" for activity in your life.
  - ○ Pray for God to bring to your mind other occurrences or issues.
    - ✔ Traumatic events that made you wonder if God was in charge or if He really cared for you.
    - ✔ Sins or questionable activities, past or present, that keep coming back to haunt you.
    - ✔ Any involvement with the occult.
    - ✔ Anything that seems generational—passed on in your lineage.
    - ✔ Negative attitudes or emotions that control you.

- Renounce
  - ○ With each item on the list, resist the devil (James 4:7).
  - ○ Say: "Satan, in the name of the Lord Jesus Christ, I renounce your using this _____ as a gateway into my life. I renounce your using it as a reason for staying. I belong to the Lord Jesus Christ. I am His child and He lives in my heart by His Holy Spirit, so you may not use _____ as ground for involvement in my life any longer. I renounce you. I command you in the name and authority of the Lord Jesus Christ to leave me and go to the Abyss where Jesus sends you."
  - ○ Recognize Satan's lies and counter them with God's truth.
  - ○ Affirm and confess the truths of the Word of God, making faith confessions.

- Reclaim
  - ○ Submit to God, and He will come near to you (James 4:7-8).
  - ○ Say to God: "I give this whole area of my life (name it—my emotions, my sexuality, my memories, etc.) to you. I love you and I want to belong to you body, soul and spirit. I want you to be Lord in this area of my life. I cannot handle it, but you can, so I give it to you."[255]

Freedom in Christ Resources by Dr. Neil T. Anderson

- *Victory Over the Darkness*
- *The Bondage Breaker*
- *Steps to Freedom in Christ*

Other Inner Healing Models

Within the Higher Life and C&MA movements, a variety of doctrines and practices can be found. The Alliance is known as a "big tent," with variations agreeing to disagree—varying views on Calvinism and Arminianism, end times and rapture, women in ministry, etc. The Alliance tries to maintain a balance within these variations, the historic position being not to create strife over one's personal beliefs and convictions. So a wide variety of healing, inner healing, and deliverance models may be used within Higher Life and Alliance churches. The list here briefly describes some of the common models used. Listing them here does not mean endorsement of everything in the model, but that at least a portion of the model is compatible with Higher Life and Alliance teaching and practice. Those with an asterisk (*) are distinctly C&MA or Higher Life sources.

Cleansing Stream Ministries, developed out of the ministry of Jack Hayford and Church on the Way in Van Nuys, California, which hosted Neil Anderson's Freedom in Christ seminars. One of Hayford's staff members, Chris Hayward, launched Cleansing Stream Ministries as a retreat ministry utilizing a combination of discipleship, inner healing, truth encounter, and deliverance models. Hayford has C&MA background and has spoken at the C&MA General Council. The Cleansing Stream model seems to be compatible with Higher Life and C&MA theology and practice.

Elijah House Model. John & Paula Sandford present a predominately charismatic inner healing approach often used in mainline churches as well through their books and seminars on *Transformation of the Inner Man* and *Healing the Wounded Spirit.* They use a combination of Scripture principles and psychological insights. Some are concerned about concepts similar to Jungian psychology, but they are also careful to distance themselves from Jung's theology. Similar to the Higher Life/Alliance distinctive of Christ as Sanctifier, they understand the important role of sanctification in inner healing of emotions and memories. Their approach can be used with discernment through the filter of sound biblical principles and Higher Life/Alliance distinctives.

*Emotional Healing Seminars. Dr. Mike Plunkett, Pastor of Risen King Alliance Church, New City, New York, and his wife Lisa, have developed emotional healing seminars, using a variety of inner healing and deliverance models, including Freedom in Christ. See his church website for more information: http://www.risenkingalliance.org/ministries/emotionalhealing/

*Emotionally Healthy Spirituality. Peter Scazzero, a C&MA pastor in New York City, developed this model out of his own experience of burning out in pastoral ministry. See Peter Scazzero, *Emotionally Healthy Spirituality: Unleash a Revolution in Your Life in Christ* (Nashville, TN: Thomas Nelson, 2006),

*Healing of Memories. Dr. David Seamands, one-time professor at Asbury Seminary, has a series of books dealing with inner healing entitled *Healing of Memories, Healing Damaged Emotions,* and *Putting Away Childish Things.* Dr. Seamands, who has been a speaker in C&MA conferences and churches, presents inner healing from an evangelical Wesleyan standpoint, which overlaps and is compatible with the Higher Life and C&MA movements. His son Dr. Stephen

Seamands, also a professor at Asbury who has attended C&MA churches, teaches seminars on inner healing and spiritual warfare.

Soul Care—Dr. Rob Reimer. Dr. Reimer is a C&MA pastor and adjunct professor at Alliance Theological Seminary. He has developed inner healing seminars especially for the C&MA context called Soul Care Equipping Conference. See his church's website for more information: http://www.southshorecommunitychurchma.com/calendar/scec/

Sozo is an inner healing model based on healing and restoring relationship with each member of the Triune Godhead. *Sozo* is the Greek term meaning "to save, to heal, to make whole." The *Sozo* model includes features from a variety of inner healing and deliverance models, including Dr. Ed Smith (Theophostic), Pablo Botari (an Argentine Baptist deliverance minister) and others. *Sozo* was formed out of the ministry of Bethel Church in Redding, California, therefore, more charismatic in orientation, but not distinctly Pentecostal. In *Sozo* ministry, the person receiving prayer is guided through a process of hearing from God concerning wounds and lies he or she has experienced. As those lies are revealed and replaced by truth from God, the person is made whole. Some Christian licensed clinical psychologists use Sozo as part of their practice.

Some Higher Life/Alliance people are comfortable with Sozo's ministry, some are not. My knowledge of Sozo ministry has been mainly through the projects of my Doctor of Ministry students, in which they have evaluated the effectiveness of the model. Those studies have shown Sozo to be effective in bringing inner healing and greater intimacy with God. Theologically, the Sozo model seems compatible with Higher Life/Alliance doctrine and practice.

Theophostic. This model was initiated by Baptist minister Ed Smith, who holds a doctorate in pastoral ministry from Midwestern Baptist Theological Seminary in Kansas City, Missouri. Theophostic means "light of God." The concept foundational to this approach is that while praying for a need God gives light or revelation upon a person's past painful experience.[256] "Adherents believe that people's current distress is rooted in past painful experiences that exposed them to accepting lies from Satan or his demons. Smith teaches that when a person's body, soul, and spirit can be freed by Jesus' truth from those lies, the distress found in the memory will go away as well."[257]

Some conventional Christian therapists such as Paul Meier and Mark Verkler of New Life Clinic in Dallas make use of Theophostic techniques. Neil Anderson's book *Christ-Centered Therapy* recommends Theophostic as a part of a "Counseling Assistance Tool Kit." Although some people have concern for dredging up false memories or too much emphasis on role of demons, with proper balanced training and discernment, this model has been used in C&MA circles. Alliance missionary and professor Dr. John Ellenberger and his wife Helen have used Theophostic in conjunction with Truth Encounter and other inner healing/deliverance models with much success.

CHAPTER 11

Pastoral Care for Those Who Are Not Healed

We believe strongly in the healing power of God. We believe God is a healer by nature and desires health and healing for His children. And yet, not everyone we pray for is healed. Even in Jesus' ministry, while in most cases all were healed, a few instances can be found in which not everyone was healed. In order to be a healing community, it means ministering to those who may not be physically healed, but who are still in need of healing of their whole person. Those who are not healed can still enjoy the love and presence and peace of God in spite of their physical conditions. They can still be overcomers through Christ. Joni Erickson Tada is an illustration of one who has overcome in spite of her disability.

How can we minister pastorally to those who are not healed? First and most important of all, we can exercise compassionate ministry. Secondly, we can enhance their understanding of healing as a process. Third, we can guide into truth, correct erroneous beliefs that can be toxic, and impart a healthy theology of suffering. Fourth, we can clarify how to discern God's purposes. Fifth, we can encourage them to persevere and not lose hope. Finally, we can encourage them to abide in Christ and to practice the presence of God.

Exercise Compassionate Ministry to the Unhealed

Assure Them of God's Love. When people are not healed, they may think, "Well, God does not love me, or He would heal me." Or, "God healed someone else, why not me?" So the first thing we need to do is assure them that God does indeed love them. It is interesting to note that Jesus commended those who "visit" the sick and "minister to" the sick (Matthew 25:36, 39, 43, 44). He did not say, "heal the sick." In Jesus' very words, He is acknowledging that some who are sick will not be healed but will need the compassionate care of the church. He was expressing His love by emphasizing the need to visit and minister to the sick even when, and especially when, they are not healed.

Believe That Everyone Can Experience the Love and Presence of God Even When Not Healed. We not only assure them of God's love, but through our ministry we can demonstrate the Manifest Presence of the love of God. When we pray for them, we expect God to touch them in some way with His love. When Jesus exhorted to visiting the sick, the word "visit" does not mean just to care for. It is the word that is used the vast majority of times in Scripture of the special "visitation" of God. God does not merely care for us when He visits us—He does something remarkable, out of the ordinary, supernatural, a movement of the Holy Spirit. The old revival writers of centuries past wrote of "visitations" of God pouring out revival.

Dr. Deena Van't Hul, a missionary to China who works with orphans, noted of the parallel passage in James 1:27 about visiting orphans and widows, that "as Christ the Hope of Glory resides in the believer, this action [visiting] becomes not only a representation, but a release, as Jesus in the believer meets the orphan [or sick or other person in need] face-to-face. This becomes a power-packed visitation releasing supernatural effects."[259]

In other words, even when healing does not come, something remarkable happens when we "visit" the sick. People are encouraged, strengthened, given hope, power to persevere—that is the abundant life. A.B. Simpson himself acknowledged that sometimes people are not healed, but they are empowered to endure, to persevere, to overcome in the midst of infirmity. They are given the strength to carry on when they thought they could not—that is the abundant life.

Pastoral care for the unhealed in body can still provide health and healing for the spirit, emotions, attitudes, and personality. They can experience the love and peace of Jesus in a supernatural way.

Be Empathetic, But Don't Coddle. As mentioned earlier, Carrie Judd Montgomery would normally only allow people to stay a week in her healing home, so that they would not get complacent and just settle in, not dealing earnestly with the issues in their lives that might impede healing. In a similar thought, Oswald Chambers declared, "We have no business being sickly, unless it is a preparatory stage for something better, or God is nursing us through some spiritual illness."[260]

Sarah Lindenberger stressed the importance of not being too overly sympathetic when God is wanting to breakthrough in a person's issues or attitudes: "It is necessary to dwell deep and to stand alone in a certain sense, and not think it is necessary to run to some worker to be babied, petted and carried. God is calling foot soldiers to stand in the fight, and for souls that are ready to drop every weight that holds down to earth and that would interfere with a close walk with God. It is necessary to be willing and ready for self-denial and to endure hardness as good soldiers."

Enhance Understanding of Healing as a Process

It can be an encouragement to the unhealed to know that healing is often a process that takes place over a period of time, not always instantaneously. In Chapter 10 of my book *God's Healing Arsenal* I have a chapter on "Understanding Healing as a Process." From the illustration of Jesus' healing of the blind man with a second touch (Mark 8:22-25), we can see a five-fold process of healing:

1. *Tentative Healing Change.* Sometimes change in our distress or disease is rather tentative, and we are not sure anything is happening. Yet there are signs of God's working.

2. *A Healing Glimpse.* So we get a glimpse, a blip on the screen, of the healing God is bringing to our life. We are seeing change, even if ever so briefly.

3. *Healing Taking Shape.* The healing is beginning to take shape. The person can see forms of or degrees healing. There is light on the horizon.

4. *Healing Depth Inwrought.* At this stage, the healing now has some depth to it; it has become three-dimensional and real. The healing is no longer tentative or superficial, but it has worked through the person's entire being. So the healing is wrought within us; it changes us and affects us deeply.

5. *Healing Complete.* The healing had partially begun earlier, but now emerges a new and final stage of seeing—with clarity. The healing is fully manifest. Finally, the healing becomes complete and clear.

Encourage the unhealed person to read Chapter 10 of *God's Healing Arsenal* for more insights and meditate upon the process of healing as it relates to their own lives.

Guide into Truth—Correct Erroneous Beliefs

Healing Myth #1: Healing in the Atonement Means Guaranteed Universal Healing. It is often claimed that because Scripture says, "By His stripes you were healed," means that you are absolutely healed, and to say otherwise is to say Scripture is not true.

- *Vs. Biblical Truth: Scripture never claims the atonement guarantees healing; that claim is a human inference.* The Apostle Paul cautions us, "Do not go beyond what is written"

(1 Corinthians 4:6, NIV). No Scripture can be found that makes this claim. This is a conclusion that some people come to by saying that this is implied or inferred, in other words, what they think it means. They go beyond what is written to what they infer it means by their interpretation, instead of limiting their claims to what Scripture actually says.

Higher Life leader Dr. Keith Bailey explains, "The doctrine of healing in the atonement says not that universal healing is therefore available, but rather that physical healing is available to believers on the ground of the blood atonement."[261]

Healing Myth #2: All Provisions of the Atonement Are for This Life, Which Includes Healing. Dr. J. Hudson Ballard shows the flaws in this logic: "Absolute sinlessness. . . is ours through the atonement, but it is to be ours in fullness only in the future life. Again, a condition of the body not subject to weariness is purchased by the atonement, but will not be enjoyed in this life."[262]

- *Vs. Biblical Truth: We get the first fruits in this life, but not the full fruits.* Higher Life leader R.A. Torrey believed in healing in the atonement, but recognized the "here now, but not fully yet" characteristic of the kingdom of God: "But while we do not get the full benefits for the body secured for us by the atoning death of Jesus Christ in the life that now is but when Jesus comes again, nevertheless, just as one gets the first fruits of his spiritual salvation in the life that now is, so we get the first fruits of our physical salvation in the life that now is. We do get in many, many, many cases of physical healing through the atoning death of Jesus Christ even in the life that now is."[263]

Healing Myth #3: Jesus Healed All the Sick. Several passages of Scripture do say that Jesus healed all on those particular occasions: Matthew 4:23-24; 8:16 (same as Luke 4:40); 9:35; 12:15-16; 14:34-36; Luke 6:17-19; 9:11; 10:9; 17:12-19.

- *Vs. Biblical Truth: Jesus healed most, but not all.* Other passages indicate that Jesus healed *many*, not necessarily all (Mark 1:32-34; Luke 7:21). On one occasion, Jesus healed only a few due to unbelief (Mark 6:5). Following a day in which Jesus healed many, He spent the night in prayer. The next morning, the disciples told Jesus more were seeking Him, but He said, "Let's go to another place" (Mark 1:35-38). He did not continue to heal the sick there but went on to another town.

  Further, if you compare Matthew 21:14 and Acts 3:1-8, we observe that Jesus healed the blind and lame who came to Him in the temple. However, the man who sat at the gate of the temple every day (Acts 3:1) did not get healed even though Jesus passed by him on many occasions. Also, significantly, **many** disabled were by the pool of Bethsaida but **Jesus chooses only one to heal** (John 5:2-9).

  Further, a careful reading of Luke 9:1 reveals Jesus gave disciples power and authority to casts out **all** demons and to cure diseases. Luke emphasizes at the beginning of his gospel that he was endeavoring to record the exact truth. Thus, it is important to note that Luke does not say they had power and authority to cure *all* diseases, just *all demons*. Therefore, we can rightly conclude from Scripture that in the vast majority of cases, Jesus and the apostles healed everyone, but not always. (9 times all are healed; 3 times many are healed; 3 times only few or one are healed).

When those who are sick believe these myths, they are often set up for a fall if healing does not occur. They may feel guilty or condemned, thinking that if these beliefs are true, they must fall short and something must be wrong with them. Or they may blame God, saying He does not live up to His promises. Or they may lose faith in the truth of the Bible as the Word of God because it is not true. In our pastoral care, we want to give the unhealed a sound understanding of the extent and limitations we can receive from the atonement in this life.

Impart a Healthy Theology of Sickness and Suffering

Ironically, many beliefs about sickness, suffering, health, and healing, actually contribute to sickness or hinder healing. Pastorally, we need to counter unhealthy theologies of sickness and suffering in order to foster not only physical health and healing but also spiritual and emotional health and healing.

Unhealthy Theological Myth #1: If You Are Not Healed, You Must Be in Sin or Lack Faith. It is true that sickness is often connected with sin and disobedience in the Bible (Deuteronomy 28; James 5:14-16). It is also true that faith is an instrument of healing in some cases (Matt. 8:10; 9:28-29; 15:28; Mark 2:5; 5:34; 9:24; 10:52; Luke 17:19), and Jesus could heal few people in His hometown due to unbelief. Some have thereby concluded that people who are not healed must either lack faith or be in sin.

- *Vs. Healthy Biblical-Theological Truth: Some people in Scripture were not healed, but no hint of sin or unbelief is found.* Although sin or lack of faith can be factors for lack of healing, it is error to teach that it is always the fault of the unhealed person. Only in one-third (eight of about two dozen) of the accounts of healing in Jesus' ministry is faith mentioned as a factor in healing. In half of those, it is not the faith of the sick person, but the faith of others. Paul does not berate Timothy for his stomach ailments or Epaphroditus for his sickness. Understanding these cases in Scripture, R. Kelso Carter counsels, "No Christian should allow the Adversary to whip him because he is not healed, when he is conscious of a perfect acquiescence in the will of God."[264]

Certainly, we encourage people to pray, "Search me, O God, and know my heart. Try me and know my thoughts. See if there be any hurtful way in me, and lead me in the way everlasting." However, the unhealed should not become morbidly introspective, thinking, "God must be punishing me for something I have done wrong."

Unhealthy Theological Myth #2: God Wants You Sick to Make You Holy. Some claim that God gave Paul a sickness—a thorn in the flesh, a messenger from Satan to make him holy (2 Corinthians 12:1-10).

- *Vs. Healthy Biblical-Theological Truth: God will bring growth through sickness, but He does not plan for you to be sick to make you holy.* Our Heavenly Father is not a child abuser, making us sick to make us obey. Jesus never viewed sickness as a blessing or an incentive for holiness. On the contrary, He viewed sickness as oppression of the devil (Acts 10:38). In Deuteronomy 28, sickness is viewed as a curse. Paul tells us, "Christ redeemed us from the curse of the Law" (Galatians 3:13).

  Contrary to the claim that God gave Paul a sickness, a close look at Paul's words in 2 Corinthians 12 clearly shows otherwise. We do in fact know it was NOT from God—it was a messenger (angel) of Satan. It came from Satan. Also, notice carefully the wording of Paul's use of the passive voice: "a thorn was given to me." He does NOT say, "God gave me a thorn. . ." He does not blame God for the thorn, but he does see God's purpose in allowing the thorn to remain.

  As mentioned earlier, William Stevens explained, "Sickness is contrary to the kingdom of heaven. . . . Disease is interference with His original and established laws. It is the sign of an invader somewhere in His kingdom. . . . God's answer is the restoration of His law from this daring infringement. . . . He treated sickness as a disorder in His kingdom, a menace to His honor and authority."

Unhealthy Theological Myth #3: God has Caused Your Sickness; Therefore, It is God's Will. It is true that in a few instances in Scripture, it is recorded that God causes sickness (for example, the death angel upon the firstborn Egyptians or the death of Ananias and Sapphira). Therefore, some have concluded that God has caused their sickness or the sickness of someone else.

- *Vs. Healthy Biblical-Theological Truth: God does not cause your sickness and suffering through sickness is not God's will, but it can be redemptive.* All sickness is ultimately due to the Fall. Sickness in a few instances can be a temporary chastisement, or more likely as a result of sin. A key Scripture in resolving this tension or dilemma is Jeremiah's word: "If the Lord causes grief, He will have compassion; He does not afflict willingly [from His heart]" (Lam. 3:32-33). Just as any loving father does not want to have to spank his child (in the biblical way, not abusively), so God does not want to have to spank us, but sometimes He has to in order to get through to us. He will avoid inflicting pain on us if He can, but sometimes the pain (like salt in a wound) is a part of the healing process. He redeems our sufferings and makes good out of what Satan would use for evil. Paul Billheimer exhorts, "Don't waste your sorrows."

Discern God's Purposes for the Unhealed

Once we have dispelled myths about healing and unhealthy theologies of sickness and suffering, we can help those who have not been healed to discern God's purposes during a time of sickness.

Discern God's Timing for Healing. In Acts 3, Peter healed a lame man who had been sitting at the doorway to the temple for years. Jesus must have walked right by him many times, and yet Jesus did not heal him. It was not God's time for him to be healed. And yet, healing eventually came in God's timing and through His chosen instrument of healing.

Discern God's Will in Delay or Lack of Healing. F.B. Meyers once asserted, "God's delays are not God's denials." From his own experience of being voiceless for two years, Andrew Murray recognized that God may have a purpose in delaying healing: "God does not grant healing to our prayers until He has attained the end for which He had permitted the sickness. He wills that this discipline bring us into a more intimate communion with Him. . . . God's timing is perfect. He can delay anything as He sees necessary, and then more speedily bring the answer at just the right moment."[265]

Consider the Sovereignty of God. We see in Scripture that while it is God's nature and will to heal, occasionally God exercises His sovereign will in not healing. For example, many disabled were by the pool, but Jesus chooses only one to heal (John 5:2-9). Jesus also noted that Elisha healed only one leper out of many (Luke 4:27). A.B. Simpson clarifies the Higher Life/Alliance understanding of healing in Scripture: "Divine healing fully recognizes the sovereignty of God and the state and spiritual attitude of the individual."[266]

Discern God's Finer Touches. Simpson describes how some believers receive healing in their earlier Christian experiences, "but when we meet them a little later in their life, we often find them struggling with sickness, unhealed and unable to understand the reason of their failure. It is because God is leading them into a deeper spiritual experience. He is teaching them to understand His guidance, and some people cannot be guided any other way than by a touch of pain. . . . God is teaching them His finer touches."[267]

Recognize That Sometimes God Gives Divine Strength Rather Than Healing. Alliance theologian George Pardington assures that those who are not healed can have an abundant life in spite of it:

Whatever the explanation, it is a fact that of those who take Christ as their Healer some are not healed of their diseases or delivered from their infirmities in the sense that the diseases wholly disappear or the infirmities are entirely removed. . . . Yet such persons daily experience a supernatural quickening of their bodies which gives them freshness and strength and in some instances extraordinary physical endurance. Indeed, they seem to have something more than Divine Healing; they have Divine Life. Theirs indeed is a paradoxical experience. Instead of being bedridden or helpless invalids they keep going in the strength of Jesus, not only carrying their own burdens but stretching out a helping hand to others. Surely it is one thing to sink down under the power of disease or the weight of infirmity; but it is quite another thing to rise above the power of disease and the weight of infirmity and in the strength of the ascended and glorified Christ not only have a victorious spirit but bear fruit, yea, the 'much fruit' that shall abide the day of His coming.[268]

Encourage the Unhealed to Persevere and Not Lose Hope

Pray Until You Get a Clear Answer. Citing Paul's response to his thorn in the flesh, Higher Life leaders exhort the unhealed to persevere in prayer and claiming healing unless God shows otherwise:

- "Paul certainly prayed until he got an answer from heaven, and so we should claim deliverance at the very least until we get a refusal as clear and divine as he did."—A.B. Simpson[269]

- "We have Paul's example for steadfastly praying in faith for its removal, until we get an answer from the Lord about which there can be no mistake."—Russell Kelso Carter[270]

- "Healing is to be expected. Paul himself expected healing in his own case [his thorn in the flesh] until God definitely revealed to him that it was not His will in that particular instance."—R.A. Torrey[271]

Expect as Much Healing as the Spirit Guides. Higher Life YMCA leader S.D. Gordon urges as to expect as much healing as the Holy Spirit stirs in our hearts to claim: "How far may Christ's healing be expected? . . . We may have all we can take, as His Spirit guides our taking."[272]

Claim Health and Strength Until Your Work Is Done. Puritans like Oliver Cromwell and Charles Spurgeon stirred many struggling people with the motto, "A man is immortal until his work is done."

A.B. Simpson likewise affirmed that we can claim "sufficiency of health and strength for our life-work" until we have completed all the tasks of life God intends for us.[273]

Encourage to Persevere in Faith. Delays in answers to prayer are intended to prove and strengthen our faith. Sometimes it is due to the opposition of Satan, who attempts to hinder answers to prayer, as in Daniel 10:12-13. In such cases, Andrew Murray counsels, "The only means by which this unseen enemy can be conquered is faith. Standing firmly on the promises of God, faith refuses to yield, continuing to pray and wait for the answer, even when it is delayed, knowing that the victory is sure (Eph. 6:12-13)."[274]

Maintain Assurance Even with Negative Symptoms. Carrie Montgomery asserted that once a person has heard from the Lord, "If the Devil brings his symptoms, *when the Lord has declared you to be free*, if he tries to put his tags of different diseases upon you, you have a right to refuse those tags."

Abide in Christ Daily. This was the main key for my process to overcome cancer—spending time practicing the presence of Jesus every day throughout the day. A.B. Simpson explains, "It is from close and trustful confidence alone that we can claim His healing. . . . We must get under His very wings and in the bosom of His love before faith can claim its highest victories in our inmost being. . . . This is the secret of divine healing. It is union with the One who is our physical Head as well as the source of our spiritual life."[275]

Encourage the unhealed to read Chapter 14 of *God's Healing Arsenal* on "The Key to Overcoming: Abiding in Christ."

Live Each Day One Day at a Time, Hand-in-Hand with Jesus. A.B. Simpson encourages us, "We can touch each moment that conquering Hand that never lost a battle, that never relinquished a trust, that never grows weak or weary; and strong in the strength of Christ, we can do all things hand in hand with Him."[276]

Finishing Well—Pastoral Care for Death and Dying

For the unhealed facing the possibility of death, great pastoral care and wisdom is needed. We encourage praying for and believing for healing of terminal disease, and we have seen many cases in which God does miraculously heal the terminally ill. Still, many are not healed. How do we pray in faith believing for healing and yet accepting the prospect of death as did Paul, "For me to live is Christ and die is gain"? Higher Life leaders give sound pastoral counsel for people facing mortality as well as for their families and friends.

Discern God's Specific Will for Life and Death. Like Andrew Murray, A.B. Simpson, and other Higher Life leaders, we believe that God's general will is healing, but we also understood that God may reveal upon occasion that in His sovereignty He has other plans. Andrew Murray explains, "If the Lord had some other arrangement in mind for His children whom He was about to call home to Him, He would make His will known to them. By His Holy Spirit, He would give them a desire to depart. In other special cases, He would awaken some special conviction. As a general rule, however, the Word of God promises us healing in answer to the prayer of faith."[277] Murray further counsels, "The man of faith places himself under the direction of the Spirit, which will enable him to discern the will of God regarding him, if something should prevent his attaining the age of seventy. Just as it is on earth, every rule in heaven has its exceptions."[278]

Discern God's Timing for Completing a Person's Life through Death. A.B. Simpson understood that God has His own purposes and timing for those exceptions Murray mentions: "Sometimes the Master is taking home His child and will He not, in such cases, lift the veil and show the trusting heart that its service is done? How often He does! . . . A dear young girl in Michigan who for some time claimed healing, awoke one day from sleep, her face covered with the reflection of heaven, and told her loved ones that the Master had led her to trust for life thus far, but now was taking her to Himself. It is well, and let no one dare to reproach such a heart with unfaithfulness."[279]

Assure Them That Faith and Victory Is Possible Even in Death. A.B. Simpson assures us that death can be a victory, not a defeat:

It is a beautiful picture of faith that even infirmity and approaching dissolution cannot subdue or even cloud, reminding us that the Christian's last hours may be his brightest and that the sublimest triumphs of his life should be in the face even of his foes. Have we not all seen such victories, in which the withering frame and worn out forces of nature and the very frailty of the outward temple made it more transparent to the glory that was shining out from within."[280]

Provide Additional Reading Materials to Encourage the Dying and Their Loved Ones. As led by the Spirit, have the terminally ill read the following chapters of *God's Healing Arsenal:*

- Chapter 2: "Death Angel at Our Doorstep: Facing Our Mortality"
- Chapter 6: "Death as Our Enemy and as Our Friend: A Sound Theology of Living and Dying."
- Chapter 37: "Overcoming When Death Seems Premature"

Other Ways to Provide Pastoral Care to the Unhealed

- Provide a God Squad or SWAT team as a support group and resource for counsel. See Chapter 12 of *God's Healing Arsenal* on "Gathering Your God Squad: God's Overcoming SWAT Team."
- Use Ideas from Chapter 40 of *God's Healing Arsenal* on "Developing a Community of Healing."
- Encourage the unhealed to read the following chapters from *God's Healing Arsenal:*
  - ○ Chapter 1: "Destined for Distress"
  - ○ Chapter 4: "Why Does God Allow Pain?"
  - ○ Chapter 5: "Pain Is Warfare"

- Chapter 35: "Using Your Trials to Go for the Gold: Principles on Overcoming Suffering from the Book of Job"
- Chapter 36: "What If My Miracle Doesn't Come? Reflections on Unanswered Prayer"
- Chapter 38: "Becoming an Overcomer, Not Just a Survivor"
- Chapter 39: "Becoming a Healed Wounded Healer"

Make use of these additional resources:

*Billheimer, Paul E. *Don't Waste Your Sorrows*. Ft. Washington, PA: Christian Literature Crusade, 1977.

Keefauver, Larry. *When God Doesn't Heal Now*. Nashville, TN: Thomas Nelson, 2000.

*Stumbo, John. *In the Midst: Treasures from the Dark*. Chippewa Falls, WI: Nesting Tree Books, 2012.

*Stumbo, John and Joanne. *An Honest Look at a Mysterious Journey*. Chippewa Falls, WI: Nesting Tree Books, 2012.

Yancey, Philip. *Where Is God When It Hurts?* Grand Rapids, MI: Zondervan, 1990.

Note: Asterisk (*) designates Higher Life/Alliance authors.

CHAPTER 12

Introductory Principles for Spiritual Warfare Ministry

"For we do not wrestle against flesh and blood, but against principalities,
against powers, against the rulers of the darkness of this age, against
spiritual hosts of wickedness in the heavenly places" (Eph. 6:12, NKJV).

"The nearer we get to the heavenlies, the fiercer the foes. . . .
A life of victory is not a life of freedom from the attacks of the enemy.
He is always ready to spring upon us,
and there is no victory without conflict."
—A.B. Simpson[281]

An entire manual could be devoted to the exercise of spiritual warfare in healing ministry. This chapter provides an introductory overview of principles of spiritual warfare ministry from the Higher Life/Alliance perspective as they relate to healing ministry. Much of this chapter can be used in tandem with Chapters 33 and 34 of *God's Healing Arsenal.*

The quote above from A.B. Simpson shows his recognition of the reality of spiritual warfare. The Higher Christian Life involves spiritual warfare. Since the healing ministry of Jesus involved healing people who were oppressed by the devil (Acts 10:38), it should not be surprising that healing ministry will involve spiritual warfare. The pioneers of healing homes and healing home ministries recognized that some healing involves deliverance from demons in some form.

Examples of Deliverance Ministry in the Higher Life/Alliance Context

As mentioned in Chapter 2, Johannes Blumhardt's healing ministry began with a dramatic two-year deliverance from demons. Higher Life missionaries J. Hudson Taylor and John Nevius encountered the demonic in China. C&MA missionaries, such as Robert Jaffray, Thomas Moseley, William Christie, and especially John MacMillan pioneered much of late 19th and early 20th century deliverance ministry. Alliance women like Minnie Draper and Carrie Judd Montgomery were also gifted in spiritual warfare ministry.

Ethan O. Allen—Pioneer of Higher Life/Alliance Deliverance Ministry. Ethan O. Allen (along with Johannes Blumhardt) had the greatest impact upon the development of deliverance theology and practice in the early C&MA. A.B. Simpson held him in high respect and called him the "Father of Divine Healing" in America.[282] Allen participated in C&MA and other Higher Life conventions and mentored C&MA leader William T. MacArthur in healing and deliverance ministry. Referring to Genesis 3:15 and Luke 10:19, Allen wrote a tract entitled "Satan Under Your Feet." He operated in the gift of discernment of spirits, and often practiced rebuking, binding the strong man, or "words of castin' out" evil spirits before praying for the sick. He followed what he called the "Old Commission," the words of Jesus in Mark 16:17-18.

One example of Allen's deliverance ministry is recounted by William T. MacArthur and John MacMillan: "Ethan Allen once encountered difficulty in casting a demon out of a person. At last he said the demon might go into his pig if it would leave. When he reached home his wife told him that his pig was acting very strangely. Mr. Allen said,

'Oh, I told that demon that he could go into my pig, but I did not say he could stay there.' And going to the pen, he delivered the pig from its oppressor."[283]

Deliverance Ministry by William T. MacArthur. Ethan O. Allen prophesied to MacArthur in the 1890s, "Young man, you look like somebody the Lord could use in castin' out devils."[284] His prophecy came true, as MacArthur did indeed engage in deliverance ministry through the years, on at least one occasion teaming up with Simpson in 1912.[285] Here is one example:

> The child was, to all appearance, in constant pain, especially at night. For months the mother had been broken of her rest and deprived of the means of grace, for the child would cry constantly in church. It had not grown nor increased in weight for fully eight months. The mother, now a believer, had called for the elders and requested that the child be anointed according James 5. I therefore took another brother with me, but had just kneeled to pray when the conviction seized me that there was no disease present, but simply an evil spirit. I told the mother how I felt, and suggested that we exorcise the demon instead of anointing. . . . She consented and we all three united in rebuking, while the child began to scream and struggle desperately. . . . Demons will make a desperate resistance when they are rebuked with authority. . . . The child had been . . . doing well ever since." [286]

Deliverance Ministry by A.B. Simpson. "The fire fairly flashed from Mr. Simpson's eyes as he said, 'Salvation for devils? Oh, no, hell is the place for him, let us pray.' We three kneeled, while Mr. Simpson led in prayer. . . . He became more and more intense until he burst out in a verbatim quotation from Genesis 19 where the destroying angels said to Lot, 'Escape for thy life, look not behind thee, neither stay thou in all the plain.' When he had reached these words the young woman leaped to her feet and sprang like a frightened doe in to a corner of the room."—recounted by William T. MacArthur[287]

Deliverance Ministry by Carrie Judd Montgomery. "As I cried to God He showed me that I had sinned, and opened the way for the enemy to have power over my body. . . . I asked [Mrs. Montgomery] to cast out the demons which were tormenting me, and to pray to God to heal me. . . . There was a conflict in my body as if another being was struggling within, but after a definite command in the almighty Name of Jesus, I was delivered. I heard heavenly anthems . . . with a conscious presence of the Holy Spirit. Perfect healing came to my pain-racked body."—recounted by Mrs. Frances Kies[288]

Deliverance Ministry by Paul Rader. Paul Rader, president of the C&MA following Simpson, engaged in deliverance while pastoring Moody Church in Chicago. He recalled: "One night a fellow came down the aisle barking like a dog. 'What do you do in a case like this?' I was asked. 'Prayer,' I answered, 'It is the same old dose.' That fellow was bound by the devil and barked like a dog. He is now filled with the joy of Jesus and has a hallelujah on his lips, living for Jesus, and walking with Jesus."[289]

Deliverance Ministry by John A. MacMillan. Dr. John Ellenberger, an Alliance Theological Seminary professor and C&MA missionary, remarked that "The C&MA was on the forefront of dealing with the demonic because of John MacMillan."[290] As mentioned earlier, MacMillan was the seminal writer on the authority of the believer. Here is one fascinating example of MacMillan's deliverance ministry:

> At the age of 78, John MacMillan, with the aid of others, engaged in intensive multiple deliverance session, over a three-month period expelling 171 demons from a young woman. The woman had become infested by the dark powers through living with an aunt who had practiced spiritualism. The spirits manifested violently, trying to harm her or others.
>
> Procuring her freedom entailed a long and arduous process, but step-by-step through the name and blood of Jesus, she gained total victory. On one occasion, when he walked into the room, an evil spirit manifested, addressing MacMillan in a

male voice through the woman's lips, "I know you from the Philippines." The demon recognized MacMillan from an encounter about 25 years earlier thousands of miles away on the other side of the globe.

Evidently, he had gained a reputation in the spirit world for his exercise of spiritual authority. On this occasion, MacMillan, in his characteristic quiet manner, commanded the spirit to be silent, and in the name of Jesus expelled it from the woman immediately.[291]

For numerous examples of MacMillan's deliverance ministry, see my book *A Believer with Authority: The Life and Message of John A. MacMillan.*

Spiritual Warfare Principle #1:
Exercise Spiritual Discernment of Spirit, Flesh, and Demonic

Do Not Attribute Every Affliction to Demons Nor to the Flesh. The sections on the "Using the Gift of Discernment of Spirits" in Chapter 7 and "Discernment and Manifestations" in Chapter 8, discussed the need to distinguish between that which is of the Spirit, that which is of the flesh, that which is demonic, and that which is a mixture. Those same principles apply in every aspect of spiritual warfare. Higher Life leaders stressed the importance of discernment in these matters.

Diagnose through the Spirit Whether Evil Spirits Are Afflicting Body and Mind. William C. Stevens noted that while Scripture is vital for discernment, we also need to hear from the Holy Spirit: "Very common are vexing conditions of body and of mind, and torments of body and mind; and it is noticeable that just such conditions are attributed in Scripture to demoniacal presence and afflictions. Yet such explicit rules of diagnosis are not given as to dispense with the need of the Spirit's gifts of discernment, by which to detect the evil spirits, their lodging places, and their particular operations."[292]

Sometimes Demons Will Need to Be Dealt with First. Stevens explains, "Very many conditions commonly viewed as disease are not such and cannot be dealt with as such, at least without first casting out the spirit directly producing and lodged in those symptoms."[293]

Distinguish the Sources of Mental Illness through the Holy Spirit. William T. MacArthur had a keen sense of discernment of spirits and could distinguish between demonic manifestations and human mental illness that did not involve demons: "Having met the insane frequently, . . . I can detect the symptoms [of insanity or demons] more quickly that most people, and I do hereby testify that I found no trace of insanity, or lack of mental poise in either of these cases [of demonization]."[294] Contrary to some popular misconceptions, he found that many who were mentally ill had no demonic influence and some who were demonized were quite sane.

Early in my involvement with deliverance ministry, I came across a book called *Pigs in the Parlor*, which claimed that all mental illness was caused by demons, presenting an elaborate explanation and plan of how to exorcise the demons. In my misguided ignorance and earnest enthusiasm, I tried to cast demons out of a paranoid schizophrenic woman. No demons manifested, and if she was not paranoid before, she was by the time I got done with her!

Puzzled by the disastrous attempt to do what I thought was good and right, I sought the Lord and wise counsel. I came to realize that her condition (and the mental illness of many others) was biological and generational, not directly caused by demons. Demons would take advantage of her vulnerability, harassing and deceiving her, but there were no demons to be cast out. God, who is the Divine Physician, knows the proper prescription. He showed me that His prescription for her condition was medication, praying for freedom from generational bondage, and binding spirits that would try to harass her. I have seen this frequently as well with godly people who suffer from bi-polar disorder.

Understand Principles of Distinguishing between the Flesh and Demonic. See Chapter 34 of *God's Healing Arsenal* on "The Overcoming Power of Deliverance" for a chart on "Distinguishing between Flesh and Demonic."

Spiritual Warfare Principle #2:
Be Christ-Conscious, Not Devil-Conscious.

A.W. Tozer provides strong and wise counsel about being careful not to put our focus on the devil, but on Jesus:

I know Christians so engrossed with the fight against evil spirits that they are in a state of constant turmoil. Their touching effort to hold the devil at bay exhausts them nervously and physically, and they manage to stay alive only by frantically calling on God and rebuking the devil in the name of Christ. These are innocent spiritists in reverse and are devil-conscious to a point of being borderline neurotics. They grow sensitive and suspicious and always manage to locate an evil spirit as the cause back of everything that irritates them; then their hackles stand straight up and they begin to order the devil about in a loud voice, but their nervous gestures tell how deeply frightened they are. . . .

The scriptural way to see things is to set the Lord always before us, put Christ in the center of our vision, and if Satan is lurking around he will appear on the margin only and be seen as but a shadow on the edge of the brightness. . . .The best way to keep the enemy out is to keep Christ in. The sheep need not be terrified by the wolf; they have but to stay close to the shepherd. It is not the praying sheep Satan fears but the presence of the shepherd.

The instructed Christian whose faculties have been developed by the Word and the Spirit will not fear the devil. When necessary he will stand against the powers of darkness and overcome them by the blood of the Lamb and the word of his testimony. He will recognize the peril in which he lives and will know what to do about it, but he will practice the presence of God and never allow himself to become devil-conscious."[295]

Spiritual Warfare Principle #3:
Understand Demonization in Christians

One of the most common and controversial questions is, "Can a Christian be demon-possessed?" Some early Higher Life and Alliance leaders used the ancient and archaic language of "possession" as used in the King James Version of the Bible, but they did not mean that a Christian can be *owned* by a demon, only *controlled* by a demon. This is a vital distinction.

William T. MacArthur, an associate of A.B. Simpson who was active in deliverance ministry, categorically stated, "It is a serious mistake to say that Satan possesses any child of God,"[296] meaning that a believer in Jesus Christ cannot be owned by a demon. At the same time, he cast demons out of Christians. For some people, this seems to be a contradiction. However, Higher Life/Alliance leaders clarify the distinction.

The Soul or Body May Be Occupied By Demons—But Not a Believer's Human Spirit. V. Raymond Edman, one time president of Wheaton College who also served as a C&MA missionary and editor of *The Alliance Witness* following A.W. Tozer, provides sound biblical and theological understanding of demonization in believers:

Being born again of the Spirit means that the Holy Spirit dwells in the human spirit. This does not guarantee that a child of God may not be attacked and indwelt by an evil spirit in soul or body. . . . According to Scripture the believer is the temple of the Holy Spirit (2 Cor. 6:16). The Holy Spirit inhabits the holy of holies, which no evil spirit can enter. The holy place, which corresponds to the soul, and the outer court, to the body, are subject to occupation by a foreign spirit."[297]

One practical way of understanding this is that when roaches infest a house, they do not own the house, but in some ways take control of and influence what happens in the house. Similarly, when termites infest a house, they do not own it, but they take up residence and can do damage to the house. Therefore, house needs to be fumigated in order to get rid of the roaches or termites. Similarly so the case often is of demonic infestation.

Example of Demonic Infestation of Believers. During the July 1903 Nyack Convention, toward the end of the altar ministry led by Minnie Draper, "suddenly the working of demons appeared in a dear and devoted sister." She had a partial deliverance earlier, but this session took about four hours for total deliverance and full victory.[298]

Spiritual Warfare Principle #4:
Distinguish Varying Degrees of Demon Presence and Power

William C. Stevens illuminates the need to distinguish between various degrees of demonic presence and power:

Demon presence and power in a person's life and being is by no means confined to the actual and entire surrender of the inmost personality to the demon's abode and sway. . . . More generally demonism in a life does not preclude salvation, although sometimes exorcism is necessary before salvation can take place, and often demonism is found in the experiences of saved one without the loss of fellowship with Christ. There is a very wide range of demon presence and power, which, in manifold ways and degrees, involves the brain, the senses, and the bodily members and functions. Very many conditions commonly viewed as disease are not such and cannot be dealt with as such, at least without first casting out the spirit directly producing and lodged in those symptoms."[299]

Luke records that the woman bent over for 18 years (Luke 13) had an infirmity caused by an unclean spirit. Yet Jesus did not cast out the spirit. Instead, He pronounced the woman loosed from her infirmity. Demons were involved with her sickness at some level, but not at the level of habitation within her, thus no need for casting out a demon.

For more detailed information, refer to *God's Healing Arsenal* Chapter 34 for a Chart on "Levels of Demonic Involvement."

Spiritual Warfare Principle #5:
Identify Doorways to the Demonic

Paul warns, "Do not give the devil an opportunity" (Ephesians 4:27). The Greek word for "opportunity" here is *topos*, from which is derived our English word "topography." It can be translated as "foothold" or "ground." What Paul is saying is, "Do not let the devil find ground for getting into your life." Do not give him an inch of space. Take back the territory from him. People can allow demonic infiltration of their lives in a wide variety of ways:

Occult Involvement. John MacMillan, a seasoned pioneer in deliverance ministry describes the demonization of a young Christian woman due to contact with Spiritism, unaware of the danger:

In one instance, a Christian girl whose mother to whom she was greatly attached had passed away, was told that it was possible to contact the spirit of the mother by means of a medium. Not aware of the evil of such approach, she was soon entangled in the mysteries of the séance. Before long the medium, realizing that the young woman had an unusual degree of psychic attainment, invited her to join her in the work of benefiting humanity in which she was herself engaged. The invitation was accepted, and soon the young woman became, unwittingly to herself, quite under the power of the spirits.

Still unconscious of the fact that they controlled her, she entered a well-known Bible school. There, under spiritual influences, she began to realize that something was wrong with her. She confided in the wife of one of the faculty, and it was not long until her condition became known. At once steps were taken for her deliverance. Over a period of three months some thirty-three demons were expelled, and she was delivered."[300]

Getting in Over One's Head. Significantly, a major Alliance leader found himself attacked by demons. Dr. George Peck, one of the Vice Presidents of the Alliance and author of the premier book *Throne Life* on the highest Christian life, and his fellow C&MA friend and colleague, C. W. Morehouse, had both earlier been praying for greater power to heal and cast out demons. Being relatively new in the art of spiritual warfare and not realizing the scope of what they were taking on, Peck himself was attacked by demonic forces. In January 1890, he became severely ill with pneumonia accompanied by insanity and demonic manifestations. Morehouse prayed for his healing and cast out the demons. As a result, Peck launched into a greater ministry, devoting most of his time to healing and deliverance.[301]

Transmission of Unclean Spirits. Earlier in Chapter 4, under Biblical Practice #9, I shared the concerns of Pastor Schrenck, a German Higher Life leader involved with the healing home ministry of Otto Stockmayer, warning about the laying on of hands by those who are not themselves sanctified: "I see great danger in this; and in faithfulness to my Lord and to the Church of God, I do not hesitate to warn every Christian to beware, and to not receive anointing from every man or woman whom you may meet with, but only from those who are really sanctified."[302]

Generational Bondages. A.B. Simpson called this a "Hereditary Cloud" of sickness and death." John MacMillan especially pioneered understanding and practice of deliverance from generational bondage.

Chaplain Jay Smith, who sat under MacMillan's ministry while a student at Nyack, describes MacMillan's teaching: "Breaking family curses was not a concept articulated in those words in the 1950s; but John MacMillan felt strongly that demonic hold on some had its roots in family history, in spiritism, occult, drugs, etc., and referenced the Old Testament Scripture that speaks to the iniquity of the fathers being visited on the children."[303]

MacMillan himself called it the "Principle of Heredity": "'Visiting the iniquities of the fathers upon the children' [Exod. 20:5]. The principle of heredity is involved here. . . . Because of sin, the sinner entails to his offspring sometimes a weakened body, always a tendency to worldliness and departure from God."[304] He further explains that our sins do not die with ourselves: "Nor does it end with himself; the drunkard transmits a poisoned frame to his offspring; the loose woman has a daughter who is hurrying in the ways of shame. Our sins do not die with ourselves; they scatter themselves over the society about us like the winged seeds of the thistle and the dandelion, impossible to catch, settling down in choice places to reproduce their kind."[305]

Territorial Spirits. Herman Williams, a Native American pastor with C&MA among the Navajos in Arizona, experienced an intense pain and left the reservation to go see a doctor. After he left the reservation, the pain disappeared and the doctor could find nothing wrong. When he went back on the reservation, the pain returned. He realized that there was a territorial spirit over the reservation.

That night a spirit appeared to him in his bedroom. He rebuked the spirit in the name of Jesus, and it disappeared along with the pain. He found out the next day that the medicine man had tried to put a curse on him to kill him. Instead, the curse boomeranged back on him and the medicine man died. The power of the territorial spirit was broken, and other medicine men came to Herman to assure him that they were on his side and would not try to put curses on anyone else.

Sometimes people are attacked physically or oppressed spiritually or emotionally through getting in over their head by inappropriately trying to directly engage territorial spirits in spiritual warfare. For examples of this danger, see John Paul Jackson, *Needless Casualties of War* (North Sutton, NH: Streams Publications, 1999).

Other Doorways to the Demonic. Along with these above, other doorways to demonic influence and oppression which can affect health and healing include the following:

- *Misuse of Scripture*
- *Soul (Psychic) Power*
- *Mental Attacks (depression, neuroses)*
- *Guilt and Condemnation*
- *Excessive Fear*
- *Involvement with Drugs*
- *False Guidance*
- *Passivity*
- *Seeking Experiences or Manifestations Rather Than God Himself*
- *Traumatic Experiences*
- *Curses*
- *Bitter Roots (Unforgiveness)*

These doorways are described more fully in Chapter 34 of *God's Healing Arsenal* on "The Overcoming Power of Deliverance."

Spiritual Warfare Principle #5:
Use Discretion If You Suspect Demonic Involvement

These principles are adapted from Chapter 34 of *God's Healing Arsenal* on "The Overcoming Power of Deliverance."

First of all, do not panic. "Greater is He (Christ) who is in you, than he who is in the world" (1 John 5:4).

Seek confirmation. Seek counsel and confirmation from a mature Christian that demonic forces are indeed involved.

Bind any spirit you suspect might be at work. Follow the guidelines for binding and loosing mentioned earlier.

Urge the afflicted person to repent and renounce their involvement with any of these doorways to the demonic. Instruct the person to follow the instructions for renouncing their past and breaking strongholds.

If you do not know how to proceed, seek out a balanced and knowledgeable deliverance team to help the person get set free.

Seek God about whether to pray and fast over the demonic intrusion in the person's life. I have found, in the deliverance ministry, in some cases do require fasting to exorcise the entrenched powers of darkness.

Additional Resources

Arnold, Clinton E. *3 Crucial Questions about Spiritual Warfare.* Grand Rapids: Baker Books, 1997.

Foster, K. Neill, and Paul L. King. *Binding and Loosing.* Camp Hill, PA: Christian Publications/Wingspread, 1998.

King, Paul L. *A Believer with Authority: The Life and Message of John A. MacMillan.* Camp Hill, PA: Christian Publications, 2001.

MacMillan, John A. *The Authority of the Believer.* Camp Hill, PA: Christian Publications, 1997.

APPENDIX 1

Frequently Asked Questions

What about the use of prayer cloths?

Anointed prayer cloths taken to people and placed upon the affected part of the body has been frequently used in Pentecostal and charismatic circles. What about their use in Higher Life and Christian and Missionary Alliance circles?

C&MA Leaders Recognized Some Validity in the Practice. Historically, such prayer cloths were occasionally used in C&MA meetings and by C&MA leaders but much less frequently than in Pentecostal circles. William T. MacArthur, a close associate of A.B. Simpson, recognized "some semblance of truth," for prayer cloths, wishing, "Would God that we were so filled with the Holy Spirit that our very clothing might possess the healing virtue!" However, he did not view their use as common, but as led by the Spirit on rather occasions as special miracles for a special purpose.[306]

Prayer Cloths Were Occasionally Used in Alliance Meetings. In April 1921, A. E. Funk reported on the Pittsburgh C&MA Convention in conjunction with F.F. Bosworth, saying it was like the 5th and 19th chapters of Acts with extraordinary meetings and special miracles.[307] Acts 5 is uniquely significant for supernatural revelatory knowledge, signs and wonders, healings, and exorcisms. Acts 19 records speaking in tongues, prophesying, healing, and exorcism through the use of cloths as a point of contact of faith. By pointing out these particular chapters of Acts, Funk seems to be indicating that phenomena unique to these chapters had occurred in these meetings.

But Don't Go into the Handkerchief Business. While recognizing their validity, William T. MacArthur nonetheless also cautioned, "Some have quite gone into the handkerchief business. . . . While I was in the West large packages of letters addressed to the sick were brought for my blessing, also bundles of handkerchiefs to be prayed over and some asked that the handkerchiefs might be anointed. From all this we humbly asked to be excused. We cannot reconcile this wholesale handkerchief business with the unostentatious behavior of the apostles. It savors of an unwholesome love for the spectacular."[308]

Clothing Charged with Power of Spirit Comes Only Through Contact with Jesus Himself. William T. MacArthur explains, "The charging of clothing with the power of the Holy Spirit was by no means unknown, for when Jesus went about doing good, there were times when His clothing was so filled with power that it was only necessary to touch the fringe of His garment, and as many as touched were made perfectly whole. More than that, when on the Mount of Transfiguration, His raiment was so surcharged with the Spirit from within His holy body that it was ablaze with heavenly light. But on no occasion was power manifested in a fabric which was not in contact with His sacred person."[309]

It would thus appear from Scripture and Alliance history that such points of contact as prayer cloths may be appropriate on some occasions as aids to faith, but they cannot be used indiscriminately or magically. Nor should they be used as fundraising gimmicks. They can be made available as aids to faith as led by the Holy Spirit.

How Do We View the Use Medicine and Doctors?

God Uses Doctors and Medicine, as Well as Divine Healing. Some people have mistakenly believed that A.B. Simpson was against the use of medicine. On the contrary, Simpson affirmed, "Medical Science has a place in the Natural Economy."[310]

Andrew Murray was not opposed to doctors and medicine, but believed that Jesus Himself is the first, best, and greatest Physician.[311] Throughout his life, Murray sometimes relied solely on God for healing, and at other times made use of doctors and medicine. One time during one of his evangelistic tours, Murray was thrown from a cart and broke his arm. He prayed for God's healing, bandaged his arm and applied cold compresses, then preached that evening! Sometime later he showed the arm to a doctor friend who was amazed and commented that it was "most remarkably and perfectly set and healed."

Yet on other occasions of illness or accident, he received medical treatment from doctors. Regarding the use of medicine Murray advises, "Does the use of remedies [medicine] exclude the prayer of faith? To this we believe the reply should be no, for the experience of a large number of believers testifies that, in answer to their prayer, God has often blessed the use of remedies, and made them a means of healing."[312] Still, Murray considered the prayer of faith without medicine is the best way to obtain the grace of God. His counsel is as timely today as more than a century ago: "Let the Word of God be your guide in this matter. . . . Seek to know what God Himself speaks to you in His Word."[313]

Use Medicine and Doctors Thankfully. "Let us avail ourselves of all that science has revealed as contributory to our best estate. Let us use these things thankfully. But never forget that they only help the natural."—Kenneth MacKenzie[314]

"There is no faith in merely refusing a physician. There must be the direct touching of the heavenly physician."

—A.B. Simpson[315]

Don't Abandon Medicine Unless God Clearly Indicates. "We do believe God heals His sick and suffering children when they can fully trust Him. At the same time we believe that no one should act precipitously or presumptuously in this matter, or abandon natural remedies unless they have an intelligent, Scriptural and unquestioning trust in Him alone and really know Him well enough to touch Him in living contact as their Healer."—A.B. Simpson[316]

He encouraged the development and perfecting of "every possible human remedy against all forms of disease so long as they do not exclude or antagonize His higher way. . . . It would be most un-Christlike for us to denounce it or oppose it wherever it has its true place."—A.B. Simpson[317]

"Unless they have been led to trust Christ entirely for something higher and stronger than their natural life, they had better stick to natural remedies."—A.B. Simpson[318]

In Many Cases God Does Not Give Faith to Abandon Medicine. "We do not mean to imply . . . that the medical profession is sinful, or the use of means always wrong. There may be, there always will be, innumerable cases in which faith cannot be exercised," and there is "ample room for employment" of such "natural means."—A.B. Simpson[319]

Simpson's Mentor in Divine Healing Used Medicine upon Occasion. "Dr. Cullis believed in setting broken bones and in taking medicine except where faith was perfectly free and spontaneous, notably in incurable cases. . . .Taking a little bottle from his pocket, [Cullis] said, 'Now I know that this will stop my headache in a few minutes. Knowing that, I think it would be wrong to trouble the Lord about it, or expect Him to effect the cure in any unusual way.'"—R. Kelso Carter, associate of A.B. Simpson, writing of Dr. Charles Cullis, through whose teaching Simpson was healed[320]

Most Missionaries Use Medicine and Health Principles. "Most of the [C&MA] missionaries have used quinine and other remedies freely and are instructed to observe most carefully the rules of the climate for rest and food and clothing."—R. Kelso Carter[321]

God Uses a Variety of Methods for Healing. "Christ heals human bodies today by his own direct supernatural touch, sometimes through the physicians and medicine, sometimes without medicine, sometimes when medicine is confessedly powerless, and sometimes overcoming the unwise use of medicine. The Holy Spirit's leading is the touchstone."—S.D. Gordon, C&MA Convention speaker[322]

Ask the Divine Physician for His Prescription. "What about the use of means? . . . The answer is this: Ask Christ. Get in touch, if you are not already. Then when the need comes, ask him. He will tell you. . . . He is a true physician, for he advises."—S.D. Gordon[323]

Divine Healing Is Receiving Christ Our Strength, Not Giving Up Medical Care. "Divine Healing is not giving up medicines, or fighting with physicians, or against remedies. It is not even believing in prayer, or the prayer of faith, or in the men and women who teach Divine Healing. . . . But it is really receiving the personal life of Christ to be in us as the supernatural strength of our body, and the supply of our life."—A.B. Simpson[324]

APPENDIX 2

Healing Scripture and Prayer Resources

(excerpt from Appendix 2, pp. 377ff. in *God's Healing Arsenal*)

Encourage afflicted persons, not only to read these Scripture verses, but to recite them aloud, to pray them daily during their distress, to memorize those that are the most meaningful to them, and meditate upon those verses word by word.

General Scriptures on Overcoming: John 16:33; 2 Corinthians 1:3-4; Hebrews 13:8; 1 John 5:4-5

General Scriptures on Sickness and Healing: Exodus 15:25-26; Psalm 103:3; Psalm 106:20; Psalm 107:20; Proverbs 4:20-22; Isaiah 53:4-5; Jeremiah 33:6; Matthew 8:16-17; Mark 16:18; James 5:14-16; Hebrews 13:8; 1 Peter 2:24

Bitterness, resentment, unforgiveness: Matthew 18:21-35; Mark 11:25, 26

Broken family relationships: Malachi 4:6

Demonic harassment: Isaiah 54:17; Matthew 12:28-29; Matthew 16:19; Acts. 10:38; 2 Corinthians 10:4-5; James 4:7-8; 1 John 3:8; 1 John 5:4; Revelation 12:11

Depression: Nehemiah 8:10; Psalm 42; Proverbs 17:22; Philippians 4:4-8

Distress: Job 23:10; Psalm 18:6; Psalm 30:2; Psalm 31; Psalm 59:16; Psalm 107:19-20; 120:1; Isaiah 33:2

Divine health: Proverbs 4:20-23; John 10:10; 3 John 2

Emotional/inner healing: 1 Chronicles 6:4-6; Romans 12:1-2; 1 Corinthians 13:11

Failure: Joshua 1:8; Psalm 1:1-3; Proverbs 24:16; Jeremiah 29:11; Habakkuk 3:17-19; Philippians 4:13

Fear and anxiety: Psalm 27:1-3; Psalm 46:10; Psalm 131:2; Proverbs 28:1; Jeremiah 29:11; Philippians 4:4-8; Colossians 3:15; 2 Timothy 1:7

Fear of death: Psalm 90:12; Psalm 116:15; 1 Corinthians 15:55; Philippians 1:21

Feeling overwhelmed: Psalm 143:4-11; Matthew 11:28-30; Romans 8:31-39; 1 Corinthians 10:13; Ephesians 3:16

Financial distress: Jeremiah 29:11; Habakkuk 3:17-19; Philippians 4:19; 3 John 2

Generational curses or bondage: Psalm 79:8; Ezekiel 18:14-32; Galatians 5:13; 1 Peter 1:18-19

Guilt/condemnation: Psalm 51:10; Psalm 139:23-24; Matthew 18:21-35; Mark 11:25, 26; John 8:11; Romans 8:1; 2 Corinthians 5:21; Philippians 3:9; 1 John 1:9; Revelation 12:11

Inadequacy: Proverbs 28:1; John 1:12; John 15:5; John 16:33; Romans 8:37; 1 Corinthians 10:13; 2 Corinthians 4:7; Ephesians 1:19-23; 2:6; Ephesians 3:16; Philippians 1:6; Philippians 4:13

Loneliness: Deuteronomy 31:6; Psalm 37:25; Revelation 3:20

Mental illness: Romans 8:1-14; Romans 12:1-2; 2 Corinthians 10:4-5; Philippians 4:4-8

Negative thoughts: 2 Corinthians 10:4-5; Philippians 4:4-8

Pain: Lamentations 3:32-33; Romans 5:3-5; 2 Corinthians 12:9; 2 Timothy 2:1

Weakness/Tiredness/Fatigue: Psalm 138:7; Isaiah 40:31; Matthew 11:28-30; 2 Corinthians 12:9; Ephesians 3:16

Scriptures for Specific Illnesses

Abdominal: Proverbs 3:7-8

Acne: 2 Samuel 14:25

Arthritis: Job 4:3; Psalm 145: 14; Luke 13: 11, 13

Asthma: Lamentations 3:56; Acts 17:25

Back Troubles: Psalm 145:14; Psalm 146:7-8

Barrenness: Psalm 113:9; Deuteronomy 7:9, 13, 14

Blood: Ezekiel 16:6; Joel 3:21; Mark 5:29

Bones: Psalm 34:20; Proverbs 3:8; Isaiah 58:11; Isaiah 55:2

Burns: Isaiah 43:2

Cancer: Matthew 15:13; Mark 11:23

Ears: Job 36:15; Proverbs 20:12; Isaiah 35:5; Isaiah 29:18 (roaring & noises)

Eyes: Psalm 146:8; Proverbs 20:12; Isaiah 32:3; Isaiah 35:5; Isaiah 42:18

Feet: 1 Samuel 2:9; Proverbs 3:23

Fever: Luke 4:39

Hands: Isaiah 35:3

Heart Attack/Disease: Psalm 16:1, 8, 9; Psalm 22:26; Psalm 27:14; Psalm 28:7; Psalm 57:2, 7; Psalm 73:26; Psalm 147:3

Knees: Job 4:4; Hebrews 12:12

Lameness: Isaiah 35:6

Nerves: John 14:27; Philippians 4:8; 1 Peter 5:7

Poisoning: Mark 16:18

Spine: Isaiah 55:2

Skin: Job 10:11-12; Proverbs 4:22

Stuttering: Isaiah 32:4; Mark 7:32, 33, 35

Sun Stroke/Heart: Psalm 121:5-6; Isaiah 49:10

Teeth: Song of Solomon 6:6; Amos 4:6

Tumors: Matthew 15:13

Ulcers: Matthew 15:13

Withered Hand: Mark 3:3-5

Wounds: Psalm 147:3; Jeremiah 30:17

Recommended Prayer Resources for Overcoming

Agreeing in prayer: Ecclesiastes 4:9-12; Matthew 18:18-20

Binding and loosing: Matthew 12:28-29; Matthew 16:18-19; Matthew 18:18-20

Praying a hedge of thorns: Hosea 2:6-7

When you don't know how to pray: Romans 8:26; 1 Corinthians 14:2, 4, 15; James 1:5

Copeland, Germaine. *Prayers That Avail Much.* Tulsa, OK: Harrison House, 1997.

Hunter, Joan. *Healing the Whole Man Handbook: Effective Prayers for Body, Soul, and Spirit.* Kingwood, TX: Joan Hunter Ministries, 2005, 2006.

Resources for
Healing Ministries

Other Higher Life/Alliance Resources on Biblical Healing Principles and Practices. These include classic and contemporary Higher Life and C&MA sources as well as other contemporary sources compatible with Higher Life and C&MA teaching. Note: Some of these sources may be out of print, but they may be available online, through Interlibrary Loan, or as used books. Sources designated with an asterisk (*) indicate a C&MA or other classic Higher Life author.

On Biblical Healing Principles 1 and 2—
The Supernatural Today

Deere, Jack. *Surprised by the Power of the Spirit.* Grand Rapids: Zondervan, 1993.

Greig, Gary and Kevin Springer, eds. *The Kingdom and the Power.* Ventura, CA: Gospel Light (Regal), 1993.

Grudem, Wayne A., ed. *Are Miraculous Gifts for Today? Four Views.* Grand Rapids: Zondervan, 1996.

Keener, Craig S. *Miracles: The Credibility of the New Testament Accounts.* 2 Volumes. Grand Rapids: Baker Academic, 2011.

*King, Paul L. *Genuine Gold: The Cautiously Charismatic Story of the Early Christian and Missionary Alliance*. Tulsa, OK: Word and Spirit Press, 2006.

* King, Paul L. "Holy Laughter and Other Phenomena in Evangelical and Holiness Revival Movements," *Alliance Academic Review 1996*, Elio Cuccaro, ed. (Camp Hill, PA: Christian Publications, 1998), 107-122. Accessible at www.allianceacademicreview.com.

*King, Paul L. *Nuggets of Genuine Gold: Experiencing the Spirit-Empowered Life—Teaching and Testimony from Simpson, Tozer, Jaffray, and Other Christian and Missionary Alliance Leaders*. Tulsa, OK: Word and Spirit Press, 2010.

Ruthven, Jon Mark. *On the Cessation of the Charismata*. Tulsa: Word & Spirit Press, 2011.

*Schroeder, David E. *Walking in Your Anointing*. Bloomington, IN: Author House, 2007.

On Biblical Healing Principles 3 and 4— God Is a Healer and Healing in the Atonement

*Bailey, Keith M. *Divine Healing: The Children's Bread*. Harrisburg, PA: Christian Publications, 1977.

Blue, Ken. *Authority to Heal*. Downers Grove, IL: InterVarsity Press, 1987.

*Bosworth, Fred F. *Christ the Healer*. Old Tappan, NJ: Revell, 1973.

Brown, Michael L. *Israel's Divine Healer*. Grand Rapids: Zondervan, 1995.

*Gordon, A.J. *The Ministry of Healing*. Harrisburg, PA: Christian Publications, 1982.

*Gordon, S.D. *The Healing Christ*. New York, NY: Fleming H. Revell; Ann Arbor, MI: Vine Books, [1924] 1985.

*King, Paul L. *God's Healing Arsenal: A Divine Battle Plan for Overcoming Distress and Disease*. Alachua, FL: Bridge-Logos, 2011.

*McCrossan, Thomas J. *Bodily Healing and the Atonement.* Tulsa: Kenneth Hagin Ministries, 1982. (don't let publication by Kenneth Hagin Ministries fool you or scare you—this is a reprint of a C&MA/Higher Life author)

*Simpson, A.B. *The Gospel of Healing.* New York: Christian Alliance Publishing Co., 1896. Reprinted 1955.

*Simpson, A.B. *The Lord for the Body.* Camp Hill, PA: Christian Publications, 1996.

*Sipley, Richard M. *Understanding Divine Healing.* Wheaton, IL: Victor, 1986.

Stanger, Frank Bateman. *God's Healing Community.* Nashville, TN: Abingdon, 1978.

*Murray, Andrew; A.J. Gordon; A.B. Simpson. *The Three Classics on Divine Healing.* Compiled and edited by Jonathan Graf. Camp Hill, PA: Christian Publications, 1992.

*Travis, Drake. *Healing Power Voice Activated.* Lake Mary, FL: Creation House, 2009.

Wimber, John and Kevin Springer. *Power Healing.* San Francisco, CA: HarperSanFrancisco, 1987.

On Biblical Healing Principles 5, 6, and 7— Role of Faith, Role of Attitude, Atmosphere of Faith

*King, Paul L. *A Believer with Authority.* Camp Hill, PA: Christian Publications, 2001.

*King, Paul L. *Moving Mountains: Lessons in Bold Faith from Great Evangelical Leaders.* Grand Rapids: Chosen Books, 2004.

*King, Paul L. *Only Believe: Examining the Origin and Development of Classic and Contemporary Word of Faith Theologies.* Tulsa, OK: Word and Spirit Press, 2008.

*Müller, George. *The Autobiography of George Müller.* Springdale, PA: Whitaker House, 1984.

*Price, Charles S. *The Real Faith.* Pasadena, CA: Charles Price Publishing Co., 1940, 1968.

*Simpson, A.B. *Seeing the Invisible.* Camp Hill, PA: Christian Publications, 1994.

On Biblical Healing Principles 8 and 9— Whole Person Healing and Root Causes

Anderson, Neil T. *Discipleship Counseling: The Complete Guide to Helping Others Walk in Freedom and Grow in Christ.* Ventura, CA: Regal, 2003. (Truth Encounter approach to spiritual warfare and inner healing)

Anderson, Neil T. *Steps to Freedom in Christ.* Ventura, CA: Regal Books, 1995.

Anderson, Neil T. "Who I am in Christ" bookmark.

Anderson, Neil T., Terry E. Zuehlke, and Julianne S. Zuehlke. *Christ Centered Therapy: The Practical Integration of Theology and Psychology.* Grand Rapids, MI: Zondervan, 2000.

Backus, William. *The Healing Power of a Healthy Mind: How Truth Strengthens Your Immune System.* Minneapolis: Bethany House, 1996.

Hunter, Joan. *Healing the Whole Man Handbook: Effective Prayers for Body, Soul, and Spirit.* Kingwood, TX: Joan Hunter Ministries, 2005, 2006.

McMillen, S. I. *None of These Diseases.* Old Tappan, NJ: Fleming H. Revell, 1963.

*Reimer, Rob. "Soul Care." Teaching on inner healing from a C&MA pastor's perspective and experience.

*Scazzero, Peter. *Emotionally Healthy Spirituality.* Grand Rapids, MI: Zondervan, 2006.

*Scazzero, Peter. *The Emotionally Healthy Church.* Grand Rapids, MI: Zondervan, 2003.

Seamands, David. *Healing of Damaged Emotions.* Wheaton, IL: Victor, 1981.

Seamands, David. *Healing of Memories.* Wheaton, IL: Victor, 1985.

Seamands, David. *Putting Away Childish Things.* Wheaton, IL: Victor, 1982.

*Smith, David J. *How Can I Ask God for Physical Healing?* Grand Rapids, MI: Chosen Books, 2005.

On Spiritual Warfare

Anderson, Neil T. *Discipleship Counseling: The Complete Guide to Helping Others Walk in Freedom and Grow in Christ.* Ventura, CA: Regal, 2003.

Anderson, Neil T. *Helping Others Find Freedom in Christ.* Ventura, CA: Regal Books, 1995.

Anderson, Neil T. *Living Free in Christ.* Ventura, CA: Regal Books, 1993.

Anderson, Neil T. *Setting Your Church Free.* Ventura, CA: Regal Books, 1994.

Anderson, Neil T. *The Bondage Breaker.* Eugene, OR: Harvest House, 1992.

Anderson, Neil T. *Victory over the Darkness.* Ventura, CA: Regal Books, 1990.

Anderson, Neil T. *Walking in the Light: Discerning God's Guidance in an Age of Spiritual Counterfeits.* Nashville: Thomas Nelson, 1992.

Anderson, Neil T., Terry E. Zuehlke, and Julianne S. Zuehlke. *Christ Centered Therapy: The Practical Integration of Theology and Psychology.* Grand Rapids, MI: Zondervan, 2000.

Arnold, Clinton E. *3 Crucial Questions about Spiritual Warfare.* Grand Rapids: Baker Books, 1997.

Bounds, E.M. *Satan: His Personality, Power, and Overthrow.* Grand Rapids, MI: Baker Book House, 1972. (A classic 19th century book on the devil.)

Boshold, Frank S., trans. *Blumhardt's Battle: A Conflict with Satan*. New York, NY: Thomas E. Lowe Publishers, 1970.

*Foster, K. Neill, and Paul L. King. *Binding and Loosing: Exercising Authority Over the Dark Powers*. Camp Hill, PA: Christian Publications, 1998.

*MacMillan, John A. *The Authority of the Believer*. Harrisburg, PA: Christian Publications, 1980.

Murphy, Edward F. *The Handbook on Spiritual Warfare*. Nashville, TN: Thomas Nelson, 1992, 1996.

Warner, Timothy. *Spiritual Warfare: Victory Over the Dark Powers of Our World*. Wheaton, IL: Crossway Books, 1990.

Resources on Discerning Counterfeit or Questionable Healing Beliefs and Practices

Anderson, Neil T. and Michael Jacobson, D.O. *The Biblical Guide to Alternative Medicine*. Ventura, CA: Regal, 2003.

Brown, Candy Gunther. *The Healing Gods*. New York: Oxford University Press, 2013.

Clark, Randy, and Sue Thompson. *Healing Energy: Whose Is It?* Mechanicsburg, PA: Global Awakening, 2013.

Clifton, Sandra. *From New Age to New Life*. Lake Mary, FL: Creation House, 2007. (by a former New Age psychic who became a Christian).

Clifton, Sandra. *New Age Lies Exposed*. Alachua, FL: Bridge-Logos, 2009.

On the Baptism with the Spirit and Use of Spiritual Gifts

Deere, Jack. *Surprised by the Power of the Spirit*. Grand Rapids: Zondervan, 1993.

Deere, Jack. *Surprised by the Voice of God*. Grand Rapids: Zondervan, 1996.

*Gilbertson, Richard. *The Baptism of the Holy Spirit: The Views of A.B. Simpson and His Contemporaries*. Camp Hill, PA: Christian Publications, 1993.

*Harrison, Randall A. *Overwhelmed by the Spirit: A Biblical Study on Discovering the Spirit*. Entrust Publications, 2013.

Hayford, Jack. *The Beauty of Spiritual Language*. Dallas: Word Publishing, 1992.

*King, Paul L. *Nuggets of Genuine Gold*. Tulsa, OK: Word & Spirit Press, 2010.

Lloyd-Jones, David Martyn. *Joy Unspeakable*. David Cook Dist. Kingsway, 2008.

*Murray, Andrew. *Absolute Surrender*. New Kensington, PA: Whitaker House, 1981.

*Packo, John E. *Find and Use Your Spiritual Gifts*. Chicago: Wingspread, 2014.

*Reimer, Rob. *River Dwellers: Living in the Fullness of the Spirit*. Franklin, TN: Carpenter's Son Publishing, 2015.

*Schroeder, David E. *Walking in Your Anointing*. Bloomington, IN: Author House, 2007.

*Tozer, A.W. *How to Be Filled with the Holy Spirit*. Camp Hill, PA: Christian Publications, n.d.

Questionnaire for Seekers

Name _____

Address _____

Phone _____

Email _____

Home church _____

Have you received Jesus Christ as your Savior?

Have you experienced the filling with the Holy Spirit?

What are you coming to receive prayer for today?

Endnotes

1   Frank Bateman Stanger, *God's Healing Community* (Wilmore, KY: Francis Asbury Publishing Co, 1985), 121.

2   Stanger, 121.

3   Stanger, 121.

4   A.B. Simpson, Editorial, *Christian Alliance & Missionary Weekly (CAMW)*, Feb. 28, 1890, 129.

5   A.B. Simpson, *Christ in the Bible (CITB)* (Camp Hill, PA: Christian Publications, 1992), 5:413-414.

6   A.B. Simpson, "Earnests of the Coming Age," *Alliance Weekly (AW)*, June 23, 1917, 178, 180.

7   A.B. Simpson, "Divine Healing and the Lord's Coming," *AW*, Sept. 22, 1917, 386.

8   A.B. Simpson, "The Four-fold Gospel, or the Fullness of Jesus," *AW*, July 28, 1911, 228.

9   A.B. Simpson, "The Gospel Its Own Witness, *The Word, the Work, and the World (WWW)*, Feb. 1, 1887, 66.

10 A.B. Simpson, "The Highest Christian Life," *AW*, Dec. 23, 1911, 179.

11 A.B. Simpson, *The Holy Spirit* (Harrisburg, PA, Christian Publications, n.d.), 1:204.

12 A.B. Simpson, "A New Missionary Alliance," *WWW*, June 1, 1887, 365, 367.

13 A.B. Simpson, Editorial, *CAMW*, Oct. 31, 1890, 257-258.

14 Walter Turnbull and C. H. Chrisman, "The Message of the Christian and Missionary Alliance," 1927, accessed at http://online.ambrose.edu/alliancestudies/ahtreadings/ahtr_s2.html

15 For more on Dora Dudley and the Beulah Healing Home, see Nancy A. Hardesty, *Faith Cure: Divine Healing in the Holiness and Pentecostal Movements* (Peabody, MA: Hendrickson Publishers, 2003), 65-67.

16 J. Hudson Taylor, cited in *World Shapers: A Treasury of Quotes from Great Missionaries* (Wheaton, IL: Harold Shaw Publishers, 1991), 107.

17 A.B. Simpson, *CITB* (1992), 1:123.

18 A.W. Tozer, *I Talk Back to the Devil* (Camp Hill, PA: Christian Publications, 1990), 143.

[19] A.B. Simpson, *Christ in the Bible: Gospel of John and the Acts of the Apostles* (Christian Alliance Publishing Co., 1891), Vol. X, 256.

[20] Friedrich Zuendel, *The Awakening: One Man's Battle with Darkness* (Farmington, PA: Plough Publishing House, 1999), 78.

[21] A.B. Simpson, Editorial, *CAMW*, July 6, 1907, 313.

[22] Simpson, *The Gospel of Healing* (Harrisburg, PA: Christian Publications, 1915), 57.

[23] A.B. Simpson, Editorial, *Living Truths*, Apr. 1906, 198.

[24] A.W. Tozer, *Tragedy in the Church: The Missing Gifts* (Harrisburg, PA: Christian Publications, 1978), 33, 42.

[25] A.B. Simpson, *Present Truths or the Supernatural* (Harrisburg, PA: Christian Publications, reprint 1967), 53.

[26] See George Eldon Ladd, *A Theology of the New Testament* (Grand Rapids: Eerdmans, 1974), 70-80.

[27] W.T. MacArthur, "Fabrics Filled with Power," *AW*, Sept. 14, 1912, 390..

[28] A.B. Simpson "Gifts and Grace," *Christian & Missionary Alliance Weekly (CMAW)*, June 29, 1907, 302.

[29] Etta Wurmser, "Chosen in the Furnace of Affliction," *Latter Rain Evangel*, Jan. 1917, 21.

[30] A.B. Simpson, "How to Receive Divine Healing," *WWW*, July-Aug., 1885, 203.

[31] Armin R. Gesswein, "Dispensationalism," *AW*, Mar. 1, 1941, 135, 138.

[32] Simpson, *Christ in the Bible* (1992), 1:44.

[33] W.C. Stevens, "The Cross and Sickness," *The Pentecostal Evangel*, Aug. 23, 1924, 6.

[34] Andrew Murray, *Divine Healing* (Springdale, PA: Whitaker House, 1982), 73-74.

[35] Andrew Murray, *With Christ in the School of Prayer* (Springdale, PA: Whitaker House, 1982), 82.

[36] Simpson, *Christ in the Bible: Luke* (n.d.), 178.

[37] A.B. Simpson, "Divine Healing in the Atonement," *CAMW*, Aug. 1890, 122, 124.

[38] Murray, *Divine Healing*, 72.

[39] Simpson, "Divine Healing in the Atonement," 123.

[40] Simpson, *The Gospel of Healing*, 15.

[41] R. Kelso Carter, cited in Keith M. Bailey, *Divine Healing: The Children's Bread* (Harrisburg, PA: Christian Publications, 1977), 44.

[42] Stevens, "The Cross and Sickness," 6.

[43] Simpson, *The Lord for the Body* (New York: Christian Alliance Publishing Co., n.d.),, 79.

[44] A.J. Gordon, cited in Keith M. Bailey, *Divine Healing*, 45.

[45] T.J. McCrossan, *Bodily Healing and the Atonement* (Tulsa: Kenneth Hagin Ministries, 1982), 25, 28.

[46] F.F. Bosworth, *For This Cause* (New York: Christian Alliance Publishing Co., n.d.), 19-20.

[47] Simpson, "Divine Healing in the Atonement," 123-124.

[48] A.B. Simpson, "Inquiries and Answers," *WWW*, Nov. 1886, 294; "Inquiries and Answers" was published later in A.B. Simpson's book, *The Lord for the Body*, accessed at http://online.ambrose.edu/alliancestudies/ahtreadings/ahtr_s2.html.

[49] R.A. Torrey, cited in Bailey, *Divine Healing*, 49.

[50] Simpson, *Present Truths or the Supernatural*, 15.

[51] A.B. Simpson, *A Larger Christian Life* (Camp Hill, PA: Christian Publications, 1988), 6, 11.

[52] A.B. Simpson, "According to Your Faith," *CMAW*, Sept. 8, 1906, 146.

[53] Simpson, *The Gospel of Healing*, 54, 127.

[54] Simpson, *The Four-fold Gospel* (Harrisburg, PA: Christian Publications, n.d.), 62.

[55] A.B. Simpson, "Editorial," *CAMW*, Nov. 1890, 274.

[56] A.W. Tozer, *Faith Beyond Reason* (Camp Hill, PA: Christian Publications, 1989), 34, 42.

[57] Simpson, *A Larger Christian Life*, 19.

[58] A.W. Tozer, *Of God and Men* (Harrisburg, PA: Christian Publications, 1960), 57.

[59] Simpson, "How to Receive Divine Healing," *WWW*, July-Aug., 1885, 205.

[60] Simpson, *The Gospel of Healing*, 89.

[61] Simpson, *The Life of Prayer*, 70.

[62] Simpson, *The Gospel of Healing*, 88-89.

[63] Simpson, *The Gentle Love of the Holy Spirit* (Camp Hill, PA: Christian Publications, 1983), 135.

[64] Montgomery, *The Secrets of Victory* (Oakland, CA: Triumphs of Faith, 1921), 28.

[65] Simpson, *The Four-fold Gospel*, 62.

[66] Simpson, *The Gospel of Healing*, 90.

[67] Simpson, *CITB* (1992), 4:247.

[68] A.J. Gordon, *The Ministry of Healing* (Harrisburg, PA: Christian Publications, n.d.), 24.

[69] Gordon, *The Ministry of Healing*, 25.

[70] A.B. Simpson, "The Son of Man and Sickness, *Christian & Missionary Alliance Weekly*, Jan. 13, 1906, 22

[71] Murray, *Divine Healing*, 18.

[72] A.J. Gordon, *The Ministry of Healing*, 210.

[73] Simpson, *A Larger Christian Life*, 53-54.

[74] Simpson, *The Gospel of Healing*, 128.

[75] Simpson, *CITB* (1992), 3:241.

[76] John A. MacMillan, *Full Gospel Sunday School Quarterly*, Nov. 22, 1942, 25.

[77] Bosworth, *For This Cause*, 17-18.

[78] A. W. Tozer, *Born After Midnight* (Harrisburg, PA: Christian Publications, 1959), 44.

[79] A.B. Simpson, *Triumphs of Faith*, November 1921, 253.

[80] A.B. Simpson, *Christ for the Body* (Nyack, NY: The Christian and Missionary Alliance, n.d.), n.p.

[81] Sarah Lindenberger, "The Joy of the Lord Is Your Strength," *CMAW*, Oct. 28, 1905, 675.

[82] Cited in Kimberly Erwin Alexander, *Pentecostal Healing* (Dorset, UK: Deo Publishing, 2006), 57.

[83] Ronald A.N. Kydd, *Healing through the Centuries* (Peabody, MA: Hendrickson Publishers, 1998), 141.

[84] Frederic William Farr, "The Gospel Tabernacle and Its Work," *CMAW*, March 9, 1909, 112.

[85] Simpson, *CITB: Luke* (Harrisburg, PA: Christian Publications, n.d.), Vol. XIVB, 178.

[86] A.B. Simpson, "Jesus in the Psalms: The Missionary Psalm," *CAMW*, Apr. 8, 1892, 228.

[87] A.B. Simpson, *Friday Meeting Talks, Series 3: Divine Prescriptions for the Sick and Suffering* (New York: Christian Alliance Publishing Co., 1900), 30-31.

[88] A.B. Simpson, "Jesus in the Psalms: The Priest-King Psalm," *CAMW*, Feb. 5, 1892, 86.

[89] Andrew Murray, *Divine Healing* (Springdale, PA: Whitaker House, 1982), 13.

[90] S.A. Lindenberger, "Captive Thoughts," *CAMW*, Sept. 5, 1890, 133.

[91] Sarah Lindenberger, "Some Truths of Divine Healing," *AW*, May 31, 1913, 135.

[92] Andrew Murray, *The Prayer Life* (Basingstoke, Hanks, UK: Marshall, Morgan and Scott, 1968), 18.

[93] A.J. Gordon, *The Ministry of Healing*, 243-244.

[94] A.B. Simpson, "The Master Workman in Relation to Sickness and Divine Healing," *CMAW*, Nov. 27, 1909, 138.

[95] Carrie Judd Montgomery, *The Secrets of Victory* (Oakland, CA: Triumphs of Faith, 1921), 100.

[96] A.B. Simpson, "Two Stages of Divine Healing," *AW*, Jan. 28, 1953, 5.

[97] Simpson, "Two Stages of Divine Healing," 5.

[98] Simpson, "Two Stages of Divine Healing," 5.

[99] Murray, *Divine Healing*, 45.

[100] Murray, *Divine Healing*, 121.

[101] Andrew Murray, *Holy in Christ* (Toronto: Willard Tract Depot, 1888), 209.

[102] Murray, *Divine Healing*, 13.

[103] Simpson, cited in Mrs. Charles Cowman, *Streams in the Desert* (Grand Rapids: Zondervan, [1925] 1972), 31.

[104] A.B. Simpson, "The Sanctifying Influence of Divine Healing," *AW*, Sept. 17, 1952, 602.

[105] A.B. Simpson, *Days of Heaven on Earth* (Nyack, NY: Christian Alliance Publishing Co., 1897), June 18.

[106] Lindenberger, "The Work of Berachah Home," 208. C&MA Archives.

[107] A.J. Gordon, *The Ministry of Healing*, 164-165.

[108] Murray, *Divine Healing*, 52.

[109] Murray, *Divine Healing*, 52-53.

[110] Simpson, *The Gospel of Healing*, 54, 127.

[111] Simpson, "Jesus in the Psalms: The Priest-King Psalm," *CAMW* , Feb. 1892, 86.

[112] A.B. Simpson, "Jesus in the Psalms: The Pivot Psalm," *CAMW*, Mar. 25, 1892, 197.

[113] Murray, *Divine Healing*, 76.

[114] Lindenberger, "The Work of Berachah Home," 207.

[115] "Work in Pittsburgh," *CAMW*, Feb. 28, 1890, 138.

[116] A.B. Simpson, "Divine Healing: Friday Meeting New York," *CAMW*, Feb. 28, 1890, 135.

[117] Andrew Murray, cited in Howard Taylor, *Hudson Taylor's Spiritual Secret* (Chicago: Moody Press, 1932), 236.

[118] Roger Steer, *Spiritual Secrets of George Müller* (Wheaton, Ill.: Harold Shaw Publishers, 1985), 23.

[119] Simpson, *CITB* (1992), 3:241.

[120] Spurgeon, *Spiritual Warfare in a Believer's Life* (Lynnwood, WA: Emerald Books, 1993), 176.

[121] Spurgeon, *Spiritual Warfare*, 157-159.

[122] Oswald Chambers, *Daily Thoughts for Disciples* (Grand Rapids: Discovery House, [1976] 1994), Apr. 20.

[123] F.B. Meyer, *The Secret of Guidance* (Chicago: Moody, n.d.), 123.

[124] Cited in S.A. Lindenberger, *A Cloud of Witnesses* (Nyack, NY: Christian Alliance Publishing Co., 1900), 18-20.

[125] A.B. Simpson, *The Old Faith and the New Gospels* (Harrisburg, PA: Christian Publications, 1966), 60.

[126] Summarized from David J. Smith, *How Can I Ask God for Physical Healing?* (Grand Rapids: Chosen Books, 2005).

[127] Lindenberger, "The Work of Berachah Home," 207. Note that brackets are placed where the text is uncertain because the edge of the scanned page was cut off.

[128] Carrie Judd, "Faith Rest Cottage," *Triumphs of Faith*, Apr. 1888, 96.

[129] Paul E. Billheimer, *Destined for the Throne* (Ft. Washington, PA: CLC, 1975), 120.

[130] Charles Spurgeon, *1000 Devotional Thoughts* (Grand Rapids: Baker, 1976), 470.

[131] S.D. Gordon, *The Healing Christ* (New York: Fleming H. Revell; Ann Arbor, MI: Vine Books, [1924] 1985), 62-63, 104, 108.

[132] Howard Taylor, *Hudson Taylor's Spiritual Secret*, 156.

[133] Francois Fenelon, *Let Go* (Springdale, PA: Whitaker, 1973), 9.

[134] Charles H. Spurgeon, *Faith's Checkbook* (Chicago: Moody Press, n.d.), 87.

[135] Meyer, *The Secret of Guidance*, 27.

[136] Simpson, *Days of Heaven on Earth*, Apr. 8.

[137] Carrie Judd Montgomery, "The Power of the Tongue," *CMAW*, Sept. 4, 1909, 376.

[138] Murray, *Divine Healing*, 133.

[139] Simpson, *CITB* (1992), 4:207.

[140] A.B. Simpson, "The Embosomed Miracles," *AW*, Jan. 15, 1910, 250.

[141] Andrew Murray, *The Blood of the Cross* (Springdale, PA: Whitaker House, 1981), 78.

[142] Simpson, "The Embosomed Miracles," 250.

[143] Simpson, *CITB* (1993), 3:472.

[144] Simpson, *Gifts and Grace*, 302.

[145] Paul L. King, *A Believer with Authority* (Camp Hill, PA: Christian Publications, 2001), 89.

[146] King, *A Believer with Authority*, 63.

[147] Simpson, "How to Receive Divine Healing," 205.

[148] Vernard Eller, ed., *Thy Kingdom Come: A Blumhardt Reader* (Grand Rapids: Eerdmans, 1980), 84-85.

[149] Rosemary D. Gooden, "Introduction: Sarah Mix, Healing Evangelist," in Mrs. Edward Mix, *Faith Cures and Answers to Prayer* (Syracuse, NY: Syracuse University Press, 2002), xvii.

[150] Mrs. Edward Mix, *Faith Cures and Answers to Prayer*, 31.

[151] J.A. MacMillan "The Authority of the Believer in the Ephesian Epistle" *AW*, Jan. 9, 1932, 22.

[152] "Heavenly Quickening," *AW*, Sept. 21, 1946, 594.

[153] A.B. Simpson, "The Authority of Faith," *AW*, Apr. 23, 1938, 263.

[154] J.A. MacMillan "The Authority of the Believer in the Ephesian Epistle, Part VI," *AW*, Feb. 20, 1932, 116.

[155] J.A. MacMillan "The Authority of the Believer in the Ephesian Epistle," *AW*, Jan. 23, 1932, 61.

[156] A.B. Simpson, "Spiritual Talismans," *AW*, June 14, 1919, 178.

[157] A.B. Simpson, "The Authority of Faith," *AW*, Apr. 23, 1938, 263.

158 John A. MacMillan, *The Full Gospel Sunday School Quarterly*, Nov. 22, 1942, 25.

159 J.A. MacMillan, "The Authority of the Intercessor," *AW*, May 23, 1936, 327.

160 John A. MacMillan, *The Full Gospel Sunday School Quarterly*, May 3, 1936, 17.

161 Bosworth, *For This Cause*, 19-20.

162 Simpson, "Divine Healing in the Atonement," 123-124.

163 Simpson, *CITB* (1992), 1:371.

164 John A. MacMillan, "The Cooperating Spirit," *AW*, May 4, 1936, 275.

165 J.A. MacMillan "The Authority of the Believer in the Ephesian Epistle," *AW*, Feb. 27, 1932, 133, 142.

166 Murray, *With Christ in the School of Prayer*, 117.

167 John MacMillan's Diary, cited in King, *A Believer with Authority*, 90.

168 J.A. MacMillan "The Authority of the Believer in the Ephesian Epistle," *AW*, Feb. 13, 1932, 108.

169 Fred A. Hartley III, *Church on Fire* (Ft. Washington, PA: CLC, 2014), 61.

170 John A. MacMillan, "The Oppression of the Enemy," *AW*, June 21, 1947, 386.

171 John A. MacMillan, "Fasting as an Aid to Prayer, *AW*, Mar. 4, 1950, 130.

172 MacMillan, *The Authority of the Believer*, 96.

173 Pastor Schrenck, "Dangers and Warnings," *WWW*, July-Aug. 1885, 211-212.

174 Maria Woodworth-Etter, *Marvels and Miracles* (Indianapolis, IN: M.B.W. Etter, 1922), 508. See also pp. 503-508.

175 Francis Frangipane, "He Who Has Clean Hands," *Ministries Today*, May/June 1997, 49. ff.

176 Gary Greenwald, "The Dangerous Transference of Spirits," *Charisma and Christian Life*, Oct. 1990, 110 ff.

177 Adapted from Paul L. King, *God's Healing Arsenal*, 370-371.

178 John A. MacMillan, *The Full Gospel Adult Sunday School Quarterly*, May 3, 1936, 17.

179 Larry Crabb and Dan B Allender, *Hope When You're Hurting* (Grand Rapids, MI: Zondervan, 1996), 47.

180 Jennifer A. Miskov, *Life on Wings: The Forgotten Life and Theology of Carrie Judd Montgomery (1858-1946)* (Cleveland, TN: CPT Press, 2012), 191.

181 Ora Woodberry, "John Woodbury," *AW*, Oct. 22, 1938, 677.

182 "The Past Year at the Berachah Home," *WWW*, May 1, 1885, 159.

183 Hardesty, 44. Italics mine.

184 Lindenberger, "The Work of Berachah Home," 208. C&MA Archives.

185 A.B. Simpson, *The Gospel of Healing*, 95.

186 Simpson, *CITB* (1992), 4:190.

187 Used with permission.

[188] A.B. Simpson, "Jeremiah, an Example of Faith and Courage," *AW*, Nov. 14, 1914, 98.

[189] Simpson, "The Worship and Fellowship of the Church," 126.

[190] Used with permission.

[191] A.B. Simpson, "The Ministry of the Spirit," cited in Richard Gilbertson, *The Baptism of the Holy Spirit* (Camp Hill, PA: Christian Publications, Inc., 1993), 337.

[192] Mrs. A. E. Hester, "The Lord's Doings," *CMAW*, February 9, 1901, 84.

[193] Clay Anderson, "My Blessed Deliverance," CAMW, Jan. 20, 1893, 42.

[194] Mrs. N. S. Dean, "Testimony," *CMAW*, January 26, 1901, 56.

[195] Irene E. Lewis, *Life Sketch of Rev. Mary C. Norton: Remarkable Healings on Mission Fields* (Los Angeles: Pilgrim's Mission, Inc., 1954), 30-32.

[196] A.B. Simpson, *CITB: Matthew* (Harrisburg, PA: Christian Publications, n.d.), Vol. XIII, 163.

[197] A.B. Simpson, *Wholly Sanctified* (Harrisburg, PA: Christian Publications, 1925), 64-65.

[198] Used with permission.

[199] E.M. Bounds, *The Complete Works of E.M. Bounds: Book 1: The Necessity of Prayer* (Grand Rapids: Baker, 1990), 38.

[200] Cowman, *Streams in the Desert*, July 7.

[201] William T. MacArthur, "Healing from Deafness and Deliverance from Demons," *AW*, Jan. 26, 1924, 770.

[202] William T. MacArthur, "A Reminiscence of Rev. A. B. Simpson," *AW*, Aug. 21, 1920, 325-326.

[203] Simpson, Editorial, *AW*, Feb. 24, 1912, 322; MacArthur, "Healing from Deafness," 770.

[204] Simpson's Diary, May 1907.

[205] Miskov, 193.

[206] Mrs. May Evans, "Healed of Cancer," *AW*, July 10, 1915, 231.

[207] A.B. Simpson, "How to Receive Divine Healing," *WWW*, July-Aug., 1885, 203.

[208] "Berachah," *CMAW*, Sept. 2, 1905, 557.

[209] "Berachah," 557.

[210] Lizzie Elledges, "To His Glory," *CAMW*, Aug. 17, 1898, 154.

[211] A.B. Simpson, cited by a reporter in "Healing by Faith: Sick Persons Miraculously Cured," Simpson Scrapbook, p. 200, C&MA Archives.

[212] T.J. McCrossan, *The Bible and Its Eternal Facts* (Youngstown, OH: Clement Humbard, 1947), 192-194; McCrossan, *Christ's Paralyzed Church X-Rayed* (Youngstown, OH: Rev. C.E. Humbard, 1937), 258-260.

[213] Wilbur F. Meminger, "Touring New York," *CMAW*, Dec. 7, 1907, 168.

[214] Julia C. Boyd, "A Recent Healing," *CAMW*, March 27, 1891, 202.

215 Zolla McCauley, "Testimony," *CMAW*, November 17, 1900, 284.

216 Lewis, *Life Sketch of Rev. Mary C. Norton*, 27.

217 Cited in Lindenberger, *A Cloud of Witnesses*, 29-31.

218 Cited in Lindenberger, *A Cloud of Witnesses*, 90-95.

219 Cited in Lindenberger, *A Cloud of Witnesses*, 94.

220 Mrs. N. S. Dean, "Testimony," *CMAW*, Jan. 26, 1901, 56.

221 Cited in Lindenberger, *A Cloud of Witnesses*, 127-130.

222 McCrossan, *Bodily Healing and the Atonement*, 109-110.

223 Mrs. E. L. McLaine, "The Lord's Own Healing," *CAMW*, Mar. 16, 1894, 303.

224 "Field Notes," *CAMW*, June 5, 1896, 547.

225 Mrs. A.E. Hester, "The Lord's Doings," *CMAW*, Feb. 9, 1901, 84.

226 Lizzie Elledges, "To His Glory," *CAMW*, Aug. 17, 1898, 154.

227 Dallas Willard, *The Spirit of the Disciplines: Understanding How God Changes Lives* (San Francisco: HarperSanFrancisco, 1988), 179.

228 A.B. Simpson, "Editorial," *CMAW*, Jan. 23, 1909, 280.

229 Robert Jaffray, "Speaking in Tongues—Some Words of Kindly Counsel," *AW*, Mar. 13, 1909, 395.

230 Simpson, "Editorial," *CMAW*, Jan. 23, 1909, 280.

231 A.B. Simpson, Editorial, *CMAW*, May 4, 1907, 205.

232 Carrie Judd Montgomery, "Miraculously Healed by the Lord Thirty Years Ago, Baptized in the Holy Spirit One Year Ago," *The Latter Rain Evangel*, Oct. 1909, 9.

233 Rev. N. H. Harriman, "'War on the Saints': An Analytical Study, Part III," *AW*, Jan. 10, 1914, 230-231.

234 T. J. McCrossan, *Speaking with Other Tongues: Sign or Gift—Which?* (Harrisburg, PA: Christian Publications, 1927), 42.

235 May Mabette Anderson, "The Latter Rain and Its Counterfeit, A Message for the Hour: Part I," *Living Truth*, July 1907, 383.

236 Carrie Judd Montgomery, "Witchcraft and Kindred Errors," *AW*, Oct. 15, 1938, 661.

237 Joseph Smale, "The Gift of Tongues," *Living Truths*, Jan. 1907," 32-43; W.T. MacArthur, "The Promise of the Father and Speaking with Tongues in Chicago," *CMAW*, Feb. 9, 1907, 64; A.B. Simpson, Editorial, *CMAW*, Feb. 2, 1907, 99; Paul Rader, "At Thy Word—A Farewell Message," *AW*, Nov. 20, 1920, 532.

238 Simpson, *CITB* (1993), 5:209, 212.

239 Kilgour, "Ordained a Preacher," AW. 292.

240 Bosworth, *For This Cause*, 7.

241 Paul Brand and Philip Yancey, *In His Image* (Grand Rapids: Zondervan, 1984), 104.

242 Brand, 95.

243 Brand, 102-103.

[244] Bosworth, *For This Cause*, 8-9.

[245] Bosworth, *For This Cause*, 8-9.

[246] A.B. Simpson, "The Significance of the Lord's Supper," *CMAW*, May 18, 1901, 270.

[247] Simpson, "The Significance of the Lord's Supper," 270.

[248] A.B. Simpson, "Filled with the Spirit," *CAMW*, Apr. 1, 1892, 209-210.

[249] Paul Rader, *Harnessing God* (New York: George H. Doran Co., 1926), 95-96, 99.

[250] Murray, *Divine Healing*, 115.

[251] See Matthew 15:22-28; 19:13-15, 16-22; Mark 5:23; Luke 7:12-15; 13:11; 17:15-17; John 4:46-53; 5:5; 9:1-3.

[252] Simpson, CITB (1992), 2:34-35.

[253] Neil T. Anderson, *Victory Over the Darkness* (Ventura, CA: Regal, 1993), 107.

[254] Neil T. Anderson, *Living Free in Christ* (Ventura, CA: Regal, 1993), 7.

[255] Adapted from brochure "The Three R's: Remember, Renounce, Reclaim," by Dr. John and Helen Ellenberger.

[256] For more on theophostic, see www.theophostic.com; Elizabeth Moll Stalcup, "Hope for the Wounded Soul," *Charisma*, November 2007, 70ff.

[257] "Deliverance Debate," *Christianity Today*, Feb. 5, 2001, 18.

[258] Neil T. Anderson, Terry E. Zuehlke, and Julianne S. Zuehlke, *Christ Centered Therapy: The Practical Integration of Theology and Psychology* (Grand Rapids, MI: Zondervan, 2000).

[259] Deena Van't Hul, "An Orphan Care Project: A Study Relating the Effects of Caring for Orphans on the Individual Christian," D.Min. Dissertation, United Theological Seminary, Dayton, OH, 2015.

[260] Oswald Chambers, *Biblical Psychology* (Grand Rapids: Discovery House, ([1962] 1995), 76.

[261] Bailey, *Divine Healing*, 55.

[262] J. Hudson Ballard, cited in Bailey, *Divine Healing*, 56.

[263] R.A. Torrey, cited in Bailey, *Divine Healing*, 49.

[264] Russell Kelso Carter, *Faith Healing Reviewed After Twenty Years* (Boston, Chicago: Christian Witness Co., 1897), 91.

[265] Murray, *Divine Healing*, 45, 71.

[266] Simpson, "Inquiries and Answers," 294.

[267] Simpson, "Two Stages of Divine Healing," AW, Jan. 28, 1953, 5.

[268] G.P. Pardington, *Twenty-five Wonderful Years* (New York: Christian Alliance Publishing Co., 1912; New York: Garland, 1984), 59-60.

[269] Simpson, "Inquiries and Answers," 292-293.

[270] Russell Kelso Carter, *The Atonement for Sin and Sickness* (Boston, New York: Willard Tract Repository, 1884), 126; see also pp. 124-133.

[271] Torrey, *Divine Healing*, 19.

[272] S.D. Gordon, *The Healing Christ*, 90.

[273] Simpson, *The Gospel of Healing*, 64.

[274] Murray, *Divine Healing*, 69-70.

[275] Simpson, *Lord for the Body*, 102, 103, 110-111.

[276] Simpson, "Jesus in the Psalms: The Priest-King Psalm," 86.

[277] Murray, *Divine Healing*, 114-115.

[278] Murray, *Divine Healing*, 62.

[279] Simpson, "Inquiries and Answers," 294.

[280] Simpson, *Seeing the Invisible*, 177.

[281] A.B. Simpson, *The Land of Promise* (Harrisburg, PA: Christian Publications, 1969), 69-70.

[282] William T. MacArthur, *Ethan O. Allen* (Philadelphia, PA: The Parlor Evangelist, c. 1924), 1-14.

[283] John A. MacMillan, *Full Gospel Sunday School Quarterly*, Feb. 27, 1938, 28.

[284] MacArthur, *Ethan O. Allen*, 11.

[285] MacArthur, "A Reminiscence of Rev. A. B. Simpson," *AW*, Aug. 21, 1920, 325-326.

[286] William T. MacArthur, "Healing from Deafness and Deliverance from Demons," *AW*, Jan. 26, 1924, 770.

[287] MacArthur, "A Reminiscence of Rev. A.B. Simpson," 325-326.

[288] Carrie Judd Montgomery, *Under His Wings* (Oakland, CA: Triumphs of Faith, 1936), 200-201.

[289] Paul Rader, "At Thy Word—A Farewell Message," *AW*, Nov. 20, 1920, 532.

[290] Conversation with Dr. John Ellenberger.

[291] Paul L. King, *Moving Mountains: Lessons in Bold Faith from Great Evangelical Leaders* (Grand Rapids: Chosen Books, 2004), 187-188.

[292] W.C. Stevens, "The Recovery of the Sick," *AW*, Aug. 17, 1929, 535.

[293] Stevens, "The Recovery of the Sick," 533, 535.

[294] MacArthur, "A Reminiscence of Rev. A.B. Simpson," 325-326.

[295] A.W. Tozer, *Born After Midnight* (Camp Hill, PA: Christian Publications, 1959), 43.

[296] William T. MacArthur, "The Phenomenon of Supernatural Utterance," *CMAW*, Oct. 31, 1908, 73.

[297] V. Raymond Edman, "Questions You Have Asked," *The Alliance Witness*, Sept. 14, 1966, 18.

[298] "Nyack Convention," *CMAW*, July 25, 1903, 109.

[299] Stevens, "The Recovery of the Sick," 533, 535.

300 John A. MacMillan, *Encounter with Darkness* (Harrisburg, PA: Christian Publications, 1980), 82-83.

301 "Substance of Dr. Peck's Account of His Healing of Acute Mania," *CAMW*, Mar. 21-28, 1890, 192ff.; George B. Peck, "In His Name," *CAMW*, Aug. 14, 1895, 102.

302 Pastor Schrenck, "Dangers and Warnings," *WWW*, July-Aug. 1885, 211-212.

303 Chaplain Jay Smith comments on MacMillan's teaching, cited in King, *A Believer with Authority*, 170.

304 *Full Gospel Sunday School Quarterly*, Oct. 10, 1943, 6.

305 *Full Gospel Sunday School Quarterly*, Aug. 16, 1936, 22; *SSQ*, Feb. 2, 1941, 14-15.

306 MacArthur, "Fabrics Filled with Power," 390.

307 A.E. Funk, "Pittsburgh Convention," *AW*, Apr. 9, 1921, 57.

308 MacArthur, "Fabrics Filled with Power," 390.

309 W.T. MacArthur, "Fabrics Filled with Power," 390.

310 A.B. Simpson, *The Old Faith and the New Gospels* (Harrisburg, PA: Christian Publications, 1966), 59.

311 Murray, *Divine Healing*, 18.

312 Murray, *Divine Healing*, 128. Though he sometimes received treatment from a doctor, Murray likewise advised that healing by a physician misses the greater blessing: "The healing which is wrought by our Lord Jesus brings with it and leaves behind it more real blessing than the healing which is obtained through physicians." Murray, *Divine Healing*, 20.

313 J. DuPlessis, *The Life of Andrew Murray of South Africa* (London: Marshall Brothers, Ltd., 1919), 347.

314 Kenneth MacKenzie, "Healing or Helping?," *Triumphs of Faith*, Jan. 1903, 11.

315 A.B. Simpson, "Editorial," *CAMW*, Nov. 1890, 274

316 A.B. Simpson, "Editorial," *CAMW*, Nov. 1890, 274.

317 A.B. Simpson, "Editorial," *CAMW*, Nov. 1890, 274

318 Simpson, *The Four-fold Gospel*, 48.

319 Simpson, *The Gospel of Healing*, 68.

320 Carter, *Faith Healing Reviewed*, 110, 112.

321 Carter, *Faith Healing Reviewed*, 112-114.

322 S.D. Gordon, *The Healing Christ*, xi.

323 S.D. Gordon, *The Healing Christ*, 65-66.

324 A.B. Simpson, *Triumphs of Faith*, Nov. 1922, 252.

Other Titles by Paul L. King

Come Up Higher: Rediscovering Throne Life-The Highest Christian Life for the 21st Century. Classic teaching on what it means to be seated with Christ in the heavenly places, reigning in life while here on earth. "Life-changing. . . .This book will drive a person into the secret place."—Bill Johnson; "Indispensable insights"—Dr. Gary Benedict; "Brings balance. . . . I highly recommend both the book and the man."
—Randy Clark ISBN: 978-1-939250-06-3 Paperback

God's Healing Arsenal: A Divine Battle Plan for Overcoming Distress and Disease. A wide array of healing weapons God uses to bring healing and victory. Forged in the fires of the author's own personal battle overcoming cancer. "Nuggets from the whole spectrum of God's people. . . . sage advice"—Dr. Neil T. Anderson
ISBN-10: 0882700111 ISBN-13: 978-0882700113 Paperback

Finding Your Niche: 12 Keys to Opening God's Doors for Your Life. Universal biblical principles from more than 35 years of ministry experience for unlocking the gateways to your assignment from God and encountering new vistas of God's purposes for your life and calling. Discussion and study questions included.
ISBN 10: 0-9785352-8-6 [paperback] ISBN 13: 978-0-9785352-8-5

Moving Mountains: Lessons in Bold Faith from Great Evangelical Leaders. Amazing stories and teachings of bold, wise faith from George Müller, Hudson Taylor, Charles Spurgeon, Andrew Murray, A.B. Simpson, Hannah Whitall Smith, Oswald Chambers, E.M.

Bounds, Amy Carmichael, A.W. Tozer, and more! Study guide included. *"Feast on wind and fire!"—Calvin Miller*

ISBN 0-8007-9375-7 Paperback

A Believer with Authority: The Life and Message of John A. MacMillan. The ground-breaking biography and teachings of the Christian and Missionary Alliance missionary and professor who was a trailblazing pioneer in spiritual warfare and the seminal writer on the authority of the believer. *Endorsed by Jack Hayford and Neil Anderson.*

ISBN 0-87509-917-3 Paperback

Genuine Gold: The Cautiously Charismatic Story of the Early Christian and Missionary Alliance. The rediscovered and fully-documented history of the supernatural in the C&MA, featuring first-hand testimonies of early Alliance charismatic experiences (even before Azusa Street), relationships between the C&MA and the early Pentecostal movement, and evidences of historical drift and recovery. *"[A] valuable book. . . . King's research is impressive."—Pneuma: The Journal of the Society for Pentecostal Studies*   ISBN 0-9785352-0-0 Paperback

Binding and Loosing: Exercising Authority over the Dark Powers (co-author K. Neill Foster). Understanding properly the biblical and theological concept and sound practice of combating the powers that war against Christ and His Church through binding and loosing according to Matthew 16:19—when it is appropriate, when it works and when it does not. Illustrated from real life experiences. Study guide included.   ISBN 0-87509-852-5 Paperback

Only Believe: Examining the Origin and Development of Classic and Contemporary Word of Faith Theologies. "The definitive, comprehensive study of the teachings and practices of faith throughout church history. Thoroughly documented with classic & contemporary citations, it breaks new ground, uncovers new historical & theological information about the origins of faith teaching & practice; corrects inaccurate information & misinterpretations; discerns healthy & unhealthy teachings and practices in today's Word of Faith movement; &

provides sound counsel for walking by faith . . . at once scholarly, accessible, & practical." —Mark E. Roberts, Ph.D.

ISBN978-0-9785352-6-1 Paperback

Anointed Women: The Rich Heritage of Women in Ministry in The Christian and Missionary Alliance

The remarkable stories of women used by God in amazing ways, documenting hundreds of women who served as Alliance pastors, evangelists, and teachers, planted hundreds of churches, and led thousands of people to salvation in Christ, healing, and a deeper Christian life.

ISBN978-0-9819526-7-3 Paperback

Nuggets of Genuine Gold: Simpson, Tozer, Jaffray and Other Christian and Missionary Alliance Leaders on Experiencing the Spirit-Empowered Life. Quotes, testimonies, and experiences from Alliance leaders on the baptism in the Spirit, supernatural gifts and manifestations of the Spirit, Spirit-filled life and worship, spiritual discernment and warfare.

ISBN978-0-9819526-6-6 Paperback

To order copies see www.paulkingministries.com or e-mail paul@paulkingministries.com

Blog: kingsroundtable.wordpress.com

About the Author

Dr. Paul King, an ordained minister with The Christian and Missionary Alliance, served for 16 years on the faculty of Oral Roberts University as Director of Bible Institute Programs and as an adjunct professor of theology and ministry. He received the Doctor of Ministry from Oral Roberts University and Doctor of Theology from the University of South Africa. Author of eleven books, he was awarded Scholar of the Year at Oral Roberts University in 2006, and served as Scholar-at-Large at Alliance Theological Seminary, and as an adjunct professor and consultant for Crown College.

Dr. King speaks in churches, conferences, and seminars interdenominationally and internationally, teaching on healing, ministry and leadership development, the deeper and higher life in Christ, revival and the ministry of the Holy Spirit, spiritual discernment and spiritual warfare, women in ministry, elder training, and worship. He specializes in research on 19th and early 20th century movements of holiness, healing, faith, and the Holy Spirit. As a cancer overcomer, he teaches and ministers on divine healing. He consults with churches and educational institutions regarding church health and ministry and leadership training. Paul King is the founder of Higher Life/Alliance Heritage Renewal Network and Higher Life/Alliance Healing Centers.

Dr. King and his wife Kathy married in 1975, and reside in Broken Arrow, Oklahoma, where he pastors a church plant, Higher Life Fellowship. They have two adult children, Sarah and Christopher. You can find more information about Paul King on his website www.paulkingministries.com.